"How odd, given the consuming global challenge of food, that so little of the discourse of eco-social justice, let alone of political theology, has focused on the matter. With this multi-faceted yet attractively accessible work, S. Yael Dennis has rectified the situation. Reconsidering the notion of 'food sovereignty,' it provides an interdisciplinary introduction to political theology that takes the latter where it has never gone. *Edible Entanglements* makes a brilliant contribution to political, economic, and ecological studies in religion."

—**Catherine Keller**, Author of *Political Theology of the Earth: Our Planetary Emergency and the Struggle for a New Public* (2018)

"The political, religious, and philosophical thinking surrounding issues of food production and distribution are of the highest importance in the face of continued neo-liberal globalization and the return of nationalisms. Anyone concerned about food justice should read this book. S. Yael Dennis interrogates the theological and philosophical understandings of 'sovereignty' and 'anthropology,' and human-earth relations, bringing nutritional science into the discussion as well, in order to interrogate the violence of the contemporary corporate food regimes and lift up the more egalitarian food regime of the food sovereignty movements, which recognize that we are all dependent upon (and thus vulnerable to) the rest of the planetary community which sustains our lives on a daily basis."

—**Whitney Bauman**, Florida International University

"In this book, Shelley Yael Dennis develops a political theology of food that engages the important idea of sovereignty. On the one hand, sovereignty is the nation-state's unified power to decide, based on the work of Carl Schmitt. On the other hand, food sovereignty offers an important site of resistance to the onslaught of corporate capitalism and its food security regime. Dennis combines excellent theoretical analysis with valuable ecological applications. Anyone concerned about access to food in the context of climate change should read it!"

—**Clayton Crockett**, University of Central Arkansas

"This singular book explores the concepts of sovereignty, how religion has shaped and molded such concepts, as well as the direct and unyielding consequences these power structures have had, and are still having, on environmental health, food security, and global environmental politics . . . *Edible Entanglements* rips off the blinders and explores not just how religious concepts have played into power structures and thus impacted our planet, but considers how religious thought may help us get out of the mess we are in."

—**Elizabeth J. Ruther**, Coastal State-Federal Relations Coordinator, Oregon Coastal Management Program

Edible Entanglements

Edible Entanglements

On a Political Theology of Food

S. Yael Dennis

CASCADE *Books* • Eugene, Oregon

Cascade Books
An Imprint of Wipf and Stock Publishers
199 W. 8th Ave., Suite 3
Eugene, OR 97401

www.wipfandstock.com

PAPERBACK ISBN: 978-1-5326-4363-7
HARDCOVER ISBN: 978-1-5326-4364-4
EBOOK ISBN: 978-1-5326-4365-1

Cataloguing-in-Publication data:

Names: Dennis, S. Yael, author.

Title: Edible entanglements : on a political theology of food / S. Yael Dennis.

Description: Eugene, OR : Cascade Books, 2019 | Includes bibliographical refer-
ences and index.

Identifiers: ISBN 978-1-5326-4363-7 (paperback) | ISBN 978-1-5326-4364-4
(hardcover) | ISBN 978-1-5326-4365-1 (ebook)

Subjects: LCSH: Political theology. | Sovereignty. | Food—Religious aspects. |
Agriculture—Religious aspects. | Schmitt, Carl,—1888–1985.

Classification: BR115.N87 D45 2019 (print) | BR115.N87 D45 (ebook)

Manufactured in the U.S.A.   03/08/19

For Kelsey, Connor, and Ethan . . .

If not for you, there would be no me.

Contents

Tables

Acknowledgments

THIS BOOK HAS BEEN years in the making, and I cannot hope to pay adequate tribute to the many people who have played a role in its final shape. Many patients, names long forgotten, inspired my initial questions about the material effects of social inequalities upon specific bodies. Many books and articles I read early in my professional career doubtless influenced the directions of my thought. Casual conversations, passing glances at headlines, all played a role. Yet while the list of debts cannot be completed, nonetheless there are some specific individuals whose contributions were sufficiently recent or substantive to capture a few memory cells.

I am forever indebted to Hilary Giovale, without whose insistence I would never have approached Dr. Sandra Lubarsky to inquire about the Sustainable Communities Program at Northern Arizona University. In turn, Dr. Sandra Lubarsky and Dr. Marcus Ford introduced me to process philosophy—absolutely indispensable for thinking through the complex issues brought forth in this political theology. Dr. Rom Coles energized the "political" in political theology, enlightening me about the nitty gritty of grassroots, inclusive democratic processes.

Dr. Catherine Keller tirelessly guided me through the acquisition of philosophical knowledge and skills necessary to articulate what were vague—but intense!—concerns about the public health impacts of social structures I perceived as socially unjust and environmentally unsustainable. Drs. Chris Boesel, Laurel Kearns, and Summer Harrison contributed generous amounts of time and energy refining my thinking and expression in all matters theological, sociological, and food studies-related.

Friends and colleagues at Rio Salado College, where I have the good fortune of chairing a wildly interdisciplinary department, encouraged my research, including, but not limited to, assistance from Hazel David, Kirsten Thomas, and the rest of the library faculty and staff. Dr. Stephen Fomeche was an especially stellar "acountabilibuddy." And Tristan Marble kept me sane and focused on the big picture.

Numerous friends and family cheered me on from the sidelines, among them Chana Seligman, my children Kelsey, Connor, and Ethan, and my grandson William (who gave me writing breaks that were the most fun *ever!*). Elizabeth Ruther did the heavy lifting; this book would never have happened without her indefatigable support.

I would like to extend my deepest, heartfelt gratitude to the entire team at Cascade Books, who have helped shepherd me through the publishing process from beginning to end: Charlie Collier, Sallie Vandagrift, and Daniel Lanning who have entertained my seemingly endless questions, as well as the countless others who have devoted time and energy to bringing this project to fruition.

Introduction

IN THE LATE 1980s and early 1990s I completed medical school and residency on Chicago's Near West Side. During that time I became pregnant with my first child and was advised to take one milligram of folic acid daily in order to reduce the likelihood that my daughter would develop spina bifida, a condition in which the developing neural tube fails to close, a feat that typically completes by day twenty-eight of pregnancy.[1] I marveled that such a miniscule amount of any nutrient (less than a single tablet of ibuprofen spread out over twenty-eight days!) could make a visible impact on the development of the nervous system. I could only speculate about the invisible impact of malnutrition on my patients, most of whom received welfare and food stamps. It seemed to me that my patients might have been hobbled coming out of the gate by poor nutrition. What role, I wondered, does poor nutrition play in the cycle of poverty?

My concerns in this regard were not mirrored in the wider world around me. Admittedly, as a busy medical student I was only peripherally aware of the political discourse surrounding welfare reform in the early 1990s, but much of what I gleaned during my morning commute implied that America, being the land of opportunity, afforded us all equal possibilities for financial success provided we were willing to work hard. Mainstream media seemed to amplify voices of the Religious Right preoccupied primarily with denouncing homosexuality, criminalizing abortion, assuring that creationism made it into school curriculum, and preventing governments from interfering with free markets. They seemed somewhat more concerned with providing school prayer than school lunches.

---

1. Since this discovery was made in the late 1980s folate has been added to most cereal and bread products to reduce the likelihood of spina bifida.

These priorities puzzled me greatly, having been an avid reader of sacred text since early adolescence. I had been raised in a strictly secular home, however, and my reading was uninformed by the sedimentations of tradition in the thousands of years between the writing of those texts and the political milieu at the end of the twentieth century. Therefore, I was aware of the numerous biblical injunctions to feed the poor and liberate the captive, whereas I couldn't recall any injunctions insisting that we implement prayer in public schools or support free-market capitalism. I could not understand the seeming lack of concern about ecological issues; after all, Scripture held that God both created and declared this world very good. The political agenda of the Christian Right seemed—from my admittedly remote perspective—to be disconnected from the priorities I encountered within Scripture.

Furthermore, it seemed to me that if the United States of America were *really* a Christian nation, as those folks insisted, then its economic organization would reflect more concern for the disenfranchised and less resentment of them. Caring for God's creation would be a number one priority since it is among the first of God's commandments (scripturally speaking). Something seemed *off* to me. Was it possible, I wondered, that more or less secular concerns found purchase in religious communities and masqueraded as Christian dogma? At any rate, a competing worldview not entirely consistent with the economic messages of the Bible—yet somehow consistent with other tenets dear to the Christian Right—certainly seemed operative.

While these loudly conservative Christian voices drew support from the Abrahamic traditions for free-market-based agendas, or what I have come to call "neoliberal economics," I encountered within the Bible both justification of *and challenge to* their perspective. This contradiction plagued me throughout my fifteen-year medical career, most of which entailed serving the poor in public mental health facilities. Even after establishing a private practice, I noted that similar socio-political and economic forces seemed to bear heavily upon the well-being of my clients, although with differing intensities.

Those experiences planted the seeds for this political theology of food. I returned to graduate school on a vague quest to study the nexus of religion, worldview, gender, and ecology that would account for what I observed but could not express. In truth, I sought a ready-made explanation that had thus far eluded me, some well-established truth that my medical school had overlooked in its curriculum design. What I discovered instead was a mosaic of theological and philosophical perspectives that illuminate one or another aspect of this interconnection, including process philosophy, new materialisms, feminist theory, and progressive theologies. Above all, it was the discursive

field of political theology that invigorated and clarified the "armchair" observations I made about this nexus as a practicing physician.

The Theological and the Political

Scholars in the field of political theology hail from both secular and religious orientations, and concern themselves with the appearance of theological concepts in the political arena. The contemporary discourse often
engages the work of Carl Schmitt, who famously declared that "All significant concepts of the modern theory of the state are secularized theological
concepts."[2] The political and the theological draw sustenance from one another. Up close, the line between the two blurs as each seems to seep into the
other. Theologies suggest particular social arrangements. Social structures
profess theological commitments (albeit often disavowed).

As Mark Lewis Taylor describes it, the political refers to "certain mode[s]
of organizing the human practices that structure social interaction."[3] Taylor
identifies the theological as a dimension of the political. The discourse of the
theological is tasked with critical reflection upon "motions of power" in a
politics characterized by conflict.[4] Motions of power are integrally entwined
with the resolution or perpetuation of these tensions, not infrequently leaving a trail of suffering in their wake.

The full title of Taylor's volume, *The Theological and the Political: On
the Weight of the World* raises a central question: What about the weighti-
ness of the world? Taylor describes this weight as perception of the ines-
capability of participation in the system that differentially visits harm and
privilege on those within it. He goes on to say that the "weight felt" can be
regarded as a sense of shared humanity being disrupted by oppressive social
arrangements that impose heavy burdens of suffering. By this account, the
weight of each of the emaciated bodies of the nearly seven million people
who die of starvation every year is rather heavy—indeed may in fact be
heavier than the bodies of the eight million people suffering from obesity,
although in truth our global food system can be said to be serving neither
bodies very well. Drawing upon Taylor's verbiage, "motions of power" have
much to do with who starves, who becomes obese, and who retains a slen-
der, well-nourished figure.

Borrowing Taylor's terms, a political theology of food concerns itself
with "the theological" in its critical analysis of ongoing injustices in food

2. Schmitt, *Political Theology*, 36.
3. Taylor, *Theological and the Political*, 5.
4. Ibid.

politics, calling attention to the "motions of power" that perpetuate them. Although it carries distinctive theological implications, a political theology of food does not constitute a constructive theological intervention into what Taylor refers to as Guild Theology, or theology of the formal, academic, and doctrinally committed variety. Why use the world "theological," if I do not intend such an intervention? Again, I turn to Taylor for clarification: "even those who reject [Guild Theology] must work in the ruins of its failure."[5] This is a particularly salient point, since the remains of theological concepts persist within secular theories. One such failure of "Guild Theology," I contend, is the classical notion of sovereignty, particularly in its secularized versions endorsed by Schmitt.[6]

Theologically, a sovereign God is envisioned as all-powerful, unchanging, and most importantly transcendent as regards the material world. This God establishes natural laws; suspends them when a miracle is called for; metes out punishment; and guarantees justice. We may not like the decisions of this God, but those who espouse this theology assure us that even the bad things are a meaningful part of the ultimate plan. When this concept is applied in the secular arena, it supports numerous related ideas. First, the idea that a nation is territorially defined and more or less autonomous, thus entitled to self-rule. And second, the idea that a single political leader is capable of securing the borders of a nation and providing for the welfare of its citizens, with the right to rule over others (i.e., noncitizens, rebels, etc.) if they threaten the welfare of the state. Thus, the notion of sovereignty refers to concepts as divergent as autonomy and the right to self-rule on the one hand, or supremacy and the right to rule over others on the other hand.

The political concept of sovereignty has superimposed the image of a transcendent, sovereign God upon a human sovereign figure, with a similar hope of preservation of identity. As Bruno Latour notes, environmental politics are no exception; even self-proclaimed secular politics resorts to using "nature" as a transcendent that becomes sovereign.[7] Still more intriguing, the concept of national sovereignty emerged in the context of the global spice trade in order to establish the right of a governing body to rule over a bounded territory for the purposes of conducting and profiting from that

---

5. Ibid., 11.

6. More problematic from a theological, rather than political, perspective is the problem of theodicy. For example, as will be discussed in later chapters, the failure of the transcendent God to halt the brutality unleashed during the First World War decidedly scarred political theorist Carl Schmitt. But an exhaustive account of theodicy is well beyond the scope of the present study.

7. Latour, *Politics of Nature*, 12, 200.

trade,[8] yet it ironically has reached its own crisis point due in part to transnational global food trade, for reasons that will become clearer in Part I.[9] Even more to the point of a political theology of food, free-market-based economic policies are imposed upon developing nations by multilateral agencies presuming the right to rule over others—one aspect of sovereignty. Meanwhile, the food sovereignty movement has arisen in opposition to those maneuvers, claiming not so much the right to rule over others as the right to self-determination.

While attending to the conceptual dimensions of food, a political theology of food must also attend to the material dimensions of food—its production, distribution, and consumption. A political theology of food is therefore also informed by biological sciences and quantum physics. It presumes life on earth to be characterized by dynamically entangled becoming, in which no boundaries—including between one nation and another, human and nonhuman, or even between life and death, can be definitively settled once and for all. Boundaries, including national boundaries and declarations of sovereignty, remain subject to disruption. For what appear at first glance to be firm boundaries reveal themselves to be porous sites of interchange, and the "surface" appearance is perpetually in the (re)making.[10] Consequently, decisions, both large and small, must be continually made and remade. Thus the theoretical positions of process philosophy, new materialisms, and science studies constitute some of the transdisciplinary tools most useful for a political theology of food.

8. Gupta, "A Different History of the Present," 29–46.

9. Ray and Srivinas, *Curried Cultures*, 38.

10. As evidence of the consistent remaking of the bodies' boundaries, allow me to mention two biological phenomena. First, the normally very short lifespan of epithelial cells—the cells forming both the skin and the inner lining of the intestine. These cells live only a matter of days, typically three to five, after which time they are sloughed off and a new layers of cells emerges to the surface. Yet only in the case of medical emergencies does it occur that dead skin falls off without another layer present to take its place. The ongoing replication of cells maintains the appearance of an enduring surface despite frequent loss of skin cells. The second is the acute version of a pathological condition known as "disseminated intravascular coagulation," a clotting abnormality occurring at the end stage of other illnesses such as cardiogenic shock or heat stroke. In this condition, numerous tiny blood clots form throughout the vascular system, depleting the body's clotting factors. As a result, there are no clotting factors available to repair the many microscopic wounds that the body typically repairs without one's awareness. Subsequently, bleeding typically occurs from such obvious sites of recent injury as the site of yesterday's blood draw, but also from the nose, mouth, and ears. What this demonstrates is that tiny ruptures occur on multiple surfaces of our bodies many times a day, but due to the remaking of our bodily boundaries by our clotting system, we are typically unaware of these threats to bodily integrity. Peters et al. "Disseminated Intravascular Coagulopathy," 419–23.

Charting the Course

Transdisciplinary inquiry is vital to a political theology of food, since food politics operates simultaneously in several registers: individual, national, transnational, and ecological. It may seem more reasonable in some regards to tackle only one of these registers for the sake of simplicity. And indeed, much scholarship takes precisely that approach. Because sovereignty is central to political theology, a political theology of food interrogates how the concept of sovereignty permeates food politics within *each* of these registers. This analysis reveals how sovereignty comes undone within each of them around one of at least three fault lines: the suspension of law, claims to unity, or promises of security.

Theoretical disagreements between German jurist Carl Schmitt and German Jewish literary critic Walter Benjamin will form the axis around which much of this political theology of food revolves. Both men disagree passionately about the concept of sovereignty and about the proper role of the theological within the political. Schmitt espouses an orthodox theological model of divine sovereignty, and bases his description of political sovereignty upon just this notion of unilateral, top-down, absolute, authority. Benjamin also endorses something of a traditional theological model of sovereignty, but in his case this model serves to upend any pretense to human sovereignty. The underlying dilemmas to which both men point resurface as especially relevant to food politics in the context of climate change. These finer points of disagreement between Schmitt and Benjamin as relevant to a political theology of food receive concentrated attention in chapter 1.

In the aftermath of the 2011 bombing of the World Trade Center academic interest in political theology has experienced something of a renaissance, and with it a resurgence of the debate between Schmitt and Benjamin. As will become clearer in chapter 2, despite the deep divisions between Schmitt and Benjamin, the food sovereignty movement could potentially draw support from political theologians favoring either one—at least to a limited degree. The radically democratic processes and lack of formal rules in the movement resonate with radically left-leaning political theologians who tend to favor Benjamin's approach, while the food sovereignty movement's nationalist origins and demand for world-wide recognition of their nation-state would alienate those same theorists. The misalignment between the food sovereignty movement and the radically progressive political theologies that might otherwise support the movement are, I contend, related to the paradoxical motions of power exhibited in global food trade.

Paradoxical motions of power in global food trade will be accounted for by drawing upon the concept of food regimes and rhetorical framing in chapter 3. The concept of food regimes was developed by Harriet Fried-mann and Philip McMichael, and describes settled structures and practices in global food systems. In their schema, the current regime is referred to as the corporate food regime. Madeleine Fairbairn contributes an analysis of political frames in global food politics, delineating the rhetorical fram-ing of the corporate food regime and its major contender, the food sov-ereignty movement. Examining motions of power in food politics reveals that economic renditions of Schmittian sovereignty are carried out by the corporate food regime under the political frame of "food security," artfully sidestepping—or presuming?—the question of their right to the sovereign decision, while never overtly claiming to possess sovereignty. Furthermore, a disjuncture between the political frames and systemic practices of the food sovereignty movement is at least partially responsible for its enigmatic claims to sovereignty.

Connecting social injustices inherent in our contemporary global food system to enactments of sovereignty on the part of the corporate food regime will be the task of chapter 4.[11] This will involve an application of Giorgio Agamben's *homo sacer* and state of exception to the context of food politics, constituting a new approach to the analysis of motions of power in the global food system. When viewed through the lens of Agamben's *homo sacer* and state of exception, it becomes clear that despite the sovereign's promise to provide security, enactments of sovereignty can, and frequently do, increase vulnerability. Jacques Derrida's critique of Agamben will shift the site of inquiry from the political to the ethical. An examination of Judith Butler's ethic of nonviolence as a response to precarity in the global food system closes the chapter.

The materialization of human bodies in the context of the global food system receives concentrated attention in chapter 5. Feminist ethics, new materialist methodologies, and scientific data from nutritional research will contribute to an account of the social production of malnourished starving and obese bodies through the workings of an oppressive food system. The intercalation of bodies thus produced into social hierarchies retroactively reinforces and legitimates the original oppression.[12] Demonstrating the so-

11. Agamben, *Homo Sacer,* and Agamben, *State of Exception* will inform this section.

12. Bennett's vibrant materiality emphasizes the effect that food has on human behavior. Barad's agential realism is founded upon the notion that "the primary onto-logical unit is not independent objects with independently determinate boundaries and properties but rather what Bohr terms 'phenomena'" (*Meeting the Universe Halfway,* 33). According to Barad, these phenomena "intra-act" such that, for example in the case of food, neither the dinner nor the diner are considered "distinct in an absolute sense" but are "only distinct in relation to their mutual entanglement." Each will, through their intra-action, shape what the other becomes.

cial production of classed bodies calls attention to both the necessity for and possibility of shifting unjust social practices.

Not only does food's boisterous dynamism mark the vulnerability of the human body, but it also marks the vulnerability of food itself. Chapter 6 enumerates the environmental impact of the corporate food regime, and also the resulting susceptibility of global food production to those environmental impacts. Bruno Latour's *Politics of Nature* surfaces as an imperfect yet potent challenge to the concept of Schmittian sovereignty in the context of global climate instability. Pivotal to Latour's contribution is a critique of dualist metaphysics that prioritizes substance over material, expert over layperson, and Being over becoming. Latour's nondualist metaphysics lends support for a political theology of food that situates itself in a relational ontology on a planet characterized more by a dynamic becoming than by a static Being.

The theological integrity and metaphysical accuracy of Schmitt's application of orthodox theological models will be assessed in chapter 7. Schmitt's secularization of sovereignty is not at all in keeping with orthodox theologies, at least not as interpreted by Karl Barth. However, even Barth's theology no longer squares entirely with the metaphysical image of our era. Subsequently, a political theology of food must seek theological models consonant with both traditional sources and contemporary science, such as Catherine Keller's theology of becoming.

Finally, Paulina Ochoa-Espejo's popular sovereignty will be interrogated for its capacity to inspire the formation of resilient multiplicities of communities and ecosystems in the face of climate catastrophes in chapter 8. Although arguing against a top-down sovereignty operative within a tightly bounded territory, this chapter will nonetheless legitimate the demand for national sovereignty on the part of those in the food sovereignty movement while attempting to avoid the pitfalls of Schmittian sovereignty.

The questions awakened in me as a young medical student have increased in number and intensity in recent years. On a planet currently facing numerous catastrophic weather events annually due to climate change—due in part to high-input agricultural practices—I ask: does it make sense to permit the continued unification of the global agricultural system into this highly mechanized and notably destructive set of practices? Especially when climate change will make it even harder to grow food? Unification of agricultural practice is supported not only by the undeclared "sovereignty" of multilateral agencies and transnational corporations. It is also implicitly supported by the disavowed integration of secularized orthodox theological concepts into secular thought. A political theology of food questions such unification on theological, political, and ecological bases and calls attention to the threat that such unification poses in the context of climate change. While questions alone will not solve anything, they do permit a fresh perspective.

Part I

Sovereignty in Theory and Action

Chapter 1

Fertilizing the Garden

Carl Schmitt's Sovereign in Interwar Germany

DESPITE THE IMPORTANCE OF the concept of sovereignty to the politics of food, few have endeavored to trace the historical trajectory of sovereignty as a political concept as it appears in global food trade. Historian and political theorist Daniele Conversi is among the handful to do so. Conversi opens his historical contextualization of the food sovereignty movement by arguing that "the link between sovereignty and food sovereignty has scarcely been theorized across human and social science disciplines."[1] And indeed, with the notable exception of the 2015 issue of *Globalizations,* including Conversi's, there is a dearth of such analysis.

Conversi begins his account of the concept of sovereignty with the Peace of Westphalia, which established territorial boundaries within which a given monarch could legitimately rule without interference.[2] The territorially bounded nature of sovereignty carried forward as monarchical rule gave way to the nation-state, and the sovereignty of the king was supplanted by the (presumably unified) will of the people as the hallmark of legitimate sovereignty.[3] Conversi flashes forward to our current era, which he characterizes as "post-sovereign," because the contemporary transnational economic situation has differentially fortified the sovereignty of certain nation-states while eroding that of others.

Thus historically contextualized, food sovereignty appears as "the most significant incarnation of the historical notion of sovereignty" according to

1. Conversi, "Sovereignty in a Changing World," 485.
2. Ibid.
3. Ibid., 486–87.

Conversi.[4] The significance of this movement is attributed in no small part to the dual nature of the claims to sovereignty: "While sovereignty [in the food sovereignty movement] still concerns the state's right to adopt and shape food policies, the subject has moved from the state to small-scale producers mobilizing, with or without the state, to defend their 'models of production and reproduction.'"[5] Rhetorically, the food sovereignty movement deploys the term sovereignty in a new register that simultaneously fortifies, relies upon and destabilizes the sovereignty of the state itself.

According to theorists in the field of political theology, the "historical notion of sovereignty" with which Conversi concerns himself derives from theological concepts.[6] Yet Conversi situates food sovereignty within the broader historical trajectory of sovereignty in its political forms, altogether ignoring the religious motifs animating the concept of sovereignty. Similarly, the discourse of political theology has yet to grapple with the concept of sovereignty as it appears in food politics or to wrestle with the central role of global food trade as a driver of geopolitics. A political theology of food attempts to bridge that gap.

I will focus on two primary eras: an interwar Germany between 1918 and 1939 and a post-9/11 United States. Two prominent theorists emerged in interwar Germany whose conceptualizations of sovereignty and politics continue to shape contemporary discourse: German jurist Carl Schmitt and German-Jewish literary critic Walter Benjamin. This chapter will elaborate upon the finer points of contention between Schmitt and Benjamin during the interwar period, as these points largely inform the contemporary (post-9/11) conversation pivotal to this political theology of food.[7] The following chapter will hone in on facets of post-9/11 political theology most relevant for a political theology of food.

This exploration will not only reveal the theological dimension of the concept of sovereignty, but it will also reveal a cluster of concerns relevant to the politics of food as humans grapple with climate change in a post-secular,

4. Ibid., 485.

5. Ibid.

6. Ibid.

7. See for example: Agamben, *State of Exception*; Derrida, "Force of Law"; Crockett, *Radical Political Theology*; Miguez, Rieger, and Sung, *Beyond the Spirit of Empire*; Bell, *Divinations*; Kroeker, *Messianic Political Theology and Diaspora Ethics*; and Rashkover and Kavaka "Power and Israel in Martin Buber's Critique of Carl Schmitt's Political Theology." Schmitt has been more directly engaged as resource, although not without reservations, by Northcott in his *Political Theology of Climate Change*. A detailed analysis of Northcott's work is beyond the scope of the present study, but suffice to say that his emphasis on smaller local communities is much appreciated, although not unambivalently so.

allegedly post-sovereign context. These concerns exist as contrasting pairs, such as unity versus plurality; technicity versus Luddism; traditionalism opposed to progressivism; nationalism against globalism; and can be reduced to esoteric theory. However, as I will discuss, these concerns have practical ramifications that merit consideration. The trauma of World War I elicited these concerns within Schmitt, Benjamin, and many others who endured its horrors. These concerns rise to the forefront again at the outset of the twenty-first century, in some measure due to the conjunction of terrorism and the crisis of the nation-state. Schmitt's and Benjamin's wrestling with these concerns is worth revisiting, as their theoretical approaches reverberate in contemporary political theology.

Carl Schmitt's Political Theology

Carl Schmitt's political theology, and in particular his concept of sovereignty, is widely engaged in the academic discourse in political theology. Although Schmitt is by no means an uncontroversial figure, his theory holds something of fascination for anti-liberal thinkers from every position of the political spectrum, from far-left progressives to far-right conservatives.[8] As radical political theologian Clayton Crockett remarks, "On the right, Carl Schmitt's concept of the political conjoins perfectly with the neoconservative ideology of domination. On the left, it is Schmitt's analysis of the crisis of liberalism that is seen as prescient, even if his embrace of fascism is roundly rejected."[9] Schmitt perceived liberalism to be in crisis because in his view notions of freedom and equality collapsed to relativism or mere normativism with no capacity for true moral decision-making. Implicit in Schmitt's analysis of the crisis of liberalism is a critique of attempts to establish a legitimate sovereignty without the benefit of a transcendent divine. His embrace of domination, and ultimately fascism, constituted an effort to reinstate a source of transcendence capable of assuring moral order.

Carl Schmitt's *Political Theology: Four Chapters on the Concept of Sovereignty* first appeared in March 1922 and, by Schmitt's own account, remained unchanged at the time of its second publication twelve years later.[10] In his preface to the second edition, Schmitt identifies his primary

8. Examples of volumes written by left-leaning political thinkers who engage Carl Schmitt include the authors mentioned in the above note, along with Hardt and Negri, *Empire*. Neoconservative essays influenced by Schmitt include Kagan and Kristol, "What to Do About Iraq," and David Brooks, "A Return to National Greatness."

9. Crockett, *Radical Political Theology*, 49.

10. Schmitt, *Political Theology*, 1.

contention was with "liberal normativeness and its kind of 'constitutional state.'"[11] Schmitt mentions the German Weimar period (1919–1933) as his example of normativism. In Schmitt's opinion the legislators of that period did little more than authorize behaviors and attitudes that were already norms, rather than evaluate the morality, ethics, or rationale behind the particular norms themselves. The Weimar period was characterized by Schmitt as "a deteriorated and self-contradictory normativism . . . a degenerate decisionism, blind to the law, clinging to the 'normative power of the factual' and not to a genuine decision." As a consequence of its failure to cling to "a genuine decision," it proved powerless in the face of existential threats.[12]

Schmitt argues for a decisionist foundation for law—and politics— which in his opinion requires a sovereign. Schmitt opens *Political Theology* by declaring that the "sovereign is he who decides on the exception"[13] The exception, according to Schmitt, constitutes an exceptional emergency that poses an "extreme peril, a danger to the existence of the state, or the like."[14] Since the exception appears as an *unpredictable* emergency that can never be fully encompassed by the general norms, the decision as to whether or not an exception exists cannot be codified into any constitution or law. Since it poses an *existential* threat to the state, it demands a *decisive* response. When such an event occurs, it often happens that many interested parties believe they know the proper response, yet are in disagreement. Schmitt asserts that "sovereignty (and thus the state itself) resides in deciding this controversy, that is, in determining what constitutes public order and security" and having the authority to suspend law in response to the threat to order and security posed by the exception.

For example, generally Americans are protected from random searches by the fourth amendment, which prohibits searches of person

11. Ibid.

12. Ibid. It is challenging to pinpoint the precise threats to which Schmitt perceived the government incapable of responding, and he does not identify specific examples himself. To some degree Schmitt's assessment of the Weimar Republic might be regarded as rooted in Schmitt's nationalist tendencies. The Weimar Republic formed in the context of a significant defeat in World War I and a domestic revolution influenced by Bolshevism abroad. The Weimar Constitution was a valiant attempt to unify a culturally, economically, and politically diverse Germany in the form of a parliamentary democracy. Dissatisfaction arose shortly after the constitution was signed, as those on the right perceived democracy to be a "foreign import," and the Versailles Treaty made economic growth next to impossible in post-war Germany. Thus, the Weimar Republic never achieved a state of legitimacy. Please see Henig, *The Weimar Republic*.

13. Ibid., 5.

14. Ibid., 6.

or property without probable cause. Yet when boarding an aircraft in the United States, all persons are subject to search of their personal belongings, and even a highly intimate pat down. This is not in violation of the fourth amendment, however, because in 1973 the Ninth Circuit Court of Appeals determined that the existential threat posed by armed civilians entering aircraft warranted a suspension of the constitutional amendment in this situation.[15] This is a situation-specific suspension of law, demonstrating the exercise of a restricted, rather than absolute, judicial sovereignty in this case. Schmitt's point is that if no one in a nation possesses authority to suspend the laws of that nation in response to such an existential threat, the nation will succumb to the threat.

The example above involves a relatively isolated suspension of law in response to a more or less circumscribed threat. According to Schmitt, the decision on the exception and the appropriate response can only be martialed by a sovereign with unlimited authority. This unlimited authority is what distinguishes an exception from the example given above: "what characterizes an exception is principally unlimited authority," in particular the unlimited authority of the sovereign to suspend the constitution in its entirety.[16] What the decision upon the exception means is that an existential threat has arisen that warrants suspension of the law entirely, a decision that can only be rendered by a sovereign who is *above* the law. Thus, Schmitt insists that the only proof that a valid state exists is that in such a state exists one capable of determining when to suspend the laws of that very state—in order to maintain the security of the state itself. In Schmitt's opinion, "all tendencies of modern constitutional development point toward eliminating the sovereign in this sense."[17] Without the capacity to suspend the constitution—the very thing that establishes the state as such—the state cannot be secured.

Based on Schmitt's decisionist rendition of sovereignty, implicit in the avoidance of the decision is a negation of sovereignty and hence a depoliticization. As should be obvious from Schmitt's definition of both the sovereign and the exception, theories of state that do away with the sovereign or in any

15. Open Jurist. *United States vs. Davis.* n.d. http://openjurist.org/482/f2d/893/united-states-v-davis.

16. Schmitt, *Political Theology,* 7–12.

17. Ibid. Unlimited authority is decidedly what "checks and balances" are designed to prohibit. Incidentally, the decision on the exception is related to the friend/enemy distinction (Strong, "Foreword," xvi) in that the criminal "friend" necessitates the force of law, whereas the presence of the enemy warrants its suspension altogether. The friend–enemy distinction is, for Schmitt, "the criterion for the political and for a political theology" (Schmitt, *Political Theology II,* 122).

way limit the ability to decide upon the exception risk the very existence of the state because they undermine the ability to respond to the existential threat posed by the exception. More specifically, according to Schmitt, "if the individual states no longer have the power to declare the exception . . . then they no longer enjoy the status of states."[18] Schmitt is clearly suggesting that constitutional governments lacking identifiable sovereigns are unable to effectively respond to unexpected threats by suspending the law and are thus not truly sovereign. Conversely, the presence of a sovereign figure serves as guarantor of security.

History has proven Schmitt wrong in this regard. For example, even in Schmitt's own context of interwar Germany the endorsement of Hitler's unlimited authority to suspend the German constitution—in other words his sovereignty—did not catalyze the development of lasting stability for the German state. Despite this obvious fallacy, there are some theorists—both academic and armchair—who insist that the concept of the nation-state is intrinsically bound to a Schmittian-type sovereignty. If the theorist is right-leaning, their convictions in this regard lead them to wholeheartedly endorse strong executive actions they perceive vital to the interests of national security. Or, should the theorist be left-leaning and find nothing more terrifying than absolute authority, they are inclined to dismiss the importance of the state altogether, declaring the nation-state as political structure to be hopelessly entwined with oppressive power structures.

Resurgence of Nationalism

If Schmitt has so clearly been disproven by history, why even bother engaging Schmitt at all? The recent trend toward nationalism—both in Europe and the United States—is associated with the dominance of leaders exhibiting a rendition of sovereignty reminiscent of Schmitt, for example, the current president of the United States, Donald Trump.[19] Popular support for these leaders has been attributed, among other things, to the rise in immigration and economic pressures of transnational global capitalism. Reacting to what they perceive as an erosion of their "way of life"—their national identity and perceived entitlements—people in many countries have turned to nationalism, and particularly "ethno-nationalism" to shore up the boundaries of their nation-states and ward off the existential threat posed by immigration. Coincident with this turn to nationalism is the election of leaders exhibiting a Schmittian rendition of sovereignty.

18. Schmitt, *Political Theology*, 11.

19. *Economist*, "League of Nationalists."

What is less often highlighted in media coverage of immigration is the degree to which climate change and environmental degradation contribute to the rise in nationalism. For example, immigration results in part from climate change. While the more immediate cause is violent conflict, it is widely noted that these conflicts increase in prevalence due to climate change–induced drought, conflicts over access to grazable or arable land, and the food shortages that follow, as will be discussed in later chapters. What I hope to demonstrate in the coming chapters is that climate change–induced disasters will bring about—indeed, already *are* bringing about—demands for an absolute, Schmittian-type sovereignty capable of keeping the existential threat in abeyance. Yet, paradoxically the existential threat—both due to climate change and also other causes—increases when such unlimited authority as Schmitt calls for is enacted.

Although this book nears completion in Trump's first year in office, with his Schmittian tendencies everywhere evidenced, it was not written in response to Trump or Trumpism. Indeed, Trump's candidacy was not even in its infancy at the inception of this project toward the beginning of 2013. Instead my research was inspired by reading Christian Parenti's *Tropic of Chaos* in the same week I read Lester Brown's *Full Planet, Empty Plates: The New Geopolitics of Food Scarcity,* which had been a bit like reading the proverbial "writing on the wall."[20]

The regression to nationalist tendencies was predictable, despite the historical failure of nationalism in the last world war, on the basis of the geopolitical impacts of climate change Parenti documented, a situation likely to worsen given predictions for future climate-driven changes in resource availability. Even at this very early stage of manifestations of climate change we are witnessing regional drought, food shortages, and eruptions of violent conflict sufficiently widespread to warrant the descriptor "geopolitical instability."[21] In the face of this rising instability, critical masses of people are banding together in support of a dominant leader perceived as capable of assuring "national security." These are indeed ominous developments, and we are still early in the climate-change game.

Thus, while Schmitt's *Political Theology* is easily critiqued, his version of absolute sovereignty is not so easily eradicated as a fantasied solution to political chaos. Schmitt identifies features of liberal democracy held to

20. Parenti, *Tropic of Chaos.*

21. Copely, "The Big Picture Take on Geopolitical Instability." Admittedly, Copely does not trace the root causes of this instability to climate change, but rather addresses the "surface manifestations" of heightened conflict. My point is that the conflict can be traced to climate change issues, and also is so widespread (so early on) as to qualify as "geopolitical instability."

be problematic by both conservatives and progressives—albeit for different reasons. He names—and one might even say endorses—the visceral urgency for security that leads people to grant unlimited authority to a dominant leader. However, my sense is that theorists both right and left who insist that an unlimited sovereignty reminiscent of Schmitt's is inimically welded to the concept of a viable nation-state may be oversimplifying this connection. His critics on the left have identified the processes by which this version of sovereignty becomes itself an existential threat, thus countering the claims of those on the right that a strong, unilateral sovereign is a guarantor of a sovereign state. But yet I suggest that those on the left, such as Michael Hardt and Antonio Negri and others, are equally mistaken when they suggest that disbanding the nation-state will free us from tyrannical instantiations of sovereignty. Perhaps something akin to a "strategic sovereignty" based upon an iterative model of "people as process" might strike the balance required. Before launching into such a proposition, which will be undertaken in chapter 6, much more analysis of Schmittian/unilateral/top-down/absolute sovereignty—particularly its theological and metaphysical dimensions—in the context of global food politics on a planet in peril is needed.

The Unity of the Sovereign

Much of my critique of absolute sovereignty will rest upon a critique of the requirement for unity implicit in Schmitt's *Political Theology*. In later chapters, I will argue that the unity to which Schmitt appeals never in fact actualizes—not in a single human deemed "sovereign" nor in a group of people recognized as "sovereign." My critique is, in large part, a metaphysical statement embedded within the arguments of chapters 5 and 6 and based on theoretical science studies. For later chapters, it is essential to establish that the Schmittian sovereign is alleged to be a single individual characterized by unity whose decisions thereby confer unity and stability upon a collective in need of unification and stabilization. Let us begin.

Schmitt refers to the sovereign as "he." Schmitt's use of the singular masculine personal pronoun could be read as the personification of a legislative body, such as a congress or parliament, as this "he" who is sovereign. According to George Schwab, writing the introduction to *Political Theology*, despite Schmitt's acceptance of constitutional democracies, he sought to restore indivisibility to the sovereign.[22] Schmitt does so by declaring the sovereign to be "the popularly elected president."[23] Thus

22. Schwab, "Introduction," xlii.
23. Schmitt, *Political Theology*, l.

according to Schwab, Schmitt envisions the sovereign as a single human being, and not a legislative body.

Schmitt's own words on the topic might be more persuasive, if yet more challenging to unravel, than Schwabb's assessment of Schmitt's writing. Schmitt states that if the capacity to decide upon an exception "is not hampered in some way by checks and balances, as is the case in a liberal constitution, then it is clear who the sovereign is."[24] Perhaps he means to say that the system of checks and balances renders precise points of decision invisible, but that collectively the bodies that "check and balance" one another's power constitute a sovereign decision-making body. However, Schmitt says that "The essence of liberalism is negotiation . . . in the hope that the definitive dispute, the decisive battle, can be transformed into a parliamentary debate and permit the decision to be suspended forever in an everlasting discussion."[25] He is suggesting that the point of legislative assemblies is to *avoid* the decision, and thus to avoid sovereignty insofar as sovereignty *requires* a decision based upon Schmitt's earlier definition.

So perhaps what he really means to say is that if a sovereign exists in a constitutional democracy, it is not the collective of bodies that check and balance one another's power. The group as a whole is never the decision-maker, despite superficial appearances to the contrary. Behind the scenes lies an individual decider—by Schmitt's definition, a single individual enacting sovereignty. While the precise identity of the sovereign is obscured by the checks and balances, the sovereign remains nonetheless an individual decider.[26]

Additionally, against supporters of an association theory of the state—who might be said to argue for a sort of popular sovereignty or assemblage theory that expresses the "will of the people"—Schmitt is clear: "If the state is pushed into playing the role of a mere proclaiming herald, then it can no longer be sovereign."[27] He identifies such a "community, based on associations and constituted from below" as failing to account for the fact that legal concepts, in their "general universality," inevitably require a decision in order to judge "a concrete fact concretely." Such a normative concept of law as association theory merely designates "how decisions should be made, not who should decide" (and quite possibly Schmitt might say the same of

24. Ibid., 7.

25. Ibid., 63.

26. Reminiscent of Douglas Adams's line in *Hitchhiker's Guide to the Galaxy*, "The President of the Universe holds no real power. His sole purpose is to take attention away from where power actually exists." Although for Schmitt this would be more true of a parliament than of a president.

27. Ibid., 25.

popular sovereignty).[28] While these populist or assemblage-like structures theorize a process for decision-making, Schmitt—following Hobbes—declares that "what matters for the reality of legal life is who decides."[29] In other words, collective decision-making is no substitute for the sovereign; ultimately it is an individual who must decide for the state, if the state can be said to be sovereign.

Schmitt's Reliance upon a Transcendent God

Schmitt contends that his version of sovereignty is modeled on a theological concept of God. Schmitt maintains that "all significant concepts of the modern theory of the state are secularized theological concepts."[30] The relationship between the modern state and secularized theological concepts is a matter of developmental trajectory, as the state form emerged as the West became increasingly secularlized. And there is also a matter of structural analogy between "the exception in jurisprudence" and "the miracle in theology."[31] Schmitt insists that a true understanding of the development of the concepts of the state relies upon understanding the infusion of these concepts with the theological.

Schmitt's concept of immanence and transcendences is not identical to the usage of those terms as metaphysical signifiers in theology or philosophy. For Schmitt, there is a structural analogy between God as transcendent to the material world and the sovereign as transcendent to the state such that while from a metaphysical perspective the sovereign is also immanent with regards to the material, creaturely world, from the perspective of the state the sovereign can be regarded as transcendent. For Schmitt, the immanent domain of the physical world is a locus of problems in need of solutions that can only arrive from the transcendent sphere. By way of analogy, the state itself is perceived as an immanent domain in need of stabilization that can only be guaranteed by a sovereign who is unbound by the constitution that determines the boundaries of the state itself.

Schmitt goes on to say that "The metaphysical image that a definite epoch forges of the world has the same structure as what the world immediately understands to be appropriate as a form of political organization."[32]

28. Ibid., 24–33.

29. Ibid., 34.

30. Ibid., 36.

31. Ibid.

32. Ibid., 46. The metaphysical dualism inspiring Schmitt's analogy will be critiqued throughout the study albeit most often obliquely. Furthermore, Schmitt's failure to

Despite its trend toward secularity, the same holds true for the modern constitutional state, according to Schmitt:

> The idea of the modern constitutional state triumphed together with deism, a theology and metaphysics that banished the miracle from the world. This theology and metaphysics rejected not only the transgression of the laws of nature through an exception brought about by direct intervention, as is found in the idea of a miracle, but also the sovereign's direct intervention in a valid legal order. The rationalism of the Enlightenment rejected the exception in every form.[33]

Is it possible that Schmitt intends this as critique of those who would rush to endorse a form of government solely because it conforms to their metaphysical image of the world? This question is pressing, as a political theology of food will stridently argue against absolute sovereignty on the basis that it is dissonant with the metaphysical image of the world as disclosed by science studies.

If we have learned nothing from the historical trajectory of science and metaphysical images, at least we have learned that we are almost certainly incorrect regarding some aspect of the metaphysical image we currently hold. As faulty as it may be, our metaphysical image is the closest approximation we can generate of empirical experience. For example, at one point seizures were attributed to spirit possession, whereas now we understand this to be caused by disorganized firing of brain cells. To reject empirical evidence of how things (seem to) work in the material world when making important decisions seems foolhardy. Each historical metaphysical image held explanatory power in its day; it was not considered mythological or even mere image. It accounted for real experiences. I would argue against any effort to discredit metaphysical images as valid inspiration for political structure by suggesting that despite being faulty, a metaphysical image

---

recognize that the sovereign is not *in fact* transcendent to the immanent plane renders him vulnerable to critique from religious-minded thinkers such as Karl Barth (to be discussed in chapter 6) and Martin Buber, along with Walter Benjamin (discussed below).

33. Ibid., 37. Here it is important to mention that Schmitt to some degree follows in the footsteps of his teacher Max Weber. The degree to which Schmitt follows in Weber's footsteps versus upends Weber's thesis is hotly contested. There are some who use Schmitt's connection to Weber to style Weber as a proto-fascist, and others who perceive Schmitt's thesis to be a rejection of Weber altogether. Integrating both perspectives are those who affirm that Schmitt performed a double maneuver by which he solidified his legitimacy on the basis of his ties to Weber, then proceeded to dismantle Weber's liberalism once his authority had been established. See Engelbrekt, "What Carl Schmitt Picked Up in Weber's Seminar," and Magalhaes, "A Contingent Affinity."

nonetheless generally accounts for lived experience, which seems the ultimately valid basis for political and social structures.

I do not believe Schmitt was critiquing the general practice of model-
ing political arrangements on metaphysical understandings. I believe that
Schmitt is suggesting that when empirical reality (in the form of what might
be called modern science) failed to bear evidence that "miracles" occur, the
modern constitutional state rejected the idea of miracles, and the exception
right along with it. Schmitt equates the exception with decision-making,
and, hence, with sovereignty. Despite modernity's explicit rejection of the
exception, a rejection that would seem to speak against decision-making
and sovereignty, Schmitt contends that nonetheless a decision-making
power lurks beneath the surface: "there appears a huge cloak-and-dagger
drama, in which the state acts in many disguises but always as the same invisible person."[34] Schmitt likens this to the plot device of a *deus ex machina*.

What remains unclear is precisely why Schmitt insists upon preserving
the exception, the "transcendence" of God, and the concept of sovereignty
as central to his political theology. A related essay, *The Age of Neutralization and Depoliticization* might provide clues. Written in 1929, Schmitt
argued that the "central domain" of concern displayed a secularization of
theological concepts throughout four stages beginning in the sixteenth century. Schmitt's concept of a central domain refers to a framework or set of
priorities within which political discourse finds its relevance. Schmitt refers
to these domains as the theological, the metaphysical, the humanitarian-
moral, and the economic. Schmitt is clear that there is no decisive break
between these epochs, and that these do not represent any sort of progres-
sion or regression. He asserts that these domains represent:

> the fact that in these four centuries of European history the in-
> tellectual vanguard changed, that its convictions and arguments
> continued to change, as did the content of its intellectual inter-
> ests, the basis of its actions, the secret of its political success, and
> the willingness of the great masses to be impressed by certain
> suggestions.[35]

These were changes, above all, in the priorities by which values were assigned to people, actions, and circumstances.

The significance of these domains for the general populace is that these
domains lend specific content to what are otherwise ambiguous concepts.
For example, in the context of the eighteenth century, which Schmitt aligns
with the humanitarian-moral age, the ambiguous notion of progress "meant

34. Schmitt, *Political Theology*, 38.
35. Schmitt, "Age of Secularization and Depoliticization," 83.

above all progress in culture, self-determination, and education: *moral perfection*."[36] All problems and solutions are calculated in the terms provided by the central domain, in this case morality. Provided the issues related to the central domain are "in order, everything else is 'provided' by definition."[37] He goes on to say that "above all the *state* also derives its reality and power from the respective central domain, because the decisive disputes of friend-enemy groupings are also determined by it."[38] According to Schmitt, the same state cannot entertain two different formulations of the same domain: in an economic epoch "one and the same state cannot accommodate two contradictory economic systems."[39] Schmitt also contends that a state that does not "claim to understand and direct" relations based upon the central domain of the epoch "must declare itself neutral with respect to political questions and decisions and thereby renounce its claim to rule."[40]

Schmitt considered the intellectual shift from theology to "natural" science to be "the strongest and most consequential" of all epochal shifts. This is because at the core of this epoch is the "striving for a neutral domain" which Schmitt perceives to be a reaction to the enormous conflicts that characterized the theological domain with its monarchical system of rule. As Schmitt states:

> Theology, the former central domain, was abandoned because it was controversial, in favor of another—neutral—domain. The former central domain became neutralized in that it ceased to be the central domain. On the basis of the new central domain, one hoped to find minimum agreement and common premises allowing for the possibility of security, clarity, prudence, and peace.[41]

Schmitt argues that in the early part of the twentieth century it was commonly believed that the much sought-after neutral ground had at last been found in technology. Schmitt, writing in the first half of the twentieth century, observed that "the twentieth century began as the age not only of technology but of a religious belief in technology," which he refers to as technicity.[42] Thus it would appear as though the twentieth century heralded

36. Ibid., 86.
37. Ibid.
38. Ibid., 87.
39. Ibid., 88.
40. Ibid.
41. Ibid., 89.
42. Ibid., 85.

a new epoch. Schmitt regards this as problematic because technical prin-ciples and perspectives alone do not settle political disputes.[43]

In Schmitt's view, although this new epoch is neutral, it is not spirit-less. Schmitt insists that the epoch of technicity reveals "the belief in an activistic metaphysics—belief in unlimited power and the domination of man over nature, even over human nature; the belief in the unlimited 'receding of natural boundaries,' in the unlimited possibilities for change and prosperity."[44] Thus, Schmitt opines, the spirit of technicity might "be called fantastic and satanic, but not simply dead, spiritless, or mechanized soullessness."[45] This technicity is, according to Schmitt, a "torpid religion" to which "great masses of industrialized peoples" adhere because of subcon-scious belief that "the absolute depoliticization sought after four centuries can be found here, and that universal peace begins here."[46]

The final paragraphs of this essay leave me with a sense of incomple-tion, of arguments alluded to but not announced, and conclusions hinted at but not driven home. I will try to piece together what I believe Schmitt is saying, because I perceive it as exceedingly relevant to Schmitt's over-all concern with sovereignty in general. First, Schmitt names the fact that technology per se is not an unambiguous good: it is "equally available to both [peace and war]."[47] Next he asserts that "nothing changes by speaking in the name of . . . peace" and goes on to say that "the most terrible war is pursued only in the name of peace, the most terrible oppression only in the name of freedom, and the most terrible inhumanity only in the name of humanity."[48] Schmitt is difficult to dismiss in this lucid moment, identifying the tragic dimension of political life and anticipating a noteworthy concern of postsecular theorists in this observation.

Schmitt then insists that we must:

> recognize the pluralism of spiritual life and know that the cen-tral domain of spiritual existence cannot be a neutral domain . . .
> life struggles not with death, spirit not with spiritlessness; spirit
> struggles with spirit, life with life, and out of the power of an in-tegral understanding of this arises the order of human things.[49]

43. Ibid., 92.
44. Ibid., 94.
45. Ibid., 95.
46. Ibid.
47. Ibid., 95.
48. Ibid.
49. Ibid., 26.

What spirits are struggling with other spirits in this scenario? Schmitt is suggesting that the "spirit of technicity" is at odds with some other spiritual value system, never named. He is adamant that the "neutral ground" sought as a corrective to political conflict can neither eliminate conflict nor assure a moral outcome. His argument reverberates ominously, yet inconclusively.

He does not come out and *say* that neutrality per se is satanic or evil, but he leads us there by what is referred to in mathematics as the transitive property: if "a" equals "b" and "b" equals "c" then "a" equals "c." Schmitt insisted that neutrality characterizes technicity. Technicity, in Schmitt's reading, is evil; for how else might we read his assertion that the spirit of technicity is "satanic?" Thus, presumptions of neutrality may also be said to be evil. Schmitt suggests that, despite its claims to provide peace, in fact the greatest of all atrocities will be committed in the context of the technological domain *because* it is neutral, and therefore the system itself promotes no means of valuation and thus no boundaries for human behavior—moral or otherwise. Lacking an internal moral framework, technology, technicity, and neutrality with them, abandon us to the wilderness of a dog-eat-dog world. If technicity is the central domain, the new world order proves to be terrifying indeed.

According to Tracy B. Strong, in his foreword to Schmitt's *Political Theology*, "The point of the analysis of the centrality of the exception for sovereignty is precisely to restore, in a democratic age, the element of transcendence that had been there in the sixteenth and even the seventeenth centuries . . . Failing that, the triumph of non-political, inhuman technologizing will be inevitable."[50] By virtue of Schmitt's own assertion that all modern concepts of the state are secularized theological concepts, and the fact that he equates neutral technicity with evil, he recapitulates a longstanding drama between a transcendent good and an immanent (or, Schmitt might say, technological) evil.

However, as described in the following chapter, enactments of a unilateral, Schmittian-type sovereignty on the part of those who set global food policy (World Trade Organization, International Monetary Fund, World Bank) are no guarantee against "inhuman technologizing" that deploys ever more technologically intense agricultural methods with inhumane results. Thus, the reason for devoting so much time and attention to Schmitt's political theology and his theory of secularization. Schmitt's concerns about potentially deadly deployments of technology, depoliticization of contemporary life, and the need to respond decisively to chaotic events are not unique to him. These same concerns emerge in the context

50. Strong, "Foreword," xxv.

of environmental activism in general and the food movement in particular. However, Schmitt's solutions to these problems will nonetheless fail to satisfy the moral and ethical demands of those movements. These demands arise in the context of an altogether different metaphysics that does not so easily link transcendent with good and immanent with evil, as will be described in detail in the subsequent chapters.

Before going into further detail on the metaphysical and moral disputes contra Schmitt, it must be noted that Schmitt insists that resurrecting the concept of sovereignty is vital to preservation of "the political." For example, Strong observes, if "the political is in danger of disappearing as a human form of life, this can only be because sovereignty as Schmitt understands it is increasingly not a constituent part of our present world."[51] My analysis will unveil strong opposition to Schmitt's argument that the elimination of his version of sovereignty amounts to depoliticization.

The concept of "the political" is not exhausted by, nor even best represented by, decisions upon the exception that shore up the boundaries of the state, as Schmitt seems to imply. Surely "the political" describes the social arrangements *internal to the state* along with the interactions between states. Food activists would also argue quite the opposite of Schmitt's assertion. They would argue that enactments of transcendent sovereignty are short-circuiting political processes internal to the nation-states themselves. Thus, Schmitt's insistence on a single, centralized (and therefore transcendent) sovereign could be said to constitute an undermining, rather than a restoration of, the political.

For example, the chaotic events likely to occur in the context of climate change will take the form of environmental disasters and also international conflicts. Environmental disasters are regional events arguably requiring the distribution of sovereignty (decision-making authority) to address them; a centralized sovereign may impair the restoration of order in those events. For example, after Superstorm Sandy the grassroots organization Occupy Sandy demonstrated the way in which grassroots efforts can be more efficient at providing disaster relief to impoverished areas notably underserved by top-down approaches to disaster relief.[52] Ecological arguments against Schmitt's model of sovereignty will be more fully explored in later chapters.

---

51. Ibid., xxii.
52. Feuer, "Occupy Sandy."

Theologically Problematic Concepts Embedded in Schmitt's Theory

Even more important than questions about unity and ability to restore order, are the metaphysically, theologically problematic concepts that underlie Schmitt's grafting of monarchically structured sovereignty to the democratic process. It is possible that Schmitt's personal experience of World War I in some sense diminished his estimation of God's importance vis-à-vis the purpose of the state. Before World War I, Schmitt believed that the Catholic church was the moral determinant of right, and although the church preceded the state in importance, the purpose of the state was to realize the aims of the church. After the war, Schmitt "perceived the role of the state as the securing of conditions under which citizens could pursue their private wills."[53] This is a decidedly more limited role for both state and God, yet Schmitt insists on God's importance in his very formulation of political theology.

What is this about? Is his turn to this traditional, Hobbesian, absolute sovereignty the cynical move of someone who has given up on God? The move of someone who now—since he has given up on an actual God to bring order to earth and instead insists upon following a sovereign leader—will behave in a manner very much Godlike? By Schmitt's own account, his Catholic faith was "dis-placed" and "de-totalized."[54] While Schmitt lost faith in his Catholic theology, he did not gain an equal faith in liberal political progress.

Schmitt believes that a metaphysical kernel lies at the heart of all political theories, and in the technological domain he has glimpsed a metaphysical kernel with no moral statement whatsoever, a metaphysical kernel that does not assure security. He says that "In political reality there is no irresistible highest or greatest power that operates according to the certainty of natural law."[55] On the one hand, if technology is based upon natural law, nothing could be more certain—or at least certainly predictable (according to Schmitt's understanding of natural law, which differs with the one elucidated by science studies, to be described at length in later chapters). On the other hand, this would imply that if technology does not carry an implicit moral code then *neither does natural law.*

The problem Schmitt struggles with is how to fortify the political through re-enchantment:

53. Schwab, "Foreword," xxxviii.

54. Ibid., xxix–xxx.

55. Schmitt, *Political Theology*, 18.

Schmitt, who had been a student of Max Weber, accepts the idea of the "demagification" or "disenchantment" of the world. To say that all concepts in modern state theory are secularized theological concepts is not to want to restore to those concepts a theological dimension, but it is to point to the fact that what has been lost since the sixteenth ("theological") century has amounted to a hollowing-out of political concepts. They thus no longer have, as it were, the force and strength that they had earlier, and they are unable to resist the dynamics of technology.[56]

Schmitt's assessment that the immanent, neutral plane gave rise to an evil technicity has already been described in detail above. In response to his fears of this evil, Schmitt emphasizes the exception, thus restoring the transcendence of both divine and human soveriegnty to a position of centrality in his political theology, thus reenchanting the political.[57]

Unfortunately, Schmitt attempts to undo the political hollowness without addressing the problematic theological and metaphysical concepts that have been operative all along. He fails to question whether alternative concepts of God might prove more compelling, more enchanting to a modern audience in a way that might "challenge the dynamics of technology" by producing a moral framework to guide its deployment. And for that, he can be forgiven. He is not a trained theologian. He is disappointed in the transcendent God as a restraint on human behavior during World War I, and does not observe evidence of a moral framework in the immanent domain. Confidence in human sovereignty notwithstanding, he holds "the belief that man is basically dangerous and that his primary goal is physical security" so he "opted for a strong state that would ensure order, peace, and stability."[58] Here he is in good historical company, expressing sentiments surfacing in Hobbes's *Leviathan*, Augustine's *City of God*, and even the *Pirkei Avot*, a second-century rabbinic compilation.[59]

For Schmitt, national stability becomes something of a moral good in itself. On the one hand this is ironic given his anxieties about the lack of moral valuation characteristic of the immanent domain and technicity

---

56. Strong, "Foreword," xxiv–xxv.

57. Ibid. Indeed, "fears of evil" often generate or amplify desires for a transcendent sovereign capable of restoring order and providing safety. This seems to be evidenced by the general trend toward escalating nationalisms observed in world politics of the moment.

58. Ibid., xlix–l.

59. *Pirkei Avot* 3:4: "Rabbi Chanina, the deputy High Priest, said: Pray for the welfare of the government, for were it not for fear of it, people would swallow one another alive."

with it. On the other hand, because the transcendent God has been dismissed as a guarantor of order, the sovereign is permitted to fulfill not only the vacancy left behind but also to fulfill the need for moral valuation in the immanent domain. Whereas at one point Schmitt may have believed that obedience to God would assure stability because God promotes moral goods, now he insists that obedience to the sovereign leader is itself a moral good because the sovereign promotes stability, which at least passes for a moral good in Schmitt's estimation.

Schmitt does not identify his desire for order, peace, and stability as themselves imbued with theological concepts. Nonetheless, I suggest that the desire for order and peace can be read as the remnant of not only a theological doctrine of God, but also of a theological *narrative* prevalent in the West. For example, in *Reinventing Eden: The Fate of Nature in Western Culture,* Carolyn Merchant identifies this narrative as the Recovery of Eden story, which she argues is "the mainstream narrative of Western culture."[60] According to this narrative, Eden represents the once-pristine world in which humans are imagined to have originated, a world now lost due to human error. The trajectory of Western culture, according to Merchant, has been aiming at the recovery of this lost Eden, which I contend is parallel to Schmitt's desire for order, peace, and stability.

For Merchant, there are two versions of this narrative that differ regarding the source of redemption. In one version, "humanity can be redeemed through Christianity"[61] and in the other "the way upward could be found through science, technology, capitalist development, and a new vision of the modern state."[62] Schmitt's assessment of technology seems to be that the second narrative leads us down a blind alley. Schmitt "notes, as had Hobbes, that there is in Christianity a dangerous tendency to introduce rebellion into the political realm."[63] Subsequently, Schmitt backtracks to a secularized concept of God. Troublingly, in Schmitt's version, humanity will be redeemed (secured) not through Christ or Christian practice. Instead, humanity will be secured through the sovereign, configured not as God made flesh but as flesh made God when absolute sovereignty is bestowed upon a human political leader.

The recovery narrative identified by Carolyn Merchant represents not only a desire to return to our imagined paradisiacal origins, but also an *eschatological* vision of the future very much consonant with the Christian

60. Merchant, *Reinventing Eden,* 2.

61. Ibid., 11.

62. Ibid., 63.

63. Strong, "Foreword," xxxii.

tradition. The restoration of creation is very much intrinsic to images of the New Jerusalem as depicted in the Book of Revelation.[64] Indeed, contemporary interpretations of The Book of Revelation, such as those by Harry O. Meier and Barbara Rossing, understand the text as the promise of a renewed Eden.[65] Thus, one begins to hear polyphonic resonances between the backwards-looking attempt to recover a lost Eden and the forward-looking hope for the eschatologically promised establishment of a New Jerusalem as these images oscillate throughout the historical trajectory Merchant surveys.

The implicit eschatology of the recovery narrative Merchant identifies, and its involvement of not only human political structures but also the arrangement of human/non-human relationships contingent upon those structures, becomes important in the critique of political theological concepts of sovereignty put forth here. Political theology, and sovereignty in particular, are often cast with a messianic hue. The messianism implicit in both concepts has been no less responsible for the phenomena Merchant observes than has the desire to retreat to a lost Eden. In fact, eschatological hope that a lasting order can be finally achieved is what prompts Schmitt to endorse absolute sovereignty.

Before offering further critique on the messianism and eschatology implicit in the concept of absolute sovereignty, a critique that will unfold throughout the remaining chapters, let us turn to the conception of sovereignty put forth by Walter Benjamin, a contemporary of Schmitt's whose messianically-tinged work is also commonly cited by political theorists and theologians of the twenty-first century.[66]

Walter Benjamin's Critique of Sovereignty

Walter Benjamin was a German Jewish literary theorist and philosopher, and contemporary of Carl Schmitt's. Disillusioned with liberal politics, Benjamin aligned himself with the Marxist cause. Benjamin's initial foray into political theology was a 1921 essay, "Critique of Violence," penned in support of the proletarian strike of 1920. Giorgio Agamben and Jacques

---

64. Southgate, *Groaning of Creation,* 370.

65. See for example: Maier, "There's a New World Coming!," and Rossing, "For the Healing of the World."

66. See for example: Agamben, *State of Exception*; Derrida, "Force of Law," 920–1045; Crockett, *Radical Political Theology*; and Miguez, Rieger, and Sung, *Beyond the Spirit of Empire*.

Derrida both argue that Carl Schmitt likely wrote *Political Theology* in response to the depiction of sovereignty proposed in Benjamin's essay.[67]

It is likely that Schmitt and Benjamin greatly influenced one another's work. In fact, Marc de Wilde argues that "the political theologies of Benjamin and Schmitt... developed in the course of their dialogue, in which both authors respond to each other's criticism by changing and correcting their own positions in significant ways."[68] The two men rarely communicated directly, conducting their dialogue by means of academic publications. Their references to one another were oblique, and they seldom cited one another explicitly. Yet evidence exists that the two communicated directly.

For example, in 1930 Benjamin sent a copy of *The Origin of German Tragic Drama* to Carl Schmitt along with a letter reading as follows:

> You will very quickly recognize how much my book is indebted to you for its presentation of the doctrine of sovereignty in the seventeenth century. Perhaps I may say, in addition, that I have also derived from your later works, especially *Die Diktatur*, a confirmation of my modes of research in the philosophy of art from yours in the philosophy of the state.[69]

Although Benjamin expresses his indebtedness to Schmitt, this should not be construed as Benjamin's endorsement of the type of unilateral, top-down sovereignty proposed by Schmitt. Since the mid-1980s, careful research has demonstrated that "although Benjamin had borrowed Schmitt's concepts, he injected them into new contexts in which their original meanings were challenged and opposed."[70] These careful distinctions are vitally important in light of Benjamin's Jewishness and Schmitt's eventual affiliation with the Nazi Party.

Both Schmitt and Benjamin held liberalism and parliamentary democracy to be problematic forms of governance, but they approached the dilemmas from different vantage points: Benjamin from the far-left socialist perspective, and Schmitt from the extreme right.[71] Also, both men perceived the political sphere to be haunted by theological concepts that had been secularized and thus neutralized. It is precisely due to their secularization and neutralization that these theological concepts could not be publicly discussed *as* theological concepts. As a corollary to their understanding of the political as haunted by the theological, both men construed sovereignty as a messianic

67. Agamben, *State of Exception,* 52–53; Derrida, "Force of Law:"920–1045.

68. de Wilde, "Meeting Opposites," 363.

69. Ibid., 364.

70. Ibid., 365.

71. Ibid., 363–65.

project, at least initially.[72] However, according to de Wilde, in the metaphoric resonances of Benjamin, the proletariat revolutionary general strike of 1918 was the messianic moment, whereas in Schmitt's case the messianic metaphor was to be found in the image of the sovereign as transcendent figure "capable of creating a completely restored order."[73]

One preliminary point, raised by Derrida, is important to note in beginning, as keeping it in mind while reading excerpts from "Critique of Violence" raises one's awareness to the resonances and dissonances between Benjamin and Schmitt:

> Zur Kritik der Gewalt: "translated in French as "Critique de la violence" and in English as "Critique of Violence." But these two translations, while not altogether *injuste* (and so not altogether violent), are very active interpretations that don't do justice to the fact that *Gewalt* also signifies, for Germans, legitimate power, authority, public force. *Gesetzgebende Gewalt* is legislative power, *geistliche Gewalt* the spiritual power of the church, *Staatsgewalt* the authority or power of the state. *Gewalt*, then, is both violence and legitimate power, justified authority.[74]

In other words, it is not merely the use of violence that Benjamin calls into question, but the state itself, a position diametrically opposed to Schmitt's desire to shore up the state as a means to assuring stability. Thus, despite sharing anti-liberal sentiments and theological motivations, the two men position themselves differently vis-à-vis the state.

Benjamin directs his critique toward violence as a means, rather than assessing the ends it serves. Benjamin argues that to critique violence in light of the ends toward which it is directed merely illuminates appropriate instances in which violence as a principle may be applied.[75] He wishes instead to question violence *on principle*. He notes that the state attempts to subdue violence among its citizenry by settling disputes through law. The state, he believes, does not wish to hold a monopoly on violence because violence is morally wrong *per se*, but rather because extra-state violence poses an existential threat to the legal system itself.

The particular non-state violence Benjamin wishes to interrogate is the revolutionary general strike. The violence of which striking workers

---

72. Ibid., 365; Martel, *Divine Violence*, 47; Derrida, "Force of Law," 979. De Wilde argues that after 1933 Schmitt abandons the messianic vision in favor of a vision of the sovereign as parallel to Paul's *katechon*.

73. deWilde, "Meeting Opposites," 374.

74. Derrida, "Force of Law," 927.

75. Benjamin, "Critique of Violence," 277–300.

were accused was simply that of not showing up to work, *en masse*, therefore disrupting production and consumption of material goods. Benjamin asserts that the "right to strike conceded to labor is certainly not a right to exercise violence but, rather, to escape from a violence indirectly exercised by the employer."[76] However, the state would object to a revolutionary general strike, arguing that this revolutionary purpose exceeds the intentions of the legal protection bestowed upon striking laborers.[77] In Benjamin's view, it is only if the workers exercise this right "in order to overthrow the legal system that has conferred" the right to strike, that the general strike "may be called violent." Above all, according to Benjamin, the state fears the passive violence of the general strike.[78]

Benjamin elucidates two contrasting but related concepts of violence as means. Of violence as means Benjamin states "If, therefore, conclusions can be drawn from military violence, as being primordial and paradigmatic of all violence used for natural ends, there is inherent in all such violence a lawmaking character."[79] It is for this reason that the state desires a monopoly on violence: it *really* desires a monopoly on lawmaking. Benjamin goes on to declare that "all violence as a means is either lawmaking or law-preserving. If it lays claim to neither of these predicates it forfeits all validity."[80] I think here Benjamin is not endorsing violence directed toward those means, but merely observing that violence is rendered socially acceptable, if it is at all, only when it serves those purposes.

Furthermore, "lawmaking is power making, and to that extent, an immediate manifestation of violence. Justice is the principle of all divine end making, power the principle of all mythical law making."[81] Law is inherently violent and unjust, not least because it lacks the "divine" qualifier but because "ends that are for one situation just, universally acceptable and valid, are so for no other situation, no matter how similar it may be in other respects."[82] In other words, as with Schmitt earlier, laws are general and their application is particular; applications of laws in situations to which they are not suited render them unjust. For both Schmitt and Benjamin this is no small problem.

76. Ibid., 281.

77. Ibid., 282: "state will call this . . . an abuse, since the right to strike was not 'so intended.'"

78. Ibid.

79. Ibid., 283.

80. Ibid., 287.

81. Ibid., 295.

82. Ibid., 294.

For Schmitt, this problem is solved by implementing his concept of the sovereign—modeled on God; for Benjamin by setting up the sovereign's *opposition* to God. Benjamin refers to both law-making and law-preserving violence together as "mythical violence," through which the mythical foundations of lawmaking and law-preserving violence are laid bare: "Far from inaugurating a purer sphere, the mythical manifestation of immediate violence shows itself fundamentally identical with all legal violence."[83] Benjamin further distinguishes mythic violence from divine violence in a passage worthy of quoting at length:

> If mythical violence is lawmaking, divine violence is law-destroying; if the former sets boundaries, the latter boundlessly destroys them; if mythical violence brings at once guilt and retribution, divine power only expiates; if the former threatens, the latter strikes; if the former is bloody, the latter is lethal without spilling blood . . . For blood is the symbol of mere life . . . [and] . . . Mythical violence is bloody power over mere life for its own sake, divine violence is pure power over all life for the sake of the living. The first demands sacrifice, the second accepts it.[84]

Not only has Benjamin already in 1921 declared the making and reinforcing of state boundaries to be mythological rather than divine in origin, he has also introduced a theme that will be taken up by Giorgio Agamben—that of mere life.

One must read the above with caution. Certainly, Benjamin conceives of the *possibility* that divine violence might happen via human action—and the revolutionary general strike may present just such an instance. While that abstract possibility is certain, the identification of any particular concrete instantiation is less so: "For only mythical violence, not divine, will be recognizable as such with certainty . . . because the expiatory power of violence is not visible to men."[85] We cannot, therefore, legitimate revolutionary efforts to overthrow unjust laws by claiming divine origins of *those* efforts any more than we can substantiate our support of "the sovereign" on the grounds of his divinity. Divine approval of either option is not immediately forthcoming. It is this uncertainty, and the subsequent weight of responsibility, that Benjamin leaves us to grapple with.

Whether or not one concurs with Agamben, Derrida, and their followers that Schmitt wrote *Political Theology* in response to Benjamin's "Critique of Violence," more direct evidence leads us to conclude that Benjamin's 1928

83. Ibid., 296.
84. Ibid.
85. Ibid., 300.

publication *The Origin of German Tragic Drama* [*Ursprung des deutschen Trauerspiels*] was a response, and perhaps a rebuttal, to Schmitt's *Political Theology*.[86] In fact, Benjamin cites Schmitt's *Political Theology* verbatim:

> If one wishes to explain how 'the lively awareness of the signifi-cance of the state of emergency, which is dominant in the natu-ral law of the seventeenth century' disappears in the following century, it is not therefore enough simply to refer to the greater political stability of the eighteenth century.[87]

In the above, Benjamin directly quotes Schmitt regarding the "lively aware-ness of the significance of the state of emergency," and proceeds to just as directly disagree with him. Whereas Schmitt indicates that this "disappear-ance" of "lively awareness" occurred "when a relatively lasting order was established,"[88] Benjamin frankly doubts the establishment of a lasting order to be an explanation for the significance of the state of emergency in the seventeenth century, and urges the examination of additional facts.

If such forthright disagreement is noted in his engagement with Schmitt, in what way can Benjamin be said to be indebted to him? Accord-ing to philosopher Samuel Weber, the debt owed was related to "a certain *methodological extremism*" found in the work of both men, insofar as both took as their subject of inquiry the limit case—the state of exception.[89] Fur-ther, Benjamin and Schmitt agree that "the modern doctrine of sovereignty originates in the Counter-Reformation's 'ideal of a complete stabilization' and longing for an 'ecclesiastical and political restoration.'"[90] While both men endorse a sort of methodological extremism, and place the roots of the modern concept of sovereignty in the Counter-Reformation, Benjamin's goal in *Trauerspiel* is to demonstrate how the German baroque dramatists were critiquing the modern doctrine of sovereignty at its inception.[91]

Benjamin insists that "whereas the modern concept of sovereignty amounts to a supreme executive power on the part of the prince, the Ba-roque concept emerges from a discussion of the state of emergency, and makes it the most important function of the prince to avert this."[92] Philoso-

86. Benjamin, *The Origin of German Tragic Drama*.

87. Schmitt, *Political Theology*, 66.

88. Ibid.,14.

89. Weber, "Taking Exception to Decision," 7, emphasis in the original.

90. de Wilde, "Meeting Opposites," 372.

91. The Counter-Reformation dates from roughly the mid-sixteenth to mid-seventeenth centuries; the German Baroque from the mid- to late-sixteenth until the mid-eighteenth centuries.

92. Benjamin, *Critique of Violence*, 65.

pher Samuel Weber finds this to be a "slight but decisive modification of [Schmitt's] theory." [93] I don't find this modification to be whatsoever slight; it immediately and efficiently dispatches with Schmitt's "sovereign is he who decides on the exception." Furthermore, the modification is *decisive*—the most essential attribute of the sovereign as defined by Schmitt. It is as if Benjamin has wrested the sovereignty to decide upon the very question of sovereignty *away* from Schmitt.

Although both seem to agree that the Counter-Reformation, in conjunction with theological ideations, led to the formulation of a modern sovereignty rather similar to Schmitt's, Benjamin indicates a shift in the underlying theology as the Baroque develops. The Counter-Reformation gave rise to the "demand for a princedom whose constitutional position guarantees the continuity of the community, flourishing in feats of arms and in the sciences, in the arts and in its Church" [94] The Baroque , by contrast is unmoved by such hopes for a paradisiacal future. Benjamin's point is obvious: it is not at all the case that Christian theology has been universally held to promise a realized eschatology that might bolster Schmitt's secularized sovereign under the pretense that some long-promised lasting world order is finally at hand.

Schmitt cannot have failed to notice that the implicit theology of his own work had been found wanting. De Wilde observes that after 1933 Schmitt shifts from portraying the sovereign as a messianic figure "capable of creating a completely restored order" to the image of the *katechon*, the one who restrains the Antichrist.[95] Nonetheless his underlying political theology remained unchanged. The sovereign, although demoted from Messiah to *katechon*, nonetheless serves the significant function of restraining evil.

In literary works referred to by Benjamin as "baroque Byzantinism" Benjamin observes that the prince is a deified, heroic figure celebrated by divine beings.[96] By contrast, "in the *Trauerspiel* the monarch does not shake off his immanence."[97] Benjamin further elaborates that the monarch encompasses the role of both the martyr and the tyrant, corresponding respectively to the "very good" or the "very bad." Of the monarch and the martyr Benjamin says:

> Seen in ideological terms they are strictly complementary. In the baroque the tyrant and the martyr are but the two faces of the monarch . . . The theory of sovereignty which takes as its

93. Weber, "Taking Exception to Decision," 12.

94. Benjamin, *Trauerspiel*, 65–66.

95. de Wilde, "Meeting Opposites," 374, 377.

96. Benjamin, *Trauerspiel*, 67.

97. Ibid., 67.

example the special cases in which dictatorial powers are unfolded, positively demands the completion of the image of the sovereign, as tyrant.[98]

Schmitt himself at least alludes to this dilemma towards the end of *Political Theology*. Ironically, he views this instance as exceptional and so scarcely worthy of consideration.

Samuel Weber, philosopher and renowned Benjamin scholar, asserts—and I agree—that "with the split of the sovereign into tyrant and martyr, what is dislocated is not just the unity of *a* character, but the unity of *character as such*."[99] For Weber, "this dislocation is of particular importance for baroque theater . . . it is precisely this consistency and unity that are undermined together with the status of the sovereign."[100] Weber pinpoints the manner in which disunity of character undermines Schmitt's concept of sovereignty, reliant as it is upon unity and oneness. This emphasis on character—the distinctive morals and personalities of an individual—is particularly relevant to the question of global food politics. Not infrequently do philosophical and religious teachings insist that character co-arises with food and body, a question taken up in later chapters.[101] Subsequently, disunity is an inescapable aspect of creatureliness even for those deemed "sovereign."

Benjamin notes that the *Trauerspiel* features an antithesis between the incapacity of the tyrant to rule, in contrast to his *authority* to do so. The incapacity of the sovereign

> can be illuminated only against the background of the theory of sovereignty. This is the indecisiveness of the tyrant. The prince, who is responsible for making the decision to proclaim the state of emergency, reveals, at the first opportunity, that he is almost incapable of making a decision.[102]

Thus, Wilde argues, Benjamin depicts the sovereign not as "he who decides the exception" but rather as "he who proves unable to decide when faced with the eschatological vision of a continuing catastrophe."[103] This incapacity

98. Ibid., 69.

99. Weber, "Taking Exception to Decision," 15.

100. Ibid.

101. In which Nietzsche and Thoreau will serve as two voices in a longer and broader conversation than space constraints will permit extensive exploration. This perspective is not unique to the Jewish tradition, with its well-known insistence on kosher dietary law as condition of sanctity. The connection between character and diet is also intertwined with Hindu and Buddhist vegetarianism; see Khare, *The Eternal Food*.

102. Benjamin, *Trauerspiel*, 70–71.

103. de Wilde, "Meeting Opposites," 374.

results from the fact that "their actions are not determined by thought, but by changing physical impulses"[104] The sovereign's rational function cannot be said to be any more under control than that of their subjects; they are liable to the same vicissitudes of fleshly life. One wonders what this might mean for the sovereign in the context of climate change.

Because of their shared humanity, the sovereign and his royal subjects alike are found morally accountable for the sovereign's failures:

> The enduring fascination of the downfall of the tyrant is rooted in the conflict between the impotence and depravity of his person, on the one hand, and, on the other, the extent to which the age was convinced of the sacrosanct power of his role. It was therefore quite impossible to derive an easy moral satisfaction . . . from the tyrant's end. For if the tyrant falls, not simply in his own name, as an individual, but as ruler and in the name of mankind and history, then his fall has the quality of a judgment, in which the subject too is implicated.[105]

This passage calls attention, much as do the concluding passages of "Critique of Violence," to the responsibility of those who follow the sovereign decree: the subject of the sovereign decree is implicated in the judgment against the sovereign. Because this decree cannot be known ahead of time—or, for Benjamin *ever*—to be of divine origin, anyone who obeys the sovereign decision is responsible for deciding to obey. The weight of this moral accountability is indeed central to a political theology of food.

The disappearance of messianic eschatology has already been mentioned. Despite this disappearance, in the context of Baroque drama "the conflicts of a state of creation without grace are resolved, by a kind of playful reduction, within the sphere of the court, whose king proves to be a secularized redemptive power."[106] However, the king nonetheless does not function as messiah, despite his capacity to redeem. Because the hoped for restoration is to come about on the earthly plane by means of a human being, the sovereign's redemptive power is necessarily limited: "However highly he is enthroned over his subject and state, his status is confined to the world of creation: he is the lord of creatures, but he remains a creature."[107] Despite possessing some capacity to bring about improvement, the king falls far short of bringing about a lasting, final order.

104. Benjamin, *Trauerspiel*, 71.
105. Ibid., 72.
106. Ibid., 81.
107. Ibid., 85.

Benjamin observes that "the redemption of mankind" did not cease to be a concern of the increasingly secularized Baroque. As the hope for world restoration transferred to an increasingly secularized means of redemption, two shifts occurred. The first is that the vision of "redemption" expanded "to immeasurable proportions." The second was that rebellion against power structures almost by necessity spared the church.

> Heresy, the mediaeval road of revolt, was barred: in part precisely because of the vigour with which Christianity asserted its authority, but primarily because the ardour of a new secular will could not come anywhere near to expressing itself in the heterodox nuances of doctrine and conduct. Since therefore neither rebellion nor submission was practicable in religious terms, all the energy of the age was concentrated on a complete revolution of the content of life, while orthodox ecclesiastical forms were preserved.[108]

The secularization of eschatological visions inflated them beyond all reason, yet denied them religious fulfillment. Secular language, lacking the subtlety of religious discourse, subsequently deprived "men . . . [of] all real means of self-expression."[109]

What I understand Benjamin to be saying here is that the baroque passion for political rebellion could not express itself through the nuanced means of heretical or heterodox theological discourse. Thus, it could not grapple with potential theological inadequacies or corruptions of ecclesiastical forms; all this passion could do was reject the church and rebel against secular authority. This would, by necessity, leave unexamined the expectations for "the redemption of mankind" that must have, in part, informed this passion for political rebellion. My additional supposition would be that the theology implicit not only in the hope for redemption but also in the understanding of power structures was thus left unexamined. It would seem that Benjamin argues that the secularization of the eschatological hope for redemption and stability leads *secular politics* to rely upon—if not demand—a sort of *religious orthodoxy*.

---

108. Ibid., 79.

109. Ibid. Benjamin neglects to mention the irony in that their access to heterodox nuance was clipped at least in part by their own reactions against the Protestant Reformation. Had these "Baroque byzantinists" freed themselves from the grip of the Catholic Church's Counter-Reformation by studying the theological critiques central to the Protestant Reformation's rejection of ecclesial power structures, they may have unearthed a significant resource for theological critique not only of the ecclesial forms spared by the Counter-Reformation, but also the eschatological hopes embedded in their political rebellion.

If Benjamin is correct then hybridizations such as "political theology," "public theology" and "secular theology" appear as potent discursive methods for enhancing the capacity for theorization of "heterodox nuances of doctrine and conduct" in the *saeculum* in our own era. This potency is not expressed in public proclamations of doctrinally correct theology, but in exposing the reliance of the *saeculum* upon unconsciously assimilated orthodox theologies that, especially because they are not recognized *as* theologies, limit the ability of political discourse to grapple with subtleties and paradoxical realities—particularly around issues of food and ecology, as I will argue in later chapters.

Schmitt heard Benjamin's critique of his eschatology implicit in *Trauerspiel* and afterwards depicted his sovereign as *katechon* and not Messiah, but he did not seem to fully understand the magnitude of Benjamin's point, nor did he seem to make the connection to Benjamin's earlier "Critique of Violence." In *Trauerspiel*, Benjamin had argued that the sovereign's duties to restore order outstripped his actual capacity to do so, "leading to indecision and despair on the part of the sovereign." Schmitt attempts to counter Benjamin in his 1956 *Hamlet or Hecuba*. Schmitt contends that "instead of falling prey to indecision and despair, the sovereign turns out to be capable of transforming a 'desperate moment of catastrophe and crisis' into a powerful myth that supports his claims to power."[110] De Wilde maintains that Schmitt critiqued Benjamin "for having underestimated the power of myth: although Benjamin was right to relate the doctrine of sovereignty to the vision of a permanent catastrophe he did not acknowledge the power of myth that made this vision instrumental to the sovereign's claims to legitimacy and power."[111] De Wilde argues that while Benjamin had hoped to reveal this sort of strong, unilateral sovereignty as a precursor to unending chaos, Schmitt demonstrated that the mythology propping up sovereignty draws sustenance *precisely from the chaos*.

What Schmitt, and de Wilde, seem to overlook is that even Schmitt's own revised concept of sovereign-as-*katechon* functions *only* as a myth. Thus, any violence perpetrated by the sovereign would be mythical, and thus cannot be figured as divine by Benjamin's definition. Argue as Schmitt might that "the state of exception was necessary to protect the existing legal order," the mythological basis of sovereign legitimacy underscored Benjamin's point that sovereignty "was mobilized instead to legalize an essentially unrestricted and lawless violence."[112] Schmitt's acceptance of myth

110. de Wilde, "Meeting of Opposites," 376.

111. Ibid.,

112. Ibid., 377.

as foundation for sovereign authority stems from his desire to "justify the continuing violence in light of a future event, that is, the end-time that, announced by a period of anarchy and lawlessness, is to be restrained at all costs."[113] Consequently, Schmitt minimizes episodes of human suffering as only so many plot twists in the story of man's salvation.[114]

Schmitt responds to Benjamin's critique by recasting the sovereign in the role of *katechon*, or restraining force, as envisioned in Paul's writing. The state, in this configuration, is merely responding to the lawlessness and violence of these end times, and is staving off the looming catastrophe of the revelation of the antichrist. In doing so, Schmitt misses the point that Benjamin's perspective is completely the opposite: "the worst is already taking place, not despite but because of the willingness to accept state violence as a temporary measure."[115] Or, perhaps more to the point, the state itself might *be* the antichrist.

Myths are understood to be fact by people whose mythologies lead to violence. Schmitt's fears of ultimate disaster lead him to rationalize intense suffering caused by the attribution of mythological salvific properties to unjust power systems in the *now* moment that was his life. In light of his affiliation with the Nazi party, this is not inconsequential. Schmitt joined the Nazi party shortly after Hitler took power, led by his own concept of sovereignty and messianic hopes to support Hitler's assumption of power. The state of exception decided upon by Hitler did not bring about the promised stability, despite having killed approximately eleven million people between 1941 and 1945 (an average of 2.75 million per year).[116] In the end, Germany was defeated and divided and was to remain so for nearly fifty years. Reliance upon myth as a foundation for political power proved ineffective at inducing *real* stability.

Benjamin, by contrast, opposed state power. He suggests that the workers' strike was motivated by a desire to "escape from a violence indirectly exercised." Thus it would seem that Benjamin was guided by a hope for redemption founded upon a desire to protect the vulnerable, a desire theologically moored in Jewish tradition.[117] However, the socialist revolu-

113. Ibid, 378.

114. Ibid.

115. Ibid.

116. United States Holocaust Memorial Museum, *Documenting Numbers of Victims of the Holocaust and Nazi Persecution.*

117. Taubes, *The Political Theology of Paul* identifies Benjamin's political thought as Pauline while simultaneously reading Paul within the historical trajectory of traditional Jewish thought. In *The Time That Remains*, Agamben follows much of Taubes's reading, drawing a somewhat more direct connection between Benjamin and Paul, and omitting

tion, much like its fascist counterparts of the early twentieth century, failed to materialize equitable or stable political systems.

The desire to protect the vulnerable from an indirectly applied violence also motivates my own research. Currently, over 7.5 million people die of starvation annually.[118] The political narrative implies that these deaths are in some sense necessary to assure economic order; feeding them for free would wreak economic havoc. We are told that ever more industrialized agricultural methods, including GMO crops, will ultimately feed us all. The impact of these farming methods on the planet—and the resultant consequences to the already oppressed—are not examined in this equation. Nor, for that matter, is the assumption that food is a commodity that can legitimately be withheld from someone without financial means to purchase it. Their destruction counts at best—if it counts at all—as a necessary loss on the road to a final restoration. In other words, we are fed a version of Schmitt's *katechon* theory: the enactment of these destructive practices on the part of sovereign forces is necessary in order to prevent even worse destruction from occurring.

The wild hope leading many to endorse a dictatorial sovereign is the "utopian goal" of replacing "the unpredictability of historical accident with the iron constitution of the laws of nature."[119] We will say much more about the political function of the construct of nature—including the construct that would lead one to believe that natural law has an "iron constitution" in the first place—in later chapters. For now it is enough to know that secularization did nothing to relieve these hopes; it merely "denied them a religious fulfillment, demanding of them, or imposing upon them, a secular solution instead."[120] The secular solution Benjamin names as inadequate dovetails with the technicity Schmitt identifies as satanic.

The collective hope, especially in the West, is for technological solutions to our problems—redemption through technology, if you will. Indeed, often our hopes are realized. Take for instance vaccines, antibiotics, and refrigeration. The successes do not imply that technology is an unambiguous good, however, and Schmitt is right to caution us not to uncritically accept technology as the organizational priority of human societies. While often beneficial, technology also often brings unintended and unforeseeable consequences. Agricultural technologies have been

the historical contextualization present in Taubes. Britt's *The Political Theology of Paul* disrupts Agamben's easy linkage, taking great pains to once again situate Benjamin's thought within the broader historical trajectory of Jewish tradition.

118. World Hunger Education Service, *2015 World Hunger and Poverty Facts.*

119. Benjamin, *Trauerspiel,* 74.

120. Ibid., 79.

essential to supporting population growth; even greater suffering would be unleashed were they suddenly halted. Yet, as it turns out, the ecological destruction left in the wake of technicity—including the reliance upon technological agriculture—has revealed that the constitution of nature may be more whirlwind than iron.

The connections between amplification of fleshy vulnerability and enactments of Schmittian-type sovereignty will be examined in later chapters. Should the structures upholding the global food system be conceptually buttressed by a unilateral sovereignty accompanied by an "exception," or suspension of law, it is my hope to lay bare their mythological underpinnings. Hope of shifting global food politics toward a more sustainable and just model might emerge if these practices become more clearly legible as promoted by mythological faith in an exceptional figure to resolve existential threats. For now, suffice to say, the validity of political and economic structures that perceive such death and destruction as inextricably entwined with their salvific powers should at least be called into question. Particularly if these structures propel us toward a predictably dismal future.

Conclusion

As Conversi insists, the political significance of the food sovereignty movement is elucidated by situating this movement in the historical trajectory of the concept of sovereignty. While some are beginning to examine the historical trajectory of the *political* concept of sovereignty as applied to food politics, at the time of this writing no one has undertaken an analysis of sovereignty as a theological concept as applied to food politics. This is a significant omission, since the concept of sovereignty carries not only political but also theological implications. The political statements one endorses under the name "sovereign" cannot be neatly separated from theological concepts, whether or not explicitly identified.

Liberal democracy has been regarded as theoretically and practically problematic by thinkers both right and left, exemplified by Carl Schmitt and Walter Benjamin, respectively, and those who follow in their wake. While these thinkers concur that liberal democracy poses significant dangers, they starkly disagree as to how those weaknesses can be remedied. These disagreements, much like the concept of sovereignty itself, are often theologically tinged.

Carl Schmitt's response was to reinforce the sovereign as a sole decision-maker capable of restoring and preserving the unity of the state, enacting a secularized version of an orthodox theology insofar as the

sovereign is "above the law" in much the same way that an orthodox theology holds that God transcends the laws of physics.[121] But an orthodox
theological concept cannot necessarily be transposed onto a human sovereign, a point to which Benjamin alludes in his deconstruction of Schmittian
sovereignty.

Benjamin asserts that sovereign power is mythological and therefore
illegitimate. He also argues that the sovereign is incapable of deciding, and
when faced with the forces of nature the result is a permanent state of exception. Failure to recognize the infusion of more or less orthodox images
of God into more or less secular images of sovereign political leadership
obscures the unrealistic nature of the hopes often pinned on our political
leaders, and minimizes the very realistic nature of the fears of their potential
for despotism. These points of contention will be central to the exploration
of food politics in the context of climate change.

While in many regards the academic conversation has moved away
from Schmitt's definition of sovereignty toward thinking through the possibility of multiple sovereignties and even non-sovereignties, nonetheless
Schmitt's theories are addressed either directly or indirectly by a significant
number of scholars in this area. Thus, his work is evaluated as something
of a primary source pivotal to understanding what is at stake in a political
theology of food. The conflict between those on the one hand who would
bestow absolute authority on a political sovereign in exchange for security
and those who on the other hand find nothing so threatening as an absolute
sovereign—mirroring that between Schmitt and Benjamin—has resurfaced
with increasing intensity over the past two decades. This resurgence is in
large part due to the crisis of sovereignty posed by liberal democracy's inability to rein in transnational neoliberal capitalism. We turn now to more
recent treatments of political theology.

121. This version of a figure external to a given order, authorized to suspend the
rules of that order so as to assure preservation in the face of an existential threat will
be referred to as "strong sovereignty," "unilateral," "top-down," "absolute," or "Schmittian sovereignty" throughout this book to distinguish it from the type of sovereignty
espoused by the food sovereignty movement or the type of nonsovereign sovereignty
described by Crockett.

Chapter 2

Full Bloom

The Postsecular, Postsovereign, Post-9/11
Resurgence of Political Theology

THE ONCE-LIVELY ACADEMIC DEBATES about political theology of the interwar period had quieted to mere murmurs.[1] The decades-long quiescence
of this conversation contributes to the gap in the present review of political
theology. Hent de Vries observed that in the years following the September
11, 2001, attacks on the World Trade Center, the concept of political theology again became regarded as widely relevant in academic circles. The mere
fact of such a deadly terrorist attack on American soil broadcast the crisis
of sovereignty at a volume none could ignore. This crisis, coupled with the
spike in religious rhetoric on the part of both Muslim extremists and American politicians in the aftermath of the attack, greatly augmented academic
interest in political theology.

As the 1999 date of William Connolly's *Why I Am Not a Secularist* attests, conversation approximating "political theology" was heating up even
shortly before 9/11. Connolly was one of many responding to the pressures
of transnational global capitalism and its effects on the environment, the
poor, and even on the perceived legitimacy of national sovereignty itself.
For example, Giorgio Agamben's *Homo Sacer: Sovereign Power and Bare
Life* was published in 1995, dealing directly with themes broached in the
conversation between Schmitt and Benjamin. Jacques Derrida's *Politics of
Friendship* also gives Schmitt a nod, in this case as Derrida grapples with

---

1. de Vries, "Introduction," 7. Noteworthy contributions during this quiescent period include: Soelle, *Political Theology*; Cobb, *Process Theology as Political Theology*; and
Moltman, *God for a Secular Society*.

the friend/enemy distinction so prominent in Schmitt's thinking. Just before the terrorist attacks of 9/11, Michael Hardt and Antonio Negri's *Empire*, published in 2000, articulated the shifts in sovereignty induced by transnational global capitalism, also giving Schmitt a nod. Lastly, quite relevant to the political ecology described in later chapters, Stephen B. Scharper penned his *Redeeming the Time: A Political Theology of the Environment* in 1997 (although neither Schmitt nor Benjamin is mentioned here). These studies directly or indirectly address the widespread economic, ecological, and political transformations wrought by transnational global capitalism, changes that encompass and exceed the demographic changes illuminating the "post" in the postsecular.

Political Theology in the Postsecular

The "post" in postsecular denotes the recognition that "secularism" claimed itself to be theologically neutral despite being infused with Christian reasoning. Connolly's *Why I Am Not a Secularist* argued that secularism shares many problematic tendencies with the Christianity it attempts to displace: it presents itself as a single, uncontestably authoritative concept of reason and morality. Not coincidentally, this singular concept of reason serves to maintain Christian intellectual and moral reasoning as authoritative in public discourse. This is because secularism is more informed by its Christian roots than it acknowledges, in fact lacking precisely the "neutral, value-free zone" from which to make decisions that it purports to monopolize. Connolly insisted that due to its entanglement with Kant's "rational religion" and "moral reason," Western secularism is indeed informed by a generic version of Christianity masquerading as a value-free, neutral zone.

Transnational capitalism has resulted in greater mobility, relocation, and dislocation of various populations around the planet, and urban life has become increasingly pluralistic. Not only are there multiple Christian denominations residing in most US municipalities, but there are representatives of multiple religions present in any larger urban area. Christian moral, ethical, metaphysical, and logical frameworks can no longer be presupposed in the public arena, now populated by a vast variety of religious practitioners. The somewhat sudden shift in demographics over the past few decades poses challenges to both secularists and Christian traditionalists, insofar as it challenges the Christian presuppositions inherent in both worldviews, while heightening the conflicts between the two.

Somewhat prophetically, Connolly's inquiry into the structural similarities and disavowed integration of Christian reasoning was in large part motivated by concerns about a nationalist backlash against secularism and cultural diversity in America. Connolly saw, even in 1999, that the cultural diversity of the United States challenged the idealized image of America promoted by conservatives such as William J. Bennett. So long as traditionalists perceive themselves to be engaged in a culture war against liberals and progressives, there is a risk that "nationalists will enlist the state to promote the nation by attacking itself."[2] As I write these words, the culture war Connolly observed nearly twenty years ago seems to have significantly intensified as demonstrated by the nationalist agenda touted by US political leaders.

Post-9/11 (Political) Theologies of Food

Following the terrorist attack on the World Trade Center in 2001, interest in theological themes erupted among both politicians and academicians, in large part due to then-president George W. Bush's use of religious rhetoric. Agamben and Derrida grappled again and more intensely with both Schmittian and religious themes. Theorist Judith Butler developed a specifically Jewish ethic of nonviolence in response to post-9/11 politics in *Precarious Life: The Power of Mourning and Violence.* As the first decade of the new millenium closed, academic interest in political theology produced an unweildy bibliography, requiring several compendium and introductory texts to acquaint the unfamiliar with this field such as *The Blackwell Companion to Political Theology* edited by Peter Scott and William T. Cavanaugh; *Political Theology: A Guide for the Perplexed* by Elizabeth Phillips; *Political Theology: An Introduction* by Michael Kirwan; and *Political Theologies: Public Religions in a Post-Secular World* edited by Hent de Vries and Lawrence E. Sullivan.

Despite the proliferation of political theologies emerging in the last two to three decades, there have been few efforts to apply this theoretical approach to the topic of food politics. The Jewish tradition has engaged in lengthy discussion about proper food practices for thousands of years. A few scholars, such as Arthur Waskow and Arthur Green, have revisited the halachic system in light of contemporary food politics.[3] However, even the scholars who grapple with a Jewish ethical response to the contemporary food system do not attempt a political theology per se. The Christian tradition has historically discussed food primarily as a spiritual metaphor.[4] This

2. Connolly, *Why I Am Not a Secularist,* 113.

3. Waskow, *Down to Earth Judaism.*

4. Muers and Grummett "Introduction."

has slowly changed over the last several decades, in large part as protest against what will be described in later chapters as the corporate food regime.

The Christian theologians who theologize about food do not engage in political theology directly. Or at least they do not proclaim themselves to be writing political theologies, per se, nor do they engage Schmitt, Benjamin, sovereignty, or politics writ large. However, they do typically recognize the role that social and political structures play in determining practices of production and distribution of food. Subsequently, they speak to one or more elements of the food sovereignty frame.

For example, even as far back as 1980, Jack A. Nelson's *Hunger for Justice: The Politics of Food and Faith* decried the inequities of the corporate food regime. Nelson anchored his reflections on food and faith in his interpretation of Amos, specifically Amos 8:4–7. Nelson interpreted this passage as arising "within the context of social injustice, in which the rich grew rich by exploiting the poor and small farmers become landless laborers."[5] Nelson acknowledged that the modern social setting differs significantly from that of the biblical writers, yet he identified numerous parallels. For example, Nelson noted that "Hunger in Amos's Israel was a consequence of . . . self-perpetuating . . . structures of [economic] inequality," which he also perceived as operative in the late twentieth century.[6]

In response to these self-perpetuating structures of economic inequality, the prophet Amos had a scripturally rooted theological critique. According to Nelson, there can be no doubt that Amos perceived the earth and everything on it as a product of divine creation, intended to sustain all people. Subsequently, Amos perceived every single person as entitled to share in society's productive resources. Furthermore, economic inequalities were noted to have spiritual as well as material repercussions: "the biblical writers were profoundly aware that unjust economic structures prevented a proper relationship with God."[7]

Nelson views the jubilee tradition as indicative of a theological insight that recognizes divine ownership of the land. By contrast, in our own era, rather than an institution that levels the playing field, Nelson laments that food aid to developing nations has become a "tool of neocolonialism."[8] According to Nelson, aid in our contemporary context is distributed not in

---

5. Nelson, *Hunger for Justice*, 3.

6. Ibid., 5.

7. Ibid., 6.

8. Ibid., 14. Nelson does not argue his case with substantial facts; however, Schanbacher *does* bring forth evidence supporting this perspective so Nelson is here given the benefit of the doubt.

the name of justice, but "in the name of national security."[9] While this aid has "secured benefits for a privileged few" life has become "less secure for most of us."[10] Efforts to ensure national security that render masses of lives more precarious are misguided, according to Nelson. Nelson believes that "the basis of human security is justice. We cannot expect to be safe in our neighborhoods if we tolerate poverty and social inequality."[11]

Nelson dives right into the religious/secular divide with a clear message to those who perceive themselves to be religious: they are quite likely part of the problem. It is not enough to say that one believes in God or Jesus, suggests Nelson. Instead, one must know the true God. Nelson argues that the prophets and Jesus were exiled or killed "by people who thought they were serving God. The executioners were people who *believed* in gods but *lacked knowledge* of the true God."[12] And how would one know if one is serving the true God? Here Nelson turns to Jeremiah 22:13–17: "*to know God is to do justice.*"[13] Rather than lapsing into what Nelson would refer to as an idolatrous "faith in Jesus," Christian followers are urged to place greater importance on Jesus's historical life and ministry. The religious must also get political. Christians must, if they hope to end hunger, move beyond charity and aim their efforts at persistent and self-perpetuating social structures of inequality. To the degree that structural inequalities perpetuate hunger, Christians must strive for justice within social, religious, and political systems.[14]

Angel F. Mendez-Montoya also hopes for justice in and through the food system, but takes a more theoretical and sapiential approach. Mendez-Montoya's *The Theology of Food: Eating and the Eucharist* explores what Mendez-Montoya refers to as *alimentary theology*, theology not just *about* but *as* food.[15] Theology as food, he hopes, could simultaneously raise awareness of the material dimensions of food while also reorienting Christians theologically such that they would perceive the interdependence of creation and humanity, both entwined with their shared relationship with God.

Mendez-Montoya turns to such wisdom literature as Proverbs 9:1–6, and Ecclesiasticus 24:21–22, asserting that "Sophia . . . is both hostess and cook at a lavish banquet. She nurtures creation, but, more astonishingly,

9. Ibid., 99.

10. Ibid., 98.

11. Ibid.

12. Ibid., 188.

13. Ibid.; italics in the original.

14. Ibid., 207.

15. Mendez-Montoya, *Theology of Food*, 3.

she is also food itself."[16] Mendez-Montoya describes the creation as a divine feast in terms suggestive of perichoresis, a concept referring to the mutually indwelling persons of the Christian Trinity: "In this divine feast, the immanent and the transcendent constitute one another, and this mutual constitution invites us to reflect on why, precisely, 'food matters.'"[17]

> The world becomes food that we consume and integrate into our own bodies, into our own self. By eating, we communicate and make communion with the world, and in so doing, eliminate all boundaries between interiority and exteriority.[18]

Mutual indwelling characterizes relationships among the Trinity, between God and humanity, and also between and among humans and the world. The very nature of food speaks to a relational ontology.

For Mendez-Montoya, this ontological connection between nourishment and creation means that:

> The materiality of food, far from leaving the physical world (and contingency, immanence, Being, and so forth) malnourished or starving, recalls a prior maternal sharing of God's nurturing materiality with divinity. Food matters: this should not be as marginal as it presently is to theological thought. From a theological perspective, and from the Creation narrative, food is a central theme of God's superabundant self-sharing.[19]

This superabundant self-sharing is evident not only in the Eucharistic feast as read through sapiential literature, but also in the Exodus narrative, in the form of manna from heaven, where, according to Mendez-Montoya manna is "a sign of interdependence, hospitality, and solidarity, for it is a material demonstration of God's ultimate compassion."[20] To feed the hungry is indeed divine.

Mendez-Montoya's alimentary theology remains primarily theoretical, skimming the surface of the political debate about hunger in the closing pages. The problem Mendez-Montoya diagnoses is that humans decline to care for those most in need, including those in our midst. He is aware of the structural dimension to the problem of hunger, and intends to supply a "theopolitical vision rooted in Eucharistic sharing to promote the sort of

16. Ibid., 78.
17. Ibid., 79.
18. Ibid., 94.
19. Ibid., 112.
20. Ibid., 125

structural changes" needed to end hunger.[21] A theopolitical vision is vital, in Mendez-Montoya's view, because "at the heart of the material—that is an entanglement of social, economic, cultural, and political realities—there is a theological realm, which is the co-abiding of divinity with humanity."[22] Lamentably, Mendez-Montoya remarks that "in the current era of capitalist globalization . . . the awareness of the relation between our food at the table and God's gracious sharing is virtually lost."[23] It is his hope to transform the Eucharist into a theopolitical practice sufficiently potent to challenge "the greediness of capitalist consumerism" and discipline the desires of the ecclesia such that a fuller communion between humanity and God and among humans might be established.

Similar to Mendez, for Norman Wirzba food is "about the relationships that join us to the earth, fellow creatures, loved ones and guests, and ultimately God."[24] Wirzba's conviction is that a theology of food must articulate the realities of the food system "with reference to God as the world's source, sustenance, and end."[25] For Wirzba, the trinitarian concept of perichoresis is the model of not only divine but human relationships, such that one's personal identity is always constituted through relationship. This is true of eating, which is not merely "reducible to the consumption of others" but is also "an invitation to enter into communion and be reconciled with each other."[26] When done poorly, that is, when tinged with idolatry, "the result is degraded and destroyed habitats, miserable animals, insecure and abused workers, unjust trade arrangements and lonely eaters."[27] This not only echoes Nelson's earlier concerns about idolatry, it is also a strong indictment of industrial agriculture.

Wirzba characterizes "today's global, industrial food culture" as being "in exile because it exhibits the marks of injustice, estrangement, and bewilderment."[28] Exile, for Wirzba, "marks an inability to live peaceably, sustainably, and joyfully in one's place," losing both a healthy material relationship and a sense of communion with one's geographic location. Wirzba enumerates a litany of wrongs in the global industrial food system, casting these as symptoms of a greater refusal of membership in God's creaturely

21. Ibid., 151.

22. Ibid.

23. Ibid., 154.

24. Wirzba, *Faith and Food*, 4.

25. Ibid., 7.

26. Ibid., 11.

27. Ibid., 12.

28. Ibid., 71.

community; a refusal driven by economic motives. What Wirzba refers to as "the industrial logic that governs our world today" is governed in turn by a sort of atomic individualism that views humans, animals and ecosystems as discreet things unto themselves. This logic is, for Wirzba, gravely incorrect.

Wirzba maintains that we are not "self-standing, self-legislating beings in control of our own fate [free to] do as we please [with our bodies]."[29] Instead, he insists, "each individual body is necessarily dependent on a bewildering diversity of other bodies for its nurture and life."[30] Subsequently, he calls us to remember that our individual bodies cannot be healthy when the other bodies upon which we depend—animal bodies, bodies of water, and bodies of land—are diseased. The relational ontology permeating the theologies of food just described will wend its way into a political theology of food, which draws strength from these engagements despite not sharing the doctrinal commitments of the aforementioned authors.

The elegant contribution of the political theologians mentioned above prove to be launching points, insofar as my own work could be read as response to and extension of their grappling with the materiality of food in a theological register. Two additional theologians prove to be indispensable for thinking about a *political* theology of food that reckons with its materiality in a full-throated and transdisciplinary way: process theologian Catherine Keller and radical theologian Clayton Crockett. The inclusion of new materialist thought and science studies perspective in their approach resonates strongly with the new materialist focus of my own thought, emerging as it does from my experiences as a physician.

Catherine Keller: Counter-Apocalyptic Politics

Theologian Catherine Keller is among those producing detailed analyses of the political implications of theological thought. By her own account, Keller stages a "series of theopolitical investigations" in *God and Power: Counter-Apocalyptic Journeys*. She insists that these are simultaneously too narrowly focused on "a particular historical moment" and too loosely structured to be read as "a comprehensive political theology or a systematic study of messianic imperialism."[31] The particular historical moment addressed by her work is the moment of postmodern empire in a post-9/11 America. This empire seeks a "globalization of the economy," which is "inherently transnational and comfortable with a pagan cosmopolitanism," and also seeks

29. Ibid., 103.

30. Ibid.

31. Catherine Keller, *God and Power*, xi.

"global domination" that is "inherently unilateralist, inspired by a nationalist warrior-messianism."[32] Further, she interrogates the apocalyptic spirit implicit within the national response to 9/11, a response simultaneously political and religious. Against this national response, somewhat Schmittian in flavor, she cautions that messianic imperialism cannot assure the triumph of the American Empire.

We can certainly take Keller at her word. She does not intend to write a systematic political theology—at least not in *God and Power*. Nonetheless, she *does* stage a deconstruction of the messianic and apocalyptic narratives drawn from Revelation—narratives that I contend undergird many other political theologies in some form or fashion. In doing so, she does not leave us with either dystopic wreckage or a gilded-yet-sterile utopic redemption. She inspires us with a vision of multiform re-beginnings.

Keller begins her hermeneutic approach to Revelation by inviting us to read "the text as a dream and read the dream as our own."[33] The hermeneutic she seeks is

> a theological hermeneutic of relations, that is of indeterminacy—influenced by the model of quantum theory, in which the relation of observer and observed evinces an uncontrollable and irreducible mutuality. This hermeneutical indeterminacy admits at once its kinship to deconstruction. That is, it presumes that the rhetorical constructs of Revelation reveal much more about its writers and readers than about any One sitting on a throne.[34]

This hermeneutic resonates well with a political theology of food informed by Karen Barad's agential realism, based upon the theory of quantum indeterminacy.

The kinship between hermeneutical indeterminacy and deconstruction gives Keller license to "read the text through one or two Derridian eyes, but then also, inevitably and at the same time, to read Derrida through the eyes of this text."[35] Nonetheless, Keller's hermeneutic does not give one license to read the text however one likes. She encourages all who read the text to eschew partial readings that select the hope and diminish the damnation because the text fails to resolve the bitter struggles even in the end, even despite damnation. For example, Keller cautions liberation theologians who read Revelation "against the grain of the text" to "make

32. Ibid., x.
33. Ibid., 68.
34. Ibid., 70.
35. Ibid., 71.

their ambivalence clear," suggesting they "had better thus relativize the authority of its author to the moral claims of variously oppressed publics."[36] She cautions that we cannot simply *make* the text say what we want. We cannot simply *undo* the text either because efforts to undo the text merely recapitulate its problematic aspects.[37]

Keller's deconstruction of the text of Revelation engages Derrida's messianic thought, rather than his political thought.[38] Then again, his political thought ends in a messianic democracy to come, so perhaps . . . little distinction? And, as Keller herself notes, there are those who read Derrida as indebted to "the messianism of Walter Benjamin," a messianism that, as already described, shapes his political theology. Critical to countering the potential toxicity of a unilateral sovereign, she notes the four beasts of the apocalypse traditionally correspond to the four Gospels. She suggests that our salvation may come through this steadfast retention of plurality—the defiance of the logic of the One.[39] The commitment to a hermeneutic of uncertainty does not commit her to indecision, she notes; she will "decide in favor of the multiple and in favor of some pluralities more than others."[40] This plurality immediately undoes the singularity of "the sovereign."

After reading Derrida on the apocalypse, she notes the way in which anti-apocalypticism inevitably becomes apocalypticism, and even deconstruction can mutate into an apocalypticism of sorts, masquerading as "the ultimate, final strategy of unmasking." It is finality itself that Keller hopes to elude in her final chapter, in which she returns to the beginning:

> We may read the world itself as *genesis*, a great poem of becoming. Let us then seek clues for our *theopolitics*—for the way change is initiated, the way a beginning is made—in the *theopolitics* of creation.[41]

36. Ibid., 74.

37. Ibid., 87.

38. In *God and Power*, Keller draws upon her extensive deconstructive reading of the Book of Revelation and its apocalypse detailed in *Apocalypse Now and Then* for both her use of concepts such as antiapocalypse and counterapocalypse, as well as her integration of Derridian messianism.

39. Keller does not refer to Schmitt in the text under consideration in this section. However, she is more recently directly engaging his work in "Toward a Political Theology of the Earth." Further, although the logic of the One is not a focal point of the present research, the concept of indivisibility (i.e., unity) is central to sovereignty. For example, see Derrida, *Rogues*, xiv. Also, please refer to the above argumentation that Schmitt intended a single (male) person as sovereign, and Benjamin's subsequent critique of Schmittian sovereignty by demonstrating the sovereign's lack of unity of character.

40. Keller, *God and Power*, 91.

41. Ibid., 136.

This is a decisive break with the general trajectory of the discourse in political theology, which primarily concerns itself with ends. If seeking ends—whether in terms of the lasting order of a final conclusion (Keller's concern here) or in terms of morally valid ends that justify violence (the focus of Benjamin's critique in "Critique of Violence")—leads inevitably to failure of apocalyptic fantasy to materialize as paradise, then perhaps contaminating our vision of a finally purified social order with the messy chaos of beginnings might hold more promise. Because of the "the inescapably reciprocal character of the continuum of relations, the warrior messiah" who comes to clean up the sinful, fallen world "ends up making his own bloody mess," Keller insists, using terminology evocative of Benjamin's description of mythic violence. Significantly, seeking purified endings only brings more chaos.

Fortunately, Genesis provides a creative alternative to dystopically chaotic endings. In order for Genesis to generate more fecund political theology, first its purity must also be contaminated with chaos. Keller's point is that the purity of Genesis has always already been contaminated with chaos, found right there in the first two verses of Genesis. This chaos was "swept under the carpet of the doctrine of *creatio ex nihilo*."[42] The doctrine of "creation from nothing" was conjured as a way to preserve divine omnipotence. This submersion of chaos both reflected and fueled what Keller terms *tehomophobia*, or fear of chaos.

Tehomophobia in turn fuels politically oppressive regimes in the name of order. Keller turns to Hobbes, whom she notes serves as resource for "the present regime"—that being the post-9/11 years of the Bush administration, during which *God and Power* was written. As did Schmitt after him, Hobbes believed that no amount of destruction unleashed by state sovereignty could be surpassed by its alternative: an unending war of all against all. Hobbes argues that only Leviathan can protect against chaos, but Keller notes that this image of Leviathan bears little resemblance to its biblical antecedent. In scriptural texts, Leviathan *is* the chaos monster, not the guarantor of order. She illuminates Hobbes's willingness to endorse the monstrous under the pretense that it will result in order:

> In Hobbes's twisted exegesis of Job we glimpse the (il)logic of theopolitics: an all-powerful order is always preferable to "chaos," even if the order proves to *be* the very monster of chaos! . . . So if the ideal state *is* the Leviathan, redefined as the violent imposition of order, then no wonder the destructive chaos produced, for example, by the United States in Iraq can

42. Ibid.

be scripted as the creation of order, since order after all is the
most violent monster.[43]

Although she does not cite Schmitt in *God and Power*, the above critique
of Hobbes further erodes the ground on which Schmitt stands, for Schmitt
draws support for his political vision from Hobbes, above all. And if any
regime draws support for their tactics via "successful advocacy" of Hobbesian "violent imposition of order," perhaps we had best note the Hobbesian
connection to both Schmittianism and fascism.

Fascism elicits powerful resistance to its totalizing brutality. Ultimately
the fascist regime will fall—either consequent to internal rebellion, military
defeat, or some combination of the two—leaving survivors to grapple with
the chaos that remains. Even though empires new and old may leave wreckage in their aftermath, we need not fear (too much). While Hobbes may
have viewed Leviathan as consonant with the "violent imposition of order,"
this is not true of the author of Job: "Job's Leviathan suggests neither the
terrorizing hegemony of a state nor the terrorist extremities of resistance."[44]
Fortunately, luring complexity out of chaos is God's specialty as evidenced
by Job's depiction of God in the whirlwind—a figure representative for
Keller of "the turbulent emergence of complexity at the edge of chaos."[45]
This is a God who arguably created Leviathan not as adversary, but as something of a playmate.[46]

The Western vision of Leviathan and chaos are presented by Keller as
"projects of a primal relation, an originative connection to the chaos."[47] Although this connection has been suppressed or feared for millennia, Keller
invites us to, "in a risky and ultimately creative sense," embrace it. This embrace is described by Keller as *tehomophilia*. This embrace includes allowing
the reading of Genesis to be troubled anew by readings of old—readings such
as eleventh-century French rabbi Rashi's, in which the "linear order" of the
process of creation is syntactically broken up. Once this linearity is disrupted,
"the entire process of creation reads as *co-creation*."[48] We are invited back to
this originary moment, to some degree present in all moments:

43. Ibid., 142.

44. Ibid.

45. Ibid., 144.

46. Here linked to Keller's statement that "the rabbis have emphasized certain am-
biguity of the Hebrew: verse 26 [of Psalm 104] can be translated 'Leviathan that you
formed to sport *with* you" (145).

47. Ibid., 145.

48. Ibid.

> Then feel again the intimate vibration of God the Spirit upon the face of the deep: not as polytheistic regression, but as a *theopolitical* repudiation of the Marduk style of imperial Order. Might *tehom* signify an unrealized depth of reality, an infinite *theopoetic* potentiality that may become good or evil in its actualizations but is the "stuff" from which all things come?[49]

Keller's observation that creation emerges from the depths prompts her to ask a very important question: "Can a tehomic theology help our culture outgrow the violent certainties and messianic innocence of its 'simple faith'?"[50] Here, although she does not cite Benjamin, her remarks are resonant with his closing remarks in "Critique of Violence." We can never be certain, until after the fact, yet we remain responsible.

Keller is noteworthy as one of the few political theorists not to rest on the messianic, but rather on the creative. This political theology of food is focused upon food's materiality and as such recognizes the reliance of food upon ecosystems, or creation, if you will. Given that creation emerges from chaos, and chaos results from an excess of order, one might wonder if instead of, or alongside, a linear narrative of "recovery" of Eden—a narrative that implicitly buys into the apocalyptic as salvific and necessary—one might begin to think of (re)creation from chaos, keeping in mind that creation will always require, and thus contain a trace of, the chaos inherent in the old forms. What might happen if we purge ourselves of purity while nonetheless shouldering the weight of the world? Might we want to reimagine the political task—in which we are all of us engaged at all times—as that of continual re-creation of the world out of the messes we make rather than the search for a final solution that will stabilize conditions once and for all?

Clayton Crockett: Radical Political Theology

If Keller's *God and Power* can be said to approach political theology from a theological perspective—that is to say, a perspective arising from her commitment to a particular community and a particular text, Clayton Crockett's *Radical Political Theology* can be said to approach political theology from an atheological perspective—that is to say, a perspective arising from his commitment to at least *passing* as an atheist, as I suppose I myself do.[51] His is, in his own words, a "radical theological" approach, emerging from the death of God theologies and attached to the academy, but detached from

49. Ibid., 145.
50. Ibid., 147.
51. Crockett, *Radical Political Theology*, 16.

ecclesiastical or pastoral commitments.[52] The death of God, he notes, results from the age-old problem of theodicy, that questions how an all-powerful, all-good God can permit human projects undertaken with heinous ends in mind. Crockett perceives "death of God" talk as expressive of "the result of a genuine theological yearning for God, not simply a cynical and self-serving pronouncement."[53] Thus, while not doctrinally committed, his atheological approach is at least theologically interested.

Despite God's alleged death, Crockett self-consciously recognizes that even secular political theory cannot be purged of theological concepts, such that "we cannot fully separate or distinguish political philosophy from political theology."[54] The political philosophical concept Crockett investigates is freedom, which he insists does not exist in any absolute sense. Nonetheless, the perennial quest for freedom lays bare the myriad ways in which our lives are bound by material, biological, and sociopolitical factors. Hence Crockett views freedom as "the theological problem of our time."[55] Freedom "takes the form of potentiality in Agamben, the virtual in Deleuze, and *potentia* as constituting power in Negri . . . Radical theology's epistemological and political task is to think freedom." To that end, in full awareness of the mutual contamination of theological and political constructs, Crockett argues that "sovereign power must be seen as political and theological at the same time and must be countered theologically and politically."[56] In recognizing this mutual contamination and subsequent two-pronged task, his project is resonant with my own intent.

In his desire to undermine Schmittian sovereignty, Crockett's project is also resonant with the efforts of food activists, described in later chapters. However, I fear his efforts might simultaneously pose a *challenge* to those same food activists despite the fact that both Crockett and these food activists ultimately call for a radical democracy. In his urge to "resist positive sovereign power in both political and theological terms" Crockett insists that "sovereignty, if it can still be called sovereign, will be seen as the 'power not to,' the ability to resist exercising positive power."[57]

On the one hand this could make sense for food activists demanding food sovereignty insofar as they desire the "power not to" engage in agribusiness as usual. On the other hand, this seems to subtly contrast their

52. Ibid., 10–11.

53. Ibid., 14.

54. Ibid., 22.

55. Ibid.

56. Ibid., 23.

57. Ibid., 45.

claim for the freedom to farm agroecologically. And what I mean to say here is that it is not enough to claim that a legitimate sovereignty is the "power not to do," we must insist legitimate sovereignty might also be configured as *the power to do otherwise*. Or, emboldened by a relational ontology we might venture a step further, insisting that sovereignty be recast in terms of relational rather than coercive power.

By careful argumentation, Crockett demonstrates that popular sovereignty is theoretically derivative of "absolute, monarchical sovereignty because it is the unitary will of the people that is sovereign, not the individual whims of the multitude."[58] The people, with presumably unitary will, is represented by a single agent, who is thus considered—at least by Hobbes, as Crockett demonstrates—*the* sovereign.[59] Subsequently, for Crockett, "democracy is a step in the direction of multiplicity, but in its classical liberal form it is entangled in a univocal sovereignty, the popular sovereignty of a general will or a united state(s) or people."[60] However, this version of sovereignty presumes greater unity of "the people" than can be actually verified. At any rate, these claims to sovereignty, Crockett suggests, all derive from both the sovereignty and unity of God by way of monarchical sovereignty.[61]

Crockett's challenge to popular sovereignty by demonstrating its derivation from "absolute, monarchical sovereignty" pales in comparison to the effacement of popular sovereignty in today's political landscape, in which political power is "mediated and mediatized in complex ways that render the will of the people impotent and irrelevant to the will of corporations."[62] Thus, sovereignty has been wrested from "the people"—whether or not they had any right to claim such sovereignty in the first place—and "can be seen as divided between a more naked military force and more subtle sovereign wealth, or money."[63] If sovereignty is reliant upon unification, how are we to understand *this* division? Although Crockett does not address that particular question, he does seek to undermine both of these abusive powers. He clari-

58. Ibid., 46.

59. As will become evident in chapter 6, Crockett is not alone in identifying a crucial unity to the concept of sovereignty even when it is applied to democracies—at least in theory. For example, in *Rogues* Derrida refers to this "unity" as "ipseity," calling attention to the profoundly static image of "the sovereign" and sovereignty itself. Derrida identifies this as theologically buttressed by images of an all-powerful, unchanging God. In practice we recognize that societies and national priorities shift over time. Yet it is important to note that the presumption of unity is implicit in political theories of sovereignty as will be described in more detail in later chapters.

60. Ibid., 55.

61. Ibid., 47.

62. Ibid., 46.

63. Ibid.

fies the inappropriateness of merely substituting these abusive powers with another power—whether the power of the people or any other. The task of a radical political theology is to interrogate all structures of power.[64]

In later portions of his book, it becomes clear that Crockett is not opposed to democracy as such, but is decidedly troubled by *liberal* democracy, much like Schmitt. Unlike Schmitt, Crockett hopes to construct a political theology supportive of radical democracy, a democracy independent of claims to sovereignty, a democracy that does not rely upon the notions of a nation. This does not quite yet create an opening into which the food sovereignty movement can move. And it may turn out that despite the profoundly engaged and inclusive methodology of the democratic approach used by the food sovereignty movement, this movement is overly reliant upon problematic conservative and/or liberal concepts to expect theoretical support from Crockett's new materialist radical political theology. Let us press onward to inquire of Crockett how this proposed radical democracy may differ from liberal democracy.

One point of distinction emerges from Crockett's engagement of Spinoza as read by Antonio Negri. In short, this reading reveals that some element of Spinoza's concept of democracy remains "anomalous, unassimilable, or 'savage' to the modern liberal state . . . because for Spinoza this power operates more directly via the *potentia* of the multitude than indirectly through parliamentary councils."[65] *Potentia* can be read as a distributed, immanent power possessed and exercised by "the people," as contrasted to *Potestas*, or the concentrated, transcendent power of the sovereign. It is this radically democratic, distributed power that passes for sovereignty in the food sovereignty movement, displaying a point of convergence between Crockett's radical political theology and the praxis of the food sovereignty movement.

Another point of distinction between radical political theology and liberal democracy is Crockett's attention to the non-determined elements of our biology and thus our futurity. This non-determination implies freedom, including freedom of form. Crockett is aided in his investigation by Catherine Malabou's notion of neuroplasticity, noting that Malabou overtly draws a connection between neuroplasticity and a radically decentralized politics. He clarifies that "human society is plastic not *because* human brains are neuroplastic, but human plasticity is our social brain, our ability to think and act."[66] This capacity becomes vitally important in the context of socioeconomic inequalities, climate change, and resource scarcity. It is Crockett's hope

64. Ibid., 47.

65. Crockett and Robbins, *Religion, Politics, and the Earth*, 98.

66. Ibid., 106.

that social plasticity might prevent "the struggle for diminishing resources" from "transmut[ing] liberal capitalism into something more akin to fascism" through a commitment to "material equality and willing[ness] to experiment with new forms of governmentality."[67] His is a hope I share.

Crockett might be disinclined to lend support to the food sovereignty movement, which operates via the radically democratic processes he and other political theologians support, on the basis of its call for increased *national* sovereignty, a concept to which many progressive political theologians and political theorists are opposed.[68] Perhaps Crockett's perspective is more nuanced. For example, he makes the following, somewhat enigmatic, statement:

> The modern nation-state is the locus of representative liberal democracy; to think democracy radically, we must think and practice democracy beyond or without the state as its precondition. This does not mean that states do not or will not continue to exist, but democracy cannot be shackled to the state.[69]

Perhaps what Crockett intends here is for the democratic process itself to result in decisions that the sovereign authority of the state might find objectionable. This might provide precisely the opening into which the food sovereignty movement can insert its form of radical democracy that simultaneously demands change on the part of their national "sovereign" leaders, and demands recognition of their nation's legitimate claims to self-determination in the eyes of international decision-making bodies.

Crockett turns from a radical political theology to a new materialist political theology in *Religion, Politics, and the Earth: The New Materialism*, coauthored with Jeffrey W. Robbins. This new materialist theology anchors its legitimacy in our shared togetherness; no other norm or power will suffice.[70] According to them, any concept that seeks to deny our profound interconnectedness "represents a threat of violence against us all." Subsequently, "a new materialist politics," in conjunction with Crockett's radical political theology, "would be people taking the power that is already theirs. It is the dream of democracy whereby the people might decide our own destiny."[71] I will argue, with the assistance of Bruno Latour in later chapters, that in order to take this power, "the people" must become more politically engaged, and also more ecologically and scientifically informed.

67. Ibid.

68. Crockett is troubled by popular sovereignty (46), democratic sovereignty (48), and asserts that "sovereignty, like God, does not exist" (76).

69. Ibid., 104.

70. Crockett and Robbins, *Religion, Politics, and the Earth*, 53.

71. Ibid.

Conclusion

The conversation initiated by Schmitt and Benjamin in the 1920s and 30s has been reawakened in the aftermath of the 9/11 bombings. Despite growing interest in the field of political theology and a smattering of theologies of food, thus far few if any significant applications of political theology to contemporary food politics have been undertaken. Yet, the theologies of food do at least touch upon the material dimension of food, urging justice for people who grow, distribute, and eat it, and also for the animals we eat. Since there are few other political theologies of food with which to approach my own analysis, it has been necessary to linger a bit on some of the details in the general political theology discourse before using these theories to analyze my own particular concerns.

I am greatly aided by the theology, both political and constructive, of Catherine Keller. Although not overly intending to write a political theology—at least not in her earlier work—Keller at least gestures toward a political theology inclined to invoke the creative potential nascent in chaos, rather than reactively impose order upon it. Thus, hers is a political theology oriented toward re-beginnings, about which I will say more in later chapters. This approach is helpful, since ecological stability is unlikely to emerge any time soon, and we will need to begin again after each disaster.

Clayton Crockett's radical political theology demonstrates some of the critiques currently leveled at not only Schmittian sovereignty, but also popular sovereignty and any sovereignty that might hope to attach itself to a nation-state. Problematically, these critiques are potentially applicable to the demands of the food sovereignty movement. These critiques apply because the movement demands sovereignty for their respective nation states, a political form closely aligned with the concept of sovereignty. Equipped with a detailed understanding of the political theology concepts most relevant to my analysis, a closer examination of the motions of power and the relationship of these motions of power to the concept of Schmittian sovereignty is in order.

Chapter 3

Food Drives

Global Food Trade and the Sovereign State

As PHILOSOPHER ALFRED NORTH Whitehead observed, "the true method of discovery is like the flight of an aeroplane. It starts from the ground of particular observation; it makes a flight in the thin air of imaginative generalization; and it again lands for renewed observation rendered acute by rational interpretation."[1] This chapter could be considered a landing of the plane, touching down in the fields of agricultural production and distribution to more acutely observe the politics of food in light of the discourse on sovereignty by political theologians. The transition from theory to reality is a messy one; there is no neatly paved landing strip permitting a smooth landing. Touchdown is bumpy; theoretical abstractions do not neatly map onto specific realities, and initial contact can be jarring.

Thus, this chapter traces motions of power as revealed by decision-making in transnational global food politics relative to the concept of sovereignty and its many inconsistencies. This tracing shall occur by spiraling through several historical perspectives on the entanglements between food trade and national sovereignty. Each successive loop will bring us closer to our contemporary context and increase in detail and specificity. Particular emphasis will be placed on resonances and dissonances with a unilateral, top-down sovereignty as described in the previous chapters. My approach situates the contemporary discursive frames of "food security" and "food sovereignty" within the historical trajectory of transnational global food trade, examining rhetorical usage and political-economic enactments of the concept of sovereignty as distinct phenomena. Distinguishing between rhetorical framing and political enactments reveals the paradoxical nature

1. Whitehead, *Process and Reality*, 5.

of the contemporary landscape of food politics. The inherent paradoxes are directly related to the uneasy relations of either the food security or the food sovereignty frame with either right- or left-leaning political theologies.

Food Regimes and the Sovereign State

Postcolonial anthropologist Akhil Gupta questions why the role of food and foodstuffs in globalization remains underappreciated in scholarly discourse.[2] Gupta asserts that the concept of national sovereignty "was formulated in an historical context in which rule over colonial territories and the division of such lands was already a subject of some concern to European states."[3] Central to these concerns was the trade in spices such as cloves, nutmeg, cinnamon, and sugar and beverages such as tea and coffee. Gupta argues that comprehension of global geopolitics between the fifteenth and eighteenth centuries cannot be obtained without a firm understanding of conflicts arising around trade in spices and sugar. Without an accurate account of food trade, Gupta insists that the "rich history of global connections before the rise of the sovereign states" is obscured.[4] In light of theoretical insights of political theologians, it is not surprising that the centuries-long transition from medieval monarchies to sovereign nation-states was accompanied by theologically-tinged political mythmaking intended to support the concept of national sovereignty.[5] What *is* surprising is that the role of global food trade remains to this day underexplored in the discursive field of political theology.

According to Gupta, food trade continues to shape geopolitics. He persuasively argues that, historically, food trade gave rise to the need to establish legitimate rule of bounded territories, and thus the sovereign nation. By contrast, in the current geopolitical landscape, food is integrally interwoven into the globalization processes that have opened a gap "between the territorially expansive reorganization of capital on a global scale and the nationally limited character of state regulation and of labor organization."[6] At one time food trade was a driving force behind the establishment of sovereign

2. Gupta, "A Different History of the Present."

3. Ibid., 39.

4. Ibid., 38.

5. Kantorowicz, *The King's Two Bodies: A Study in Medieval Political Theology*. Kantorowicz wrote his study in large part as response to Carl Schmitt, despite not directly addressing Schmitt's work, according to Victoria Kahn, "Political Theology and Fiction in *The King's Two Bodies.*"

6. Gupta, "A Different History of the Present," 35.

nations and the traditional (Schmittian) model of sovereignty upon which nation-states depend. However, this is no longer the case. Initially, the concept of territorial boundaries facilitated consolidation of power over global agricultural processes; at present such boundaries pose an obstacle to such consolidation. Globalization proceeding under a neoliberal economic model is a potent force that seemingly cannot be stopped by something as apparently arbitrary as a national boundary. It could rightly be said that globalization of food trade no longer drives the formation of the nation-state; it now undermines the legitimacy of the nation-states already formed.

The shifting impact of globalized food trade upon the nation-state arises because globalization cannot be described in monolithic terms. Instead, Gupta argues, globalization is best conceived as a set of "pathways for transactions or exchanges that depend on the reconfiguration of existing structural and social conditions."[7] These pathways, in which food has always figured prominently, "ensure that flows are highly unequal and asymmetrical."[8] Gupta remarks that "only in a few nation-states in the First and Second Worlds was the sovereign, territorial state and the provisioning of social welfare a convincing fiction to the majority of their populations."[9] Could it be that this chasm between "convincing fiction" and "unconvincing fiction" is what separates the Global North left-leaning political theology discourse on sovereignty—with its skepticism of nation-state—from the demands of the peasant farmers of the Global South not for the (further) dismemberment of their nation-state, but rather the fortification of its legal boundaries?[10]

7. Ibid., 32.

8. Ibid.

9. Ibid., 34.

10. The Global North-Global South terminology is something of a blunt instrument, an overgeneralization concealing numerous identifiers of social location not the least of which is the fact that there are members of the "Global South" inhabiting the geographic territories of the "Global North." In no way is my use of this terminology to be confused with a statement that such a binary generality of identity is in fact observable. It is merely a shorthand for a cluster of social-location markers generally "recognizable" in academic discourse. In fact, it is a shorthand that surfaces routinely in food studies literature. Yet it must be emphasized that "Global North" is more accurately a terminology of social status, rather than geographic location. There are those from the geographic "Global South" currently living in the Global North, such as undocumented farm laborers from Latin America. Furthermore, there are those whose life circumstances are more akin to those we typically imagine prevail in the Global South. For example, on the Navajo reservation, vast numbers of people live without running water or electricity, conditions we do not typically associate with the United States as a "Global North" country.

Despite Gupta's allegations that sovereignty is fictional—and despite the critiques of national sovereignty leveled by radical political theologians—one wonders whether there could be a kernel of truth underneath the so-called fiction of national sovereignty, a kernel that threatens to gum up the gears of an ever more totalizing form of sovereignty. Could it be that the asymmetrical flows of power characteristic of globalization currently rely upon the dissolution of the concept of national sovereignty, whereas at one time the asymmetry of these flows was predicated upon it? Is there some way in which the concept of national sovereignty simultaneously props up lethal totalitarian regimes yet *also* provides a stop-gap measure against an even *more* totalizing, absolute global sovereignty? And further, could it be the case that social location vis-à-vis the "Global North/Global South divide" underlies the different perspectives on sovereignty held by radical political theologians and those in the food sovereignty movement? Further examination of global food trade may hint at some answers to these questions.

In the context of global food trade, the "pathways of transactions or exchanges" could be summarily captured by the term "food regime." The concept of "food regimes" detailed in a 1989 article by Harriet Friedmann and Philip McMichael facilitates the exploration of the interrelationships between global food trade and geopolitical developments. In terms that echo Gupta, they describe a food regime as "the political and economic structures that undergird successive periods of stability within the world food system."[11] Rather than portray food regimes as monoliths, Friedmann and McMichael pry open the internal inconsistencies that ultimately result in the breakdown of one regime and its transition to another.[12] One might conjecture that these internal inconsistencies reflect the tensions between various "globalizations" to which Gupta referred in his essay.[13]

The first regime identified by Friedmann and McMichael begins around the year 1870 and lasts until just prior to World War I.[14] They refer to this

---

11. Fairbairn, "Framing Resistance," 15.

12. McMichael, "Food Regime Geneology," 140.

13. Ibid., 141. However, it should be noted that their analysis does not reach quite as far back into history as does Gupta's. Whereas Gupta addresses the monarchical era prior to the development of states, Friedmann and McMichael's analysis begins in the mid-nineteenth century when nation-state development was already proceeding via colonialism. Thus, they necessarily arrive at slightly different conclusions regarding globalizing processes.

14. The end date for this first regime varies and is contingent upon whether one considers the instability to be internal to the regime or to mark a transitional period. The regime concept continues to evolve in its depiction of these periods.

regime alternately as the "colonial-diasporic"[15] or "British hegemonic."[16] The interwar period was not characterized by a regime, as policies and practices never reached that degree of consolidation. The next regime, consolidated in the 1940s and 1950s, is referred to as "the surplus regime,"[17] or the "post-war regime,"[18] and is associated with US hegemony.[19] These first two regimes occur during the period of time in which the nation-state project was reaching fruition. The postwar regime was disrupted by the food crisis of 1972 giving rise to our current regime, which is referred to as the "corporate food regime."[20] This regime loosely corresponds to the period during which the crisis of sovereignty emerges, induced by the singular pursuit of the same neoliberal economic agenda that propels the corporate food regime.

The alignment of food regimes with other international developments underscores "the pivotal role of food in global political-economy," corresponding to the imbrication of food trade in geopolitics noted elsewhere by Gupta.[21] It is worthwhile to consider these developments in more detail.

The British hegemonic food regime aligns with the latter part of the colonial period and was based upon the import of colonial tropical foods as well as staple foods from settler colonies to Europe in order to provide the European industrial classes with cheap food.[22] This effectively "re-divided the world economy into vertical power blocs, subordinating agricultural hinterland to industrial metropole."[23] This exemplifies the asymmetrical flow mentioned by Gupta: centralized economic power drew resources from subordinate colonies with disproportionately low investment of resources flowing toward these colonies.

The United States, having achieved independence from Britain by this time, was able to seamlessly integrate its national agricultural system with the industrial sectors consuming the agricultural products, permitting a great deal of self-sufficiency. This model of integrated development characterized by internal relations of production and consumption of agricultural products came to represent the developmental ideal of the postwar era.[24]

15. Ibid., 16.

16. Fairbairn, "Framing Resistance," 18.

17. Friedmann, "International Political Economy of Food," 32

18. Fairbairn, "Framing Resistance," 18.

19. McMichael, "Food Regime Geneology," 146.

20. McMichael, "Global Development and the Corporate Food Regime," 1.

21. McMichael, "Food Regime Geneology," 140.

22. Ibid., 141.

23. Friedmann, and McMichael, "Agriculture and the State System," 98.

24. See Friedmann and McMichael, "Agriculture and the State System," and Friedmann, "International Political Economy of Food."

During this period when former colonies transformed into independent nations, relationships between sectors internal to each economy were restructured in an effort to achieve this ideal.[25]

This postwar food regime operated by unspoken rules that simultaneously replicated and buttressed shifting balances in international power, the motions of which resulted in "a stable pattern of production and power that lasted for two and a half decades."[26] During this period, national regulation was prioritized, authorizing both "import controls and export subsidies" resulting in perpetual surpluses of agricultural products. Surplus commodities were then used as a tool to shift the balance of power in one state's favor. During this era, the US utilized grain imports in the form of food aid to promote the formation of nation-states from former colonies. Agriculture became not only "central to the world economy," but also central to international relations, as conflicts and alliances were expressed in the form of food aid. Presently, food aid serves to force developing nations to adopt neoliberal economic policies that perpetuate asymmetrical flows of power.

The postwar regime began to falter in the early 1970s, when explosive demand coupled with a precipitous decline in production led to a food crisis. Compounding the problem, the food shortage occurred simultaneously to financial and oil crises.[27] At that time developing nations had become caught in a trap: they had become dependent upon cheap imported food, and they were losing revenue on export crops, particularly when high-fructose corn syrup and corn oils replaced sugar and palm oils.[28] In the wake of a grain deal between the US and the USSR. that removed vast quantities of grain from the international market, food prices tripled between 1972 and 1974.[29] A concurrent crude-oil crisis drove petroleum prices to triple at the same time.

Developing nations found themselves facing severe food shortages. Borrowing money on the international market, rather than directly addressing the deeper issue of dependence on imported food, helped these nations remain afloat through the food shortage. However, when the world economic situation deteriorated in the 1980s, these countries faced situations in which these debts came due and they were forced to agree to

---

25. Ibid., 98.

26. Friedmann, "International Political Economy of Food," 31.

27. Ibid.

28. Schanbacher, *The Politcs of Food,* 20.

29. Ibid.

International Monetary Fund and World Bank conditions imposed upon them in various structural adjustment programs (SAPs).

Simultaneous to these processes in developing nations, it has become the case that "American agriculture increasingly [supplies] not final consumers . . . but inputs to corporations manufacturing and distributing foods internationally."[30] Since the 1970s, the restructuring of agriculture in the US and abroad has primarily occurred "in response to the demand by transnational agro-food corporations for inputs to manufacturing and distribution networks," rather than in response to national interest or consumer demand. Although these corporations are largely US-led, their rise in power and the policies underwritten by transnational corporations has seriously "undercut the independent capacities of states to regulate domestic production and trade,"[31] rendering rather dubious any claims that nations remain the central "organizing principle of the world economy."[32]

The perspective of food regimes clarifies the profound entanglement of global food trade with the consolidation of the nation-state system, and the current "crisis of representation" attributed to that system. Global trade in food has underwritten two paradoxical developments over the past century and a half. On the one hand, global trade in food is closely associated with the "culmination of the colonial organization . . . and the rise of the nation-state system" throughout the British hegemonic and postwar regimes.[33] On the other hand, the corporate food regime has driven both the "completion of the state system through decolonization" and its "simultaneous weakening through the transnational restructuring of agricultural sectors by agro-food capitals."[34] Thus, examined in the context of food regimes, it certainly seems that asymmetrical flows of power and capitol now rely upon the dissolution of the concept of national sovereignty, whereas at one time they were dependent upon it.

The developmental trajectory toward the consolidation of nation-states would by definition seem to closely align motions of power in food politics with deployments of Schmittian sovereignty. It is more challenging to connect these motions of power with deployments of sovereignty in the context of the weakening of state sovereignty. Who, in this scenario, is the sovereign? Demonstrating that such deployments in fact occur despite no obvious claim to such sovereignty will be my task below, in conjunction

30. Friedmann and McMichael, "Agriculture and the State System," 111.

31. Friedmann, "International Political Economy of Food," 94.

32. Friedmann and McMichael, "Agriculture and the State System," 111.

33. Ibid., 95.

34. Ibid.

with the task of demonstrating that the motions of power in secular food politics are animated by theological remnants. Validating this argument requires an examination of the political frames involved. The work of sociologist Madeleine Fairbairn will assist in this endeavor.

Political Frames: Rhetorical Strategy and Expression of Worldview

Fairbairn conjoins Friedmann and McMichael's concept of food regimes with the concept of "framing" as described by Robert Benford and David Snow to describe the deployment of language and ideas on the part of social movements in order to "mobilize support for their efforts."[35] The concepts of "regime" and "frame" encompass both the practices and the worldview involved in the food movements, respectively. The concepts of both regime and frame are necessary in order to sketch a more complete portrait of the paradoxical appearance of sovereignty in food politics.

In our current, "corporate" regime, using Friedmann and McMichael's terminology, the food security frame dominates the current political and economic landscape. This frame endorses the corporate food regime's use of "capital-intensive, large-scale, highly mechanized agriculture with monocultures of crops and extensive use of artificial fertilizers, herbicides, and pesticides, with intensive animal husbandry" deemed necessary to provide sufficient food.[36] The food security frame "first entered into the official discourse in the report of the World Food Conference of 1974 . . . hosted by the [Food and Agriculture Organization] FAO in Rome."[37] The conference culminated in a call for International Undertaking on World Food Security, which, Fairbairn argues, "was conceptualized in the corridors of global power; thus while it attempts to remedy a faulty system, it does so without questioning the dominant political-economic wisdom."[38] Initially, this discourse was "rooted in the ideology of the failing postwar food regime" and relied upon powerful nation-states to provide food security for their citizens. As the postwar regime collapsed, however, the conceptual underpinnings of the rhetorical frame were transformed as new ideologies emerged.

This dramatic transformation in the food security frame occurred in the 1980s in the wake of Amartya Sen's 1981 *Poverty and Famines,* which demonstrated that economic ability to purchase food was a more significant

35. Fairbairn, "Framing Resistance," 15.

36. Beus and Dunlap, "Conventional versus Alternative Agriculture," 594, quoting Knorr and Watkins, *Alterations in Food Production,* x.

37. Fairbairn, "Framing Resistance," 22.

38. Ibid.

factor in access to food than the physical availability of food on a local or national level.[39] Sen's analysis demonstrated that national plenitude or shortage of food did not affect all groups of people within that nation equally. Instead, differential access to food within a nation reflected different "commanding powers over food" experienced by different groups. The commanding powers were found to be economic in nature, and "lack of purchasing power" rendered individuals vulnerable to food shortage regardless of global food production or national food availability.[40]

Sen's analysis, for which he was awarded the Nobel Prize in economics, shifted the understanding of food security to one that emphasized "individual access" over "national-level availability."[41] Despite Sen's clear articulation that the market often fails to deliver much in the way of food to the hungry, Fairbairn observes that Sen's work was cited as proof that neoliberal market economics would improve individual economic status and subsequent access to food.[42] Consequently, the food security frame wholeheartedly endorses transnational neoliberal economics and the corporate food regime, despite Sen's misgivings.[43] Consequently, individuals and not nations became responsible for their own food security.

Fairbairn marks the shift toward emphasis on individual access to food as an advance in the understanding of food security. She remains troubled that this focus nonetheless frames food security in terms of "microeconomic choices facing individuals in a free market, rather than the policy choices facing governments."[44] What Fairbairn finds to be "the most striking manifestation of neoliberal logic within the household food security frame" is the effortless transformation of "the need for individual purchasing power . . . into a call for liberal trade policies." She marvels at this, since Sen himself advocated "a combination of both market and public action to improve household food security."[45] Only one half of Sen's prescription is followed, as proponents of the food security frame vigorously focus primarily on the economic growth they insist results only from free markets, presuming this growth benefits all individuals equally (which it clearly does not).

Before moving on, a word about nomenclature. Throughout this political theology of food, various terms will be used to describe the dominant

---

39. Fairbairn, "Framing Resistance," 24; Sen, *Poverty and Famines*.
40. Sen, *Poverty and Famines*, 43 and 161.
41. Fairbairn, "Framing Resistance," 24.
42. Sen, *Poverty and Famines*, 160; Fairbairn "Framing Resistance," 24.
43. Fairbairn, "Framing Resistance," 24.
44. Ibid.
45. Ibid., 25.

system of agricultural production and distribution. These include but are not limited to terms such as: "the corporate food regime," "the food security frame" and "transnational global food trade." These terms will be used interchangeably to refer to a broad constellation of political and economic structures, ideological commitments, and rhetorical strategies propping up a vastly complex system. This is partially due to the various terms for this system currently used in the academic study of food. The contrasting focal point—the food sovereignty movement, to be described below—will be referred to in much more uniform terms, despite its at least equally multiform appearances, in keeping with the vast majority of food scholarship.

Several frames have arisen to contest the food security frame, such as the food sustainability frame, the food sovereignty frame, and the food justice frame. The frame of food sustainability is so poorly defined as to render it useful to proponents of the most radically polarized movements, food security and food sovereignty, yet in each instance it signifies something different.[46] Sustainable agriculture, by definition, identifies the necessity of providing food for the present generation without obstructing the ability of future generations to meet their needs.[47] Problematically, in the hands of agencies such as the World Bank it is conceived in primarily economic terms rather unconcerned with the ecological principles important to food activists.[48]

Holt-Giminez argues that "*sustainability* in and of itself is primarily a political and social concept—a normative framework within which to make decisions."[49] He goes on to suggest that the superficial consensus that sustainability is critically important to agricultural decision-making masks profound contestations over decision-making authority between institutions, agencies, businesses, countries, villages, and families with disparate stakes in the outcome. Because these areas of contestation are masked and the term glosses over the distinctive positions of various parties, food sustainability is losing traction as a mobilizing discourse.

The food justice frame critiques differential access to adequate nutrition based upon issues such as race and class, borrowing agricultural techniques developed within the food sovereignty movement to promote equal access to nutritious food.[50] According to Teresa M. Mares, the discursive frame of food

---

46. Holt-Giminez, *Campesino a Campesino*, xv.

47. Ibid., xv.

48. The aforementioned (economic and ecological) represent two of the three pillars of sustainability. The third is social sustainability.

49. Ibid,. xvi.

50. Alkon and Agyeman, *Cultivating Food Justice*, 12.

justice draws inspiration from the movements for local food security while placing greater emphasis on the structural racism and classism that inflect access to healthy food and control of the land on which food is produced.[51] Mares is troubled by the discursive strategies of some food justice proponents that rest upon notions of citizenship, arguing that such strategies presuppose a nation-state capable of guaranteeing citizenship rights. Omitted from much of this food justice discourse are the limitations of the concept of citizen itself, a significant omission in the Global North as many who grow our food are stakeholders in agricultural processes but lack the protections afforded to citizens by virtue of their immigration status, and are therefore subject to rape, violence, and other abuses with no legal recourse.[52]

Finally, the food sovereignty frame, with its emphasis on smaller, low-input farms and a radically democratic approach to agricultural decision-making, appears to be attracting much attention as the leading rival to the food security frame and is named by Fairbairn as the first counter-frame with potential to undermine the corporate food regime.[53] This frame argues that the needs of food producers should take precedence over those of transnational agricultural corporations in agricultural decision-making.[54]

The food sovereignty movement emerged in 1996, when the international peasant farmer's movement, *Via Campesina*, "launched a global call for *food sovereignty*" in protest against the food security frame and the corporate food regime.[55] Food sovereignty, simply defined, "is the ability of countries and communities to control their own food supplies: to have a say in what is produced and under what conditions, and to have a say in what is imported and exported."[56] Food security is the frame of the global elite. Meanwhile, food sovereignty is "the first frame created by the oppressed rather than the powerful in the world food systems" and is therefore "unique in attempting to demolish the regime within which it arose and to construct an entirely new one in its place."[57] The distinguishing feature of the food sovereignty movement is "the extent to which it casts off the language of

51. Mares, "Engaging Latino Immigrants," 35.

52. Ibid. Mares's comments are in reference to scholarship by Gerda Wekerle and Charles Levkoe. Wekerle argues that the "engaged citizenry" resulting from food justice organizing should be of interest to urban planners. Levkoe insists that the food justice movement can transform consumers into citizens.

53. Fairbairn, "Framing Resistance," 27.

54. Mares, "Engaging Latino Immigrants," 35.

55. Holt-Giminez and Patel, *Food Rebellions!*, 2.

56. Cohn et al., *Agroecology and the Struggle for Food Sovereignty*, 20.

57. Fairbairn, "Framing Resistance," 27, 16.

neoliberalism and creates a viable discursive alternative."[58] This discursive alternative opens a tiny space for consideration of other worldviews and theologies as organizing concepts for a political theology of food.

The "regime"—in scare quotes because it is too loosely organized to qualify as a regime—advocated and enacted by proponents of the food sovereignty movement is negotiated at the grassroots level rather than among the political elites. The agricultural methods typically deployed are variously described as low-input sustainable agriculture or agroecological methods. Agroecological methods are precisely tailored to the ecological milieu of the farm, with consideration for soil health, water, and native flora and fauna. In the *Campesino a Campesino* movement, operating under a food sovereignty frame, these methods are taught by farmers themselves in small group workshops.[59] The pedagogical methodology, although still a site of contestation, generally uses "demonstrations, games, and group activities . . . to teach a series of agroecological themes (small-scale experimentation, diversity-stability, fertility, integrated pest management, etc.)."[60] Rather than establishing hierarchical systems of training in which imported technology is taught by an expert, farmers are encouraged to experiment in their own fields in order to develop understanding of the unique dynamics of their agroecological setting.[61]

Because it rejects the globalization project and the corporate food regime, food sovereignty "can be seen as 'counterframe' to food security—an alternative schema for understanding the corporate food regime that is conditioned by the very different experience and interests of their framers."[62] Rather than targeting corporations, food sovereignty proponents target political bodies, demanding their intervention in transnational corporate efforts to restructure agricultural practices in developing nations. This calls into question the transnational corporate structure and its *modus operandi* as a whole. The food sovereignty movement's potential to undermine the corporate food regime emanates from the fact that its frame and the practices endorsed are not easily appropriated by the corporate food regime or the food security frame.

For example, the corporate food regime, and the food security frame which it employs, selectively appropriate "certain activist demands" and use "privately enforced quality standards . . . to mollify privileged consumers

58. Ibid., 16.

59. Holt Giminez, *Campesino a Campesino.*

60. Ibid., 84.

61. Ibid., 89.

62. Fairbairn, "Framing Resistance," 27.

with new products that promise higher quality or more ethical production."[63] These market-based activist techniques mimic fundamental anthropological assumption of the food security frame—the assumption that humans are primarily economic agents making individual decisions in isolation from larger contexts. According to Fairbairn, any food movement that relies upon boycotts or consumer power without *also* pursuing policy changes implicitly reinforces the power of corporate industrial agriculture.

Interventions such as shopping at farmers markets or CSAs and co-ops, or switching to vegetarian/vegan/organic diets rely upon individual consumer choice to impact the market. While a necessary component of food activism, done in isolation these efforts leave completely untouched the larger systemic structures of the market. Without corresponding political action directed at policy change, market interventions offer at best a weak challenge to the global dominance of transnational corporate agriculture.[64] As isolated efforts, they are also tinged with a deterministic, mechanistic cosmological view that ignores the importance of grazers for the health of the soil in which plants grow, fails to address the impact of monoculture crops on wildlife, and in some cases imagines that decreasing meat consumption will deterministically release more grain for human consumption.[65] While such consumer choices *might* reduce one's personal carbon footprint, they do not necessarily result in large-scale transition to low-input, low-emissions farming nor do they alone determine whether grain is released to feed the hungry.

Rather than focusing on those types of market-based strategies, the food sovereignty movement challenges neoliberal economics at its core—by questioning "the micro-economic assumptions upon which it is predicated."[66] Its advocates deploy the language of solidarity and reject

---

63. Fairbairn, "Framing Resistance," 18. This appropriation of activist demands is the most insidious feature of the food security frame/corporate food regime. Take for example McDonald's engagement with environmental issues: he wants to feed the hungry while responding to environmental degradation, and the frame of food security offers the illusion of being able to do both while still doing business as usual despite the fact that business as usual is a causative factor in both problems. See McDonald, *Food Security*.

64. Hauter, *Future of Food and Farming in America*, 3–4.

65. Keith, *Vegetarian Myth*, 8, 108. See also Pollan, *Omnivore's Dilemma*, section on Joel Salatin's farm. For an example of the position being critiqued (directly by Lierre and indirectly by Pollan), see Kalechofsky, *Vegetarian Judaism*, especially pages 166–82. While Kalechofsky's criticisms of a meat-based diet are sound, the food shortage in 2008 demonstrates that diversion of grain for the production of fuel additives can interfere with grain availability as much if not more than feeding grain to cattle.

66. Fairbairn, "Framing Resistance," 27.

the commodification of food, asserting that the value of food exceeds its economic value. The food sovereignty movement places great value upon things typically unaccounted for in the corporate food regime, such as traditional knowledge, culture, and biodiversity. The food sovereignty movement further insists that the value of food cannot be calculated apart from the traditional knowledge, biodiversity, and cultural practices with which the production and consumption of food are integrally connected.

According to Fairbairn, the mere emergence of a resistance movement with such a powerful discursive appeal as food sovereignty could signal the failure of the corporate food regime to consolidate. She notes that the failure to consolidate may be due to flaws surpassing merely the inability to alleviate hunger. These flaws include "social injustice, environmental degradation and the loss of traditional knowledge," flaws that are criticized widely and frequently within the food sovereignty frame.[67] These rather obvious flaws may be the cause of the proliferation of scholarly writing on the food crisis in the past decade.[68] Further, the wide range of problems wrought by these flaws has promoted the use of the food sovereignty frame by food activists concerned with food justice and sustainability.

Illuminating Sovereignty in the Corporate Food Regime

Utilizing Fairbairn's insights, I have distinguished between the dominant model of agriculture (the "corporate regime" operating under a "food security" frame) and the food sovereignty movement by comparing their rhetorical frames, making use of the concept of food regimes, and interpreting the underlying worldviews operative in each movement. But I have so far said little as to how either movement relates to "the sovereign" as envisioned by Schmitt. The remainder of this chapter will elucidate these relationships.

Food Security and the Decision on the Exception

It is against the pervasive existential threat of starvation that the food security frame promises protection. The food security frame has legitimated the deployment of the corporate food regime as the intervention of choice into the problem of world hunger. As remarked upon above, in our engagement with Fairbairn, this tactic flourished in the aftermath of Amartya Sen's

---

67. Ibid., 26.

68. Counihan, and Van Esterik, *Food and Culture*, 2.

Poverty and Famines, which demonstrated that the primary cause of starvation was not inadequate supply of food, but inadequate economic capacity to purchase the food available. Global organizations, such as the Food and Agriculture Organization (FAO) and the International Fund for Agricultural Development (IFAD), in conjunction with the World Trade Organization)WTO), the World Bank and the International Monetary Fund (IMF), intervened through various policies and trade arrangements intended to produce sufficient economic growth to assure food security. According to religious ethicist William Schanbacher, the common theme of these interventions is "the focus on alleviating poverty through developmental growth" in general and upon "agricultural reform, trade, and technological progress" (such as the Green Revolution) in particular.[69]

The debt crisis in the mid-1980s provided the existential threat that permitted multilateral trade organizations [the International Monetary Fund, World Bank and World Trade Organization] to impose structural adjustment programs (SAPs) on developing nations in a manner that suspended certain economic and agricultural laws in those nations. In some cases, this permitted the entry of transnational corporations into the agricultural sector of developing nations. For example, the IMF and World Bank insisted that Mexico privatize their state-controlled National Company of Popular Subsistence. When US-based Cargill entered the Mexican corn market, local mill and factory owners were hard hit as production was transitioned to larger producers.[70] Furthermore, large transnational corporations like Cargill can manipulate market prices with little consideration of how price fluctuations will impact access to food.

Some, such as Daniele Conversi, identify Exxon, Microsoft, McDonald's, Monsanto, and other transnational corporations as the new sovereigns. Conversi observes that "their sovereign decisions are taken outside any form of democratic consultation, thus projecting a vision of remote or hidden forces dominating each single nation and individual."[71] Immediately after referring to their maneuvers as enactments of sovereignty, he goes on to assert that transnational corporations are on the verge of precipitating "the implosion of the very notion of sovereignty."[72] I would concur that they are on the verge of imploding the concept of the nation-state, but I entirely disagree that they are on the verge of imploding the concept of sovereignty as envisioned by Schmitt.

69. Schanbacher, *Politics of Food*, 28.

70. Schanbacher, *Food Politics*, 43

71. Conversi, "Sovereignty in a Changing World," 488.

72. Ibid.

I would argue quite the opposite: the transnational corporations and multilaterals are enacting Schmittian sovereignty par excellence, albeit an economic version of Schmittian sovereignty disarticulated from the nation-state. The suspension of the laws in developing nations subjected to SAPs in reaction to an exceptional situation constitutes a decision upon the exception. From a Schmittian perspective, the sovereign is "he who decides upon the exception"; in this case, the multilaterals in conjunction with transnational corporations. Despite Schmitt's insistence that the sovereign be a single individual, I nonetheless contend that they are acting as a solitary sovereign insofar as they exhibit a unity of economic purpose. The impositions of SAPs on these developing nations simultaneously undermined the sovereignty of these developing nations while establishing the sovereignty of the multilaterals. This usurpation of state sovereignty does not free us from the dangers of the sovereign, to be explicated in depth in later chapters. Instead, it heightens the risk of tyranny given the scope of power possessed by global sovereigns, or, some might say, supersovereigns.

Schmitt was also concerned about totalizing supersovereignty. It was, to some degree, to thwart such global consolidation that he longed to re-inforce a clearly demarcated national sovereignty. We see this same fear of globalizing, totalizing, supersovereignty resurfacing as a resurgence of nationalism at the onset of the new millennium. But I digress.

In response to the debt crisis of the 1980s, the World Bank, for exam-ple, pressed developing countries to adopt agricultural policies it contended would fully integrate developing nations into the world economy—an economy perceived by the World Bank as inevitable in the natural course of human evolution—while also maximizing agricultural productivity.[73] The adjustments they enforced have shifted the focus away from provision of staples for domestic consumption and toward cash crops with high value in the international market.[74] Further, these adjustments involve land reform that favors the consolidation of land in the hands of those deemed most productive—as measured in terms of cash crops—which will not only as-sure that the land is held by the "most productive users" but also will "facili-tate exit [of the rural poor] from agriculture."[75]

Contemporaneous with policies resulting in the shift of agricul-tural focus from locally consumed produce to cash crops valued by the

73. Schanbacher, *Food Politics*, 16.

74. The transformations in the agricultural systems of developing nations com-bined to create a "consumer base" for the agricultural inputs (fertilizer, pesticides, and heavy equipment, for example) supplied by transnational corporations such as Mon-santo, Cargill, Caterpillar, etc.

75. Ibid., 15.

international market were the implementation of austerity measures. These measures limited, among other things, the monies that developing nations could direct toward food subsidy programs for the poor. This was particularly problematic as the retooling of agricultural practices resulted in rising prices of staple goods in developing nations, and reduced purchasing power of their neediest citizens.

The International Monetary Fund, the "financial arm of the global governance triad," insists that poor and developing nations adopt its trade liberalization policies in exchange for financial assistance.[76] The IMF argues that these policies are required in order to assure economic prosperity through full integration into the global capitalist economy. The IMF discourages any policies that it perceives might distort trade, such as export subsidies, tariffs, or any other type of "special and differential treatment." While developing nations are not permitted to subsidize their farmers under these structural adjustments, wealthier nations have continued to do so. These subsidies are primarily granted to large agribusinesses, and with the aid of these subsidies they are enabled to dump surplus agricultural goods into foreign markets at prices below the cost of production, a practice quite damaging to peasant farmers.

Economically, these maneuvers proved counterproductive. In Mexico, for example, implementation of structural adjustment programs resulted in the decrease of "real wages . . . by 41 percent between 1982 and 1988 . . . the unemployment rate rose to 20 percent" and over half of the country was forced below the poverty line.[77] From the perspective of food accessibility, these measures also brought about negative consequences. The implementation of austerity measures reduced spending on the poor by 6 percent, during a time when food prices were escalating rapidly due to the success of Mexican products on the foreign market.[78] Because of the massive debt incurred by farmers as they were forced to adopt technological farming practices, many farmers lost their land and ultimately become laborers on land they used to own.[79] Further compounding the problem, industrial wages fell by 10 percent as farmers migrated to the cities in search of jobs.[80]

It must be remembered that the "exit from agriculture" on the part of these peasant farmers was planned, at least on the part of the World Bank, IMF and WTO. This was part of their efforts to alleviate food insecurity

76. Ibid., 17–20.

77. Ibid., 41.

78. Ibid., 56.

79. Patel, *Stuffed and Starved*, 62.

80. Ibid., 53.

through economic development and increased individual purchasing power. Unfortunately, however, many of these displaced farmers were not able to find employment in urban centers either. They had transitioned from subsistence poverty to abject poverty through the imposition of trade liberalization policies. The processes involved in this oppression of farmers and peasants are so remarkably similar from country to country that farmers of one nation feel kinship with those of others. Efforts to reduce the existential threat of poverty—and the lack of economic access to food that accompanies poverty—had the net effect of worsening the problems they were intended to alleviate.

The lives of the rural poor—and indeed, as their increasing dislocation to urban areas suggests even the lives of the urban poor—are rendered increasingly precarious in the face of these policies. Naturally, faced with dispossession of their land and a life of abject poverty, peasant farmers worldwide have started to protest these measures. Even to protest comes at a high price as "peasant groups around the world are targeted, often with impunity, by local and national forces, both public and private."[81] For example, while "at least 1,425 rural workers, leaders and activists have been assassinated" in Brazil over the past two decades, "only 79 recorded cases have ever been brought to trial."[82] As I will argue in the next chapter, Agamben's theoretical concept of *homo sacer* and its relation to enactments of sovereignty helps us to identify these deaths as consequences of the enactments of sovereignty on the part of these multilateral organizations.

Distinguishing between frames and regimes begins to clarify the paradoxical nature of the concept of sovereignty as it appears in food politics. The food security frame endorsed by these agencies correlates to specific neoliberal economic and corporate agricultural interventions. Further, we note that although these multilateral agencies do not tout their sovereignty as such when implementing these policies, they do capitalize on states of exception in order to consolidate their power and push their global economic agenda forward. In the process, these enactments of sovereignty produce heightened vulnerability and precarity as one might predict based upon the philosophical engagements of such thinkers as Judith Butler and Giorgio Agamben. This assertion will be further explored in the following chapter.

How Is Food Sovereignty "Sovereign"?

Given the dominance of the corporate food regime internationally, referring to it *as* a regime is appropriate. However, the food sovereignty movement

81. Ibid., 41.
82. Ibid., 42.

lacks the cohesion or power of a regime, so we must acknowledge that the "regime" language does not quite map onto the practices. Nonetheless, the food sovereignty movement engages in decision-making and agricultural practices that serve as points of comparison with the corporate food regime. Sociologist Christina Schiavoni observes that sovereignty emerged in the context of a "perceived weakening of state control over domestic food systems" in the wake of encroachments upon state sovereignty by multilateral agencies and transnational corporations driven by a neoliberal economic agenda.[83] Their efforts to restore domestic control over food production and distribution lead them to demand that multilateral agencies and transnational corporations recognize the sovereignty of their respective nations.

Ironically, despite the rhetorical reliance upon the concept of sovereignty and the demand that transnational corporations respect the sovereignty of their respective nation-states, the practices of those utilizing the food sovereignty frame do not align with the type of sovereignty espoused by Schmitt. Internal to their respective nations, farmers committed to the practices of the food sovereignty movement operate via loosely structured communal councils. While participants must operate according to a set of general principles animating the movement as a whole, there are no formal rules or policies in place.[84] And agricultural methods are developed by the farmers themselves, tailored to their unique geographical location.

For example, *El Movimiento Campesino a Campesino* (MCAC or Farmer to Farmer Movement) encourages participation in local farmer-organized workshops where "farmers from local and regional areas participate in agricultural experimentation and share knowledge of successful agricultural techniques."[85] Subsequently culture and agriculture are "formed and reshaped in a mutual cultural praxis" of endogenous production of knowledge rather than through the adoption of externally developed practices.[86] Through these information pathways, farmers can receive information on "the potential pitfalls and dangers of genetically modified foods, such as how health risks are still under dispute, how genetically modified foods require more capital and chemical intensive inputs, and how genetically modified seeds reduce biodiversity."[87] Significantly, this "endogenous production of knowledge" results in highly specific knowledge regarding growing patterns in precise geographic locations. Ecosystem specific knowledge becomes increasingly important in the face of climate change.

83. Schiavoni, "Competing Sovereignties, Contested Processes," 467.

84. This could be seen as an enactment of resistance to unjust laws consonant with the general worker's strike Benjamin defended in his *Critique of Violence*.

85. Schanbacher, *Food Politics*, 68.

86. Ibid.

87. Ibid., 69.

The *Movimento dos Trabalhadores Rurais Sem Terra* (MST; Brazil's landless farmer's movement) promotes "practices such as local production for local consumption, agroecology, and sustainable development," reorienting the economy from the pursuit of limitless, globalized growth to the pursuit of place-based, sustainable development. It is quite possible that the place-based orientation of these landless peasant movements gives them their nationalist, and hence Schmittian, hue. And indeed, the *Campesino* movement has its roots in nationalism. Yet Schanbacher argues that "the food sovereignty movement holds a critical and strategic position in terms of theorizing policy implementation for issues of hunger and malnutrition."[88] Food sovereignty asserts that agroecological methods can be employed toward the ends of ecological and economic sustainability, while alleviating hunger and malnutrition.

The food sovereignty frame holds potential for alleviating these problems not so much for its nationalist origins, but because its decision-making practices are radically inclusive. This gives all food system stakeholders an opportunity to contribute to solutions. In other words, rather than focusing exclusively on what might be seen as distributive justice, or the equitable distribution of goods, the food sovereignty movement emphasizes what might be seen as procedural justice, or the use of fair processes in order to grant all participants access to decision-making power.

Procedural justice emerges as particularly important regarding the role of women in agricultural decision-making. Marilee Karl and Rocio Alorda argue that rural women "produce half of the world's food, and are the main producers of staple crops" making them responsible for food security on both a family and a global level.[89] Despite their significant role in food production, many food policies advocated by multilateral agencies operating under the food security frame "are biased toward men, and promote what some feminists perceive as a patriarchal paradigm."[90] Although over the past decade these agencies have started to increase support for smallholder farms, women are inadequately represented in decision-making bodies— despite the fact that they do most of the production work on smallholder farms in developing nations. By contrast, the food sovereignty movement includes women in the decision-making process as key stakeholders in agricultural processes, testifying to its procedural justice at least as far as women are concerned. Instead of pursuing development as usual, activist-scholars

88. Ibid., 74.
89. Ibid., 60.
90. Karl and Alorda, "Inseparable," 15.

increasingly advocate that multilaterals and other development agencies utilize a food sovereignty approach to redress these problems.

While most agencies operating under the model of food security promote increased production, the cause of hunger results primarily from unequal access to food rather than inadequate production of foodstuff.[91] Yet the multilateral agencies operating under the framework of food security cannot quite get at the root cause of this unequal access under the security frame alone because of the implicit assumptions about decision-making, family structure, and gender. For example, it has been demonstrated that giving men more money to raise cash crops does not necessarily increase family wealth or improve the family's access to food, especially for female family members. Karl and Alorda suggest that "equitable participation of women in decision-making and policy-making" would more effectively alleviate these problems.[92] The attainment of food security, they note, requires the integration of some tenets of the food sovereignty model—such as the right to self-determination—into the food security model.

Esperanza Santo and Margie Lacanilao describe the success of a process similar to that promoted by Karl and Alorda.[93] Sarilaya, an ecological farming project in the Philippines, is managed by women who function as capacity-builders and community organizers, and also as informal agricultural researchers. Nineteen families have participated in this project over an eight year period of time. Despite the patriarchal nature of the culture in the Imelda Valley, where the project took place, the women in these families successfully garnered leadership roles in their families and their communities with dramatically positive results. Soil was revitalized, crop yields increased, and runoff from pesticides and fertilizers ceased. In each case, net incomes increased due to decreased expenditures on inputs. This increased income relieved women's burdens overall, including sometimes the burden of maintaining a paying job alongside their unpaid agrarian labor.

The recognition of women's importance by food sovereignty practioners underscores Schanbacher's argument that the food sovereignty movement should not be confused with a regressive nostalgia for a patriarchal, agrarian past, a charge leveled by some feminist critics against the "agrarian vision" most often touted as a solution to the global food problem.[94] Yet many in the food sovereignty movement insist upon shoring up the boundaries of their respective nation-states as a means to reinforce their

91. Ibid., 9.

92. Ibid., 14

93. Santos, and Lacanilao, "Women Contributing to Food Sovereignty," 447–51.

94. Schanbacher, *Food Politics,* 75. McKenna, "Feminism and Farming," 529–34.

efforts at self-determination, a move that could be read as regressive and patriarchal in its own right, especially by critics of Schmittian sovereignty and the nation-state. The insistence upon functional nation-state boundaries emanates from a desire to thwart transnational agribusinesses efforts at privatization of ecological resources.[95] These concerns are not foreign to critics of the nation-state.

Additionally, some of these same critics of sovereignty and the nation-state might critique the food sovereignty movement for its utilization of rights language in its plea for recognition from the United Nation.[96] The very concept of rights is entangled with the notion of the nation-state and citizenry and therefore carries particular vulnerabilities in its deployment, as shall be described in greater detail below. The food sovereignty movement is in a rather uneasy relationship to major schools of thought in political theology. Their denunciation of neoliberal economics and transnational corporations might align well with the progressive discourse in political theology, but the desire for a stronger nation-state to protect their interests from external threats posed by transnational corporations puts them at odds with many far-left thinkers who generally reject strong sovereignty—and the nation-state along with it.

Rhetorical Disjunctures

At the root of the paradoxical appearance and enactments of Schmittian sovereignty in contemporary food politics is a disjuncture between the rhetorical framing and political, economic, and agricultural enactments of both the dominant model of agriculture and the food sovereignty movement. While the dominant model does not engage the concept of sovereignty, Schmittian or otherwise, nonetheless it endorses an economic version of sovereignty as enacted by multilateral trade organizations and transnational corporations. On the other hand, the food sovereignty movement relies heavily upon the concept of sovereignty, and in particular demands that the sovereignty of their nations be recognized, yet agricultural, political, and economic decision-making proceed in a profoundly democratic and non-sovereign—at least from a Schmittian perspective—manner. The

95. See for example articles such as Viacampesina.org, "La Via Campesina Europe in solidarity with Colombian farmers" demanding that peace agreements signed by their national governments are respected by all parties. But while they join with their national governments in opposing transnational corporations, they simultaneously work transnationally with peasants from many countries in bringing their needs to the attention of the United Nations and other development agencies—thus undermining the ability of any "sovereign" to decide on their behalf.

96. Viacampesina.org, "La Via Campesina and allies push for the Declaration on Peasants' Rights in Geneva."

following table may help to clarify the distinctions between the food sovereignty movement and what is variously referred to as conventional agriculture, industrial agriculture, the corporate food regime, and transnational agribusiness (to mention only a few of its monikers).

	Schmittian (unilateral) Sovereignty	Food Security Frame/ Corporate Food Regime	Food Sovereignty Movement
Rhetorical claim to sovereignty?	Yes	No	Yes
Rhetorical reliance upon nation-state configuration?	Yes	No; operates trans-nationally	Yes
Enactment of "state of exception?"	Yes, in response to military threat	Yes, on an economic basis	No
Enacted decision-making process	Unilateral, hierarchically imposed upon constituents	Unilateral, hierarchically imposed upon constituents	Radically inclusive and democratic
Enacted relationship to national laws	National laws, in particular the constitution, are suspended due to state of exception	Economic laws suspended due to economic "state of exception"	Calls for strengthening national law

Table 2.1 Rhetorical Disjunctures

What accounts for these rhetorical disjunctures? Food activist and scholar Christina Schiavoni argues that sovereignty in the food sovereignty movement is challenging to define because two competing versions of sovereignty are simultaneously operative.[97] She names the contradiction as that between external sovereignty and internal sovereignty. External sovereignty implies the reciprocal agreement between governments of different nations as described in the Peace of Westphalia. The competing internal sovereignty establishes sovereignty on the basis of popular will. The simultaneous operation of both external and internal sovereignties has challenged scholars attempting to identify "the sovereign" in food sovereignty.

To some degree, this can be read as a conflict between the autarchic sovereignty denounced by progressive and radical political theologians such as Clayton Crockett (externally) and the radical democracy they would prefer to see in its place (internally). It is possible that the rhetorical disjunctures

97. Schiavoni, "Competing Sovereignties," 467.

demonstrated on the chart above may result from the competing sovereignties identified by Schiavoni. The vision of "external sovereignty" operative in the food sovereignty movement accounts for their rhetorical reliance on claim to sovereignty, whereas the "internal sovereignty" operates via a (radically) democratic approach. Yet the concept of sovereignty as it is currently understood does imply greater unity that can be demonstrated among participants in the food sovereignty movement, even internally.

But even if a discrepancy between internal and external sovereignties can explain the paradoxes of the food sovereignty movement, then how can one account for the disjunctures in the transnational global food system? Is it possible that the corporate food regime suffers from its own competing sovereignties, mirror images of those encountered in the food sovereignty movement? On the one hand, they make no rhetorical claim to sovereignty, and if pressed would likely assert themselves to be defenders of democracy rather than promoters of some autarchic rule. Yet they function as sovereigns, unilaterally imposing their will upon constituent nations in order to maintain a neoliberal economic order. Most disturbingly, the globalizing mission of a neoliberal economic agenda seems content to destroy what it cannot internalize.

Conclusion

How do the political contestations over economics and agriculture relate to Schmittian sovereignty and Benjaminian resistance? As I hope I have demonstrated, corporate industrial interventions can be read as deployments of Schmittian sovereignty, albeit displaced from the nation-state to transnational corporations and multilateral agencies, and enacted through economic and development policy that suspend the economic laws and development policies of developing nations through structural adjustment programs, rather than declarations of war. These corporations and agencies place heavy emphasis on technicity and economy over ecological principles. Their agenda is legitimated, in their eyes and the eyes of many, by the need to protect humans from the threat of starvation, or, in Schmittian terms, in order to eliminate the existential threat posed by lack of access to food.

The appeal of the "food security" frame is that it promises adequate access to food, both for those in the Global North and the Global South. Problematically, it has been unable to deliver on that promise; over seven million people per year die of starvation. To the credit of the food system, the raw number of people dying of starvation has remained steady for a number of years, while the total population of the world continues to climb. Thus, from the perspective of percentages this frame and its enactments seem to be at least modestly successful. However, the neoliberal economic system operates within a mechanistic worldview that empirical scientific studies are currently revealing to be inaccurate. In the face of climate change, this inaccuracy could prove disastrous. Most tragically, its short term gains may be nearing their end, as drought in Africa and the violent conflict in its wake put twenty million people in four countries at risk of starvation in 2017.[98]

By contrast, the food sovereignty movement demands a version of national sovereignty that undercuts the legitimacy of "the sovereign" (as described by Schmitt) in their insistence on the inclusion of a variety of voices in the decision-making process. In particular, they insist on the voices typically marginalized from the decision-making process of the World Bank, WTO, and IMF: landless peasants and women smallholders. This radical inclusivity potentially mitigates the abjection produced by enactments of Schmittian sovereignty, as will be demonstrated in later chapters.

While the radically democratic decision-making processes and ecological worldview of those in the "food sovereignty" movement might find support of liberal and progressive political theologians, their reliance upon the concept of national sovereignty puts them at odds with those same theorists. As noted in the previous chapter, those who reject the concept of national sovereignty similarly reject—or at least call into serious question—concepts of popular sovereignty that might lend this movement legitimacy.

In no small measure, the urgency to support the food sovereignty movement arises from an examination of the risks of proceeding with conventional agriculture—both those already occurring and those predicted to occur in the future. At the same time, it must be stressed that the present work does not call for an abrupt cessation of conventional agriculture. Such an approach would be not only quixotic but foolhardy, as an estimated three billion people rely upon food produced by conventional, high-input means.[99] Yet conventional agriculture, pressed into the service of a neoliberal economic agenda by the corporate food regime utilizing the rhetoric of food security is proving to undermine the very security it promises. Unsustainable by definition means it cannot continue. Therefore the present work hopes to add to the growing body of literature, such as the many sources cited in this chapter, calling for the limitation of conventional agricultural practices and policies promoting the gradual transition to other, less ecologically damaging, methods.

98. Miles, "Four famines mean 20 million people may starve in the next six months." Famine appears to have been averted in Somalia as of December 2017. Eight million Yemenis continue to face extreme danger heading into 2018.

99. Barber, *The Third Plate*.

Part II

Sovereignty Undone

Chapter 4

Banished from the Sovereign's Table

Precarity in the Global Food System

IN THE PREVIOUS CHAPTER motions of power in contemporary food politics were connected with deployments of a Schmittian-type sovereignty on the part of those in the corporate food regime, operating under the rhetorical frame of "food security." The renditions of this particular form of sovereignty are economic in nature in a manner not explicitly theorized by Schmitt himself. Economic deployments of sovereignty were shown to occur despite the lack of any rhetoric staking a claim to sovereignty. That these deployments occur within a political frame of "food security" is no surprise given that Carl Schmitt's formulation of sovereignty is rooted in precisely this guarantee of security in the face of an existential threat. However, what I hope to demonstrate in this chapter is that in the case of food politics, if not all politics, such deployments of sovereignty amplify existential risks on a broad scale, despite claims to the contrary.

Giorgio Agamben's Theoretical Insights

I will draw largely upon the work of Giorgio Agamben to elucidate the risks to which we are all subjected by instantiations of sovereignty on the part of multilaterals. Of pivotal importance are Agamben's concepts of *homo sacer*; the distinction between "the people" and "the People"; and the state of exception. Criticisms of Agamben, both those of Jacques Derrida and my own, will be addressed once the utility of Agamben's theories

93

has been described. In thinking with and beyond Agamben regarding issues of food politics, the nation-state, sovereignty, and multilaterals, I will draw upon Judith Butler's assertion that a less violent politics might arise once "an inevitable interdependency becomes acknowledged as the basis for global political community."[1]

Homo Sacer

In *Homo Sacer: Sovereign Power and Bare Life*, Giorgio Agamben's argument lingers on Schmitt's assertion that "the sovereign is he who decides upon the exception." While Schmitt acknowledges that dictatorship is a risk of his version of sovereignty, he leaves the consequences of this dictatorship to the imagination. Agamben fixates on it. By grappling with potential for collapse to dictatorship head on, Agamben clarifies the manner in which absolute sovereignty amplifies rather than reduces widespread bodily vulnerability.

For Agamben, the consequence of sovereignty is represented by the figure of *homo sacer*, or "sacred man." Agamben devoted an entire volume to exploration of this figure, which he seeks to portray as "bare life," akin to his reading of the ancient Greek *zoë*, which he reads as "simple natural life." This figure represents for Agamben the status of one whose life has been disqualified, as it were, and now exists as merely "bare life" through exclusion from the law as a consequence of the sovereign decision on the exception.

Ultimately, the sovereign has the ability to cast absolutely anyone outside the law, and *homo sacer* is at the mercy of absolutely everyone. To the sovereign every other is potentially *homo sacer*, and to *homo sacer* every other is sovereign.[2] Agamben's ultimate contention is that in the context of a liberal democracy given over to a prolonged—or permanent—state of exception, everyone is susceptible to becoming—in fact *does* become—*homo sacer*. When sovereignty devolves to a dictatorship through the machinations of a permanent state of exception, the consequence is precisely the profound existential threat that sovereignty was to have prevented in the first place.

Much of Agamben's argument leans on a hypothesized originary distinction between *zoë* (bare life, corresponding to *homo sacer*) and *bios* (qualified or properly formed life) made by ancient Greek philosophers. In making this case, he draws from Foucault's citation of Aristotle.[3] Agamben argues that to refer to such qualified lives as the lives of philosophers

---

1. Butler, *Precarious Life*, xii.
2. Agamben, *Homo Sacer*, 84.
3. Michel Foucault, *La volonte de savoir*, as quoted in Agamben, *Homo Sacer*.

(*bios theoretikos*) or the properly political life (*bios politikos*) neither Plato nor Aristotle would have used the word *zoë*, which he claimed lacks the capacity to convey a properly qualified life. Derrida is one of several who raise the contention that this reading of Aristotle is inaccurate, and his critique of Agamben will be detailed below. For now suffice to say that while this distinction is pivotal for Agamben, this distinction is less so for a political theology of food.

Agamben is inspired to "analyze the link binding bare life to sovereign power" by Walter Benjamin's mention of "mere life" in *Critique of Violence*.[4] To begin with, Agamben lauds Benjamin's insight that lawmaking is "necessarily and intimately bound up with" violence, quoting Benjamin at length:

> For the function of violence in lawmaking is twofold, in the sense that lawmaking pursues as its end, with violence as the means, what is to be established as law, but at the moment of instatement does not dismiss violence; rather, at this very moment of lawmaking, it specifically establishes as law not an end unalloyed by violence, but one necessarily and intimately bound to it.[5]

Agamben appears to adopt without question Benjamin's assertion that law is intimately and necessarily bound to violence.

Agamben goes on to say that "it is not by chance" that Benjamin shortly thereafter evokes the concept of *bloße Leben*.[6] Benjamin mentions *bloße Leben* in a passage declaring that "blood is the symbol of mere life" and that "mythical violence"—the violence of sovereign lawmaking and law preserving—"is bloody power over mere life for its own sake, divine violence is pure power over all life for the sake of the living."[7] However, although Benjamin does insist that legal violence is perpetrated against "mere life," as previously indicated, he decidedly does not find "mere life" to be sacred. In fact, he takes great pains to argue *against* the sacredness of life, ultimately concluding that "however sacred man is . . . there is no sacredness in his condition, in his bodily life vulnerable to injury by his fellow

---

4. Ibid., 65. Benjamin says *Bloße Leben*, which Agamben translates as bare life; others translate as mere life.

5. Walter Benjamin, "Critique of Violence," 295, and as quoted in Agamben, *Homo Sacer*, 65.

6. Agamben translates this phrase as "bare life" but Edmond Jephcott and others translate instead as "mere life." The importance of this distinction becomes clearer when assessing Derrida's critique of Agamben.

7. Benjamin, *Critique of Violence*, 297.

men."[8] Benjamin goes on to suggest that "it might well be worthwhile to track down the origin of the dogma of the sacredness of life."[9]

Agamben perceives himself as "develop[ing] these suggestions."[10] So it is somewhat ironic that Agamben's "bare life" becomes synonymous with *homo sacer,* or sacred man, over against Benjamin's objections to just this line of reasoning. Agamben ends up affirming "bare life" as sacred because his search for the "dogma of the sacredness of life" excavates the figure of *homo sacer* in the historical record. Agamben unearths from archaic Roman law the figure of *homo sacer,* representing one who, having been judged guilty of a crime, can be killed with impunity, but cannot be sacrificed. The sheer vulnerability of this figure, as Agamben sees it, results from having been excluded from "both human and divine law" by virtue of the decision of the plebiscite, and his sacredness consists of the *"unpunishability of his killing and the ban on his sacrifice."*[11] Because Benjamin has already connected "mere life" with lawmaking violence, Agamben perceives the figure of *homo sacer*—a man rendered "sacred" through legal decision—to map onto Benjamin's "mere" life. In forging a connection between *homo sacer* and bare life, Agamben applies the "sacred" qualifier to the man so named in precisely the manner already rejected by Benjamin.[12]

The exclusion of *homo sacer* from "both human and divine law" takes the form of the "ban," according to Agamben, which is "the essential structure of sovereign power."[13] Agamben makes a somewhat tortuous argument here, but ultimately finds parallels between *homo sacer* and the bandit who, having been banished, or expelled as a wrongdoer, is now vulnerable to harm from anyone. Banishment is, for Agamben, the punishment par excellence. Described as "the power of delivering something over to itself,"[14] the ban is tantamount to a refusal to preserve the one who has been banned.

Agamben argues that the ban connects the sovereign to *homo sacer,* in part because it renders both sovereign and *homo sacer* outside the law. The sovereign is under no obligation to obey the law, and *homo sacer* no longer falls under the auspices of legal protection. Agamben goes on to say that "what has been banned is delivered over to its own separateness and at the same time consigned to the mercy of the one who abandons it."[15] Thus, the

8. Ibid., 299.

9. Ibid.

10. Agamben, *Homo Sacer,* 65–66.

11. Ibid., 73; emphasis in original.

12. Benjamin, *Critique of Violence,* 297.

13. Agamben, *Homo Sacer,* 111.

14. Ibid., 109.

15. Ibid., 110.

ban implicitly connects the sovereign with *homo sacer* not only by a shared "extra-legal" position, but also by virtue of the fact that the act of banishment itself determines who is sovereign and who is *homo sacer*.

Agamben insists that "the life of the exile . . . borders on the life of *homo sacer*,"[16] by which I think he means to say that the condition of "banishment" is not so much about a physical banishment from a geographic territory, but rather a situation in which the sovereign has cast an individual outside the auspices of sovereign protection provided by the legal system over which the sovereign presides. Agamben makes a plea for his reader to "recognize this structure of the ban in . . . the public spaces in which we still live," insisting that *"in the city, the banishment of sacred life is more internal than every interiority and more external than every extraneousness."*[17] Agamben wishes to call attention to the manner in which banishment no longer necessarily results in literal exile or geographic dislocation, but rather is a state in which "citizens can be said, in a specific but extremely real sense, to appear virtually as *homies sacri*" in the context of modern biopolitics because they have been cast outside the sphere of sovereign protection.

Insofar as the hallmark of Agamben's *homo sacer* is profound vulnerability, his sacredness directly contradicts Benjamin's assertion that whatever is sacred about life it is certainly not the bodily condition of vulnerability. Nonetheless, for several reasons, I believe Agamben's *homo sacer* offers an intriguing focal point for the examination of precarity in our current situation of transnational global corporate empire. First, Agamben tracks the history of the concept of the sacredness of life through the concept of *homo sacer*, and the implications of his inquiry connect *homo sacer* to the state monopoly on violence, another concern of Benjamin's. Second, Agamben provides a lens through which the malnourished can be seen to have been banned (without explicit declaration), or cast outside the auspices of sovereign protection. Third, Agamben's inquiry into the relationship between loss of recognizable citizenship and *homo sacer* merits thoughtful consideration as climate change, in conjunction with political responses to its impact, is already producing millions of refugees who have lost their citizenship and face radical vulnerability as a consequence.

To my first point, what Agamben accomplishes effectively, in my opinion, is articulating the linkage between the state monopoly on violence and the "dogma of the sacredness of life," both concerns of Benjamin. Benjamin notes that despite claims that "all life is sacred," which in the colloquial sense is used to convey the conviction that life is inviolable such that all killing is

16. Ibid.

17. Ibid., 111; emphasis in original.

immoral, in practice people behave as if some lives are more sacred (inviolable) that others.[18] Agamben begins to untangle this conundrum by first demonstrating that "sacred" held a different connotation in antiquity than it does in our colloquial understanding. While today we may think that the term sacred means inviolable, Agamben explains that *sacer* may have initially referred to a person or object that had been "removed from the *profanum*," but has since become "overburdened with contradictory meanings" such that its use is subject to slippage.[19]

I would suggest that one of the contradictions that has burdened the concept of sacrality arises in conjunction with the sovereign decision. Thinking with Agamben, I would propose that to say that "all life is sacred" is to say that all life acquires its *social value* in relation to the sovereign. Similarly, life loses its social value when subjected to the sovereign ban. This is because while the sovereign ban casts both the sovereign and *homo sacer* outside of the *profanum*, the impact of removal from the *profanum* produces dramatically different results for each.

For example, using Agamben's preferred circumstance of Nazi Germany, the life of the sovereign, that being Adolf Hitler, was of infinitely greater value than the lives of the millions of *homines sacri* slaughtered under his regime (notably Jews, though millions of others alongside them). To draw forth another, more contemporary example, the American president's life is so greatly valued that he is heavily guarded by Secret Service at all times. By contrast, the lives of African American prostitutes are of such low value to the state system that their murders are scarcely worth investigating.[20] The Black Lives Matter movement similarly calls our attention to inconsistent social valuing of lives.

I will spend the greater part of this and the next chapter exploring how, first of all, the sovereign ban does not arise exclusively in the form of a simple binary "in or out" position in contemporary society. That is to say, the protection offered to individual bodies varies in a graded and proportional fashion based upon identifiable markers of those bodies, markers such as race, gender, class, ethnicity, religion, and nationality creating gradations of oppressions that feminist scholars will recognize as "intersectionality." What we might think of as social status or socioeconomic class in some way represents a gradient on a spectrum of proximity to sovereign power, with protection on one end and the sovereign ban on the other. As social animals,

18. Benjamin, *Critique of Violence*, 298.

19. Agamben, *Homo Sacer*, 79–80.

20. See for example the documentary "Tales of the Grim Sleeper" by Nick Broomfield.

humans are subconsciously and perpetually able to "read" where a person is in relationship to sovereign protection and treat them accordingly. While there are numerous exceptions to the general trend, the trend is that the further from sovereign protection (i.e., the lower the social status), the slower are social responses to preserve or restore bodily well-being.

While Agamben does not say it in quite this way, I would suggest that sovereign power is not only the power to suspend the constitution, as was the "exception" with which Schmitt concerned himself, but the power to determine the one to whom the law no longer applies in the sense of assuring legal protection of rights. No longer can that person's killing be considered illegal because they are no longer under the law. An example would be the case of extrajudicial killings of black men during routine traffic stops denounced by the Black Lives Matter movement. Neither can that person's death be acknowledged as a sort of "sacrifice" that serves the stability of a given social order (as, for example, a soldier's death in the line of duty might be regarded).

Agamben's overarching concern is that "sacredness is a line of flight still present in contemporary politics," and that it is increasingly "coinciding with the biological life itself of citizens."[21] Here he specifically means sacred in the sense of "removed from the *profanum*" as opposed to the sense of "closer to God" with which we often imbue the term sacred in its contemporary use. And furthermore, I read him as insisting that the the legal order constitutes the *profanum*. Agamben is suggesting that we are all at immanent risk of a banishment that may never be explicitly declared as such and subsequently "we are all virtually *homines sacri*."[22] He observes that today we are confronted with "a life that as such is exposed to a violence without precedent precisely in the most profane and banal ways."[23] He identifies traffic fatalities as an example of this "profane and banal" violence.

I would argue that among the profane and banal sorts of violence perpetrated is the malnourishment perpetrated in the food system due to the enactments of top-down sovereignty on the part of multilateral agencies and transnational corporations already discussed in the previous chapter.[24] I submit that the malnourished—both starving and obese—have

21. Agamben, *Homo Sacer,* 114–15.

22. Ibid.,115.

23. Ibid., 114.

24. Another example could be air pollution. A 2012 study at Massachusetts Institute of Technology estimated twenty-one thousand premature deaths occurred due to air pollution in California alone. See Chu, "Study: Air pollution causes 200,000 early deaths each year in the U.S." As a point of comparison, based on 2014 statistics compiled by the Center for Disease Control (the closest year available), only cancer and

been banned, excluded, or "delivered over to [their] own separateness," in that their preservation is not ensured by the sovereign powers. Their bodily integrity no longer falls within state law to protect, and subsequently the malnourished can be killed by the withholding, by means of corporate and economic policies and practices, of adequate and safe nutrition.

In part, these bodies are excluded from legal protection through structural adjustment programs that impose austerity measures on already impoverished developing countries. These measures prohibit the distribution of food subsidies to the poor, while other provisions of the structural adjustment programs simultaneously assure that local food prices increase.[25] The starving cannot be fed for free, as that would wreak havoc upon the economic system that perceives of food as nothing more than mere commodity. Yet deaths resulting from these policies are not considered to be either murder or sacrifice.

Austerity measures are imposed in the service of a neoliberal economic "law" that has as its central promise the delivery of perpetually increasing abundance for all people. The malnourished, however, have been banned, excluded, or excepted from this economic law. They will not experience the promised abundance. As Benjamin and Agamben insist, all lawmaking and law preserving involve violence, and for the malnourished this violence will take the form of persistent hunger, nutritionally related diseases, and premature death and will never be acknowledged as violence per se. As will be discussed in the application of Margaret Urban Walker's feminist ethics, these bodies are also excluded from state protections in part through what she refers to as "privatization," in our case privatization of food choices, which as already discussed are not entirely private.

Walker's understanding of privatization will be described in greater detail below, as her theory echoes Agamben's warning that:

> One and the same affirmation of bare life leads, in bourgeois democracy, to a primacy of the private over the public and of individual liberties over collective obligations and yet becomes,

heart disease surpassed air pollution as causes of death. Whereas air pollution killed twenty-one thousand, less than two thousand died as the result of homicide.

25. Food prices increase under austerity measures as developing nations must agree to transition to cash crops, as opposed to subsistence crops, in order to generate income to repay their loans. They are also required to privatize state agricultural systems, with the result that major corporations assume control of foodways. Problematically, these corporations "manipulate supply and demand for profit-making purposes," resulting in lower wages paid to farm laborers, and higher food prices at the grocery store; Schanbacher, *Politics of Food*, 43. Furthermore, according to Raj Patel, farmers and consumers also suffer because, having transitioned to cash crops, farmers no longer provide produce for local sale. Patel, *Stuffed and Starved*.

in totalitarian states, the decisive political criterion and the exemplary realm of sovereign decisions.[26]

We in the United States may feel some relief at living in a "free democracy"
rather than a totalitarian state, and therefore free of concern about becoming *homines sacre*. But Agamben reminds us of the lightning speed at which
parliamentary democracies were transformed "into totalitarian states" at the
outset of World War II, and just as speedily transformed back again at the
war's conclusion. Even for Americans, an affirmation of bare life—in conjunction with our cultural proclivities toward individualism—paves the way
for all manner of privatization. As will be argued below, privatization serves
the ends of oppressive regimes by shielding from view both their specific
abuses and their toxic effects on those they oppress. Privatization, I contend,
is a form of internal banishment, the banishment Agamben alluded to earlier
when he said that *"in the city, the banishment of sacred life is more internal
than every interiority and more external than every extraneousness."*[27]

"The People," "the people," and Human Rights

Agamben argues persistently and effectively that "bare life" is what is at
stake in the political and is furthermore always at risk in the nation-state.
Agamben calls attention to motions of power operative as instantiations of
Schmittian sovereignty in democratic nation-states that potentially threaten
their citizens with a widespread radical vulnerability. That the vulnerability
threatened by instantiations of Schmittian sovereignty is widespread should,
I contend, trigger equally widespread concern about global food politics.
Significantly, Agamben calls attention to fragility of the concept of "human
rights" that rely upon citizenship for their protection: "In the system of the
nation-state, the so-called sacred and inalienable rights of man show themselves to lack every protection and reality at the moment in which they can
no longer take the form of rights belonging to citizens of a state."[28] This is
because rights require a guarantor.[29]

Agamben argues that refugees reveal the myth undergirding the concept of "inalienable rights" that substantiated the revolutionary movements
that formed the nation-state centuries ago. These rights were simultaneously
declared "indefeasible rights of man" arising as a consequence of birth, but

26. Agamben, *Homo Sacer,* 122.
27. Ibid., 111; emphasis in original.
28. Ibid., 126.
29. Patel, "What does food sovereignty look like?," 668.

yet were conferred exclusively upon citizens.[30] *All* humans were believed to be possessed of inalienable rights as a condition of birth, yet the nation protected *only* those rights of its own citizens. The arrival of the refugee immediately calls into question the very notion of inalienable rights as these rights that are allegedly due to all humanity come into direct conflict with the bounded nature of the nation-state and the interests of its citizens. Subsequently, for Agamben, refugees "put the originary fiction of modern sovereignty in crisis" by "bringing to light the difference between birth and nation."[31] The refugee reveals the contingent nature of the allegedly inalienable rights upon which democracies are founded. Consequently, the sovereign ban—the exception, so to speak—was (at least partially) codified into law in order to explain how it happens that some humans are nonetheless not afforded rights conceived to be inalienable.[32]

In the context of the present conversation concerning food politics, the contingency of rights upon citizenship is exceedingly problematic given the conjunction of a fragile global food system and a fragile planetary ecology. The past decade has already resulted in millions of refugees, either directly from climate-related events or indirectly as the result of displacement due to violent conflict (itself partially driven by climate change). The refugee crisis is expected to worsen dramatically as temperatures (and sea levels) continue to rise dislocating millions of people living in coastal areas and as desertification renders arable land—and food—increasingly scarce. Agamben remarks:

> What is essential is that, every time refugees represent not individual cases but—as happens more and more often today—a mass phenomenon, both these [multinational] organizations [such as the UN] and individual states prove themselves, despite their solemn invocations of the "sacred and inalienable" rights of man, absolutely incapable of resolving the problem and even of confronting it directly.[33]

This should give us all pause as we consider the potential for cruelty and suffering as climate change progresses. The recent Syrian refugee crisis may be but a foretaste of what is to come. Moreover, in its reliance upon "rights" language, the food sovereignty movement (and even the food justice movement) also fails to confront this problem directly.

30. Agamben, *Homo Sacer,* 126–30.

31. Ibid., 131.

32. Agamben also details how this same line of reasoning applied to women and slaves, relevant insofar as these indicate marginalized groups, a matter of concern for a political theology of food.

33. Ibid., 133.

While gesturing toward an ominous future, though not one overtly inflected with concerns about climate change, Agamben argues that interwar Germany serves as an historical example of an instance in which bare life became synonymous with the political. Agamben warns that our democracies are at risk of transforming into fascist totalitarian regimes if we remain wedded to the concept of the nation-state. He argues that the juridico-political structure of the camp is the offspring of the state of exception and martial law, even more likely to occur when the state of exception is no longer exceptional, but has become the norm.

Not only was the camp a zone of exception, in which normal law did not apply, but any Jew entering the camp had already been declared a noncitizen—*homo sacer*, one to whom the protections of the law no longer applied. Agamben insists that the most useful inquiries into the Holocaust are not how such atrocities could be committed against human beings but rather an inquiry into "the juridical procedures and deployments of power by which human beings could be so completely deprived of their rights and prerogatives that no act committed against them could appear any longer as a crime."[34] The atrocities committed in Nazi Germany were all perfectly legal according to German law at the time.

More pressing than concerns about historical events that do not constitute a site for intervention is Agamben's chilling insistence that Nazi Germany was the prototype for contemporary politics. Nazi fascism arose in large part thanks to a conundrum at the heart of the nation-state itself. Agamben attributes this flaw to the notion of "the People as a whole political body." The concept of "the People" animated the revolutionary process that culminated in the development of democratic nation-states. The process of nation-state formation was to have united all people within a national boundary and assured their rights. Yet despite the emergence of democratic nation-states, there exists within each nation a subcategory Agamben refers to as "the people," in contrast to "the People." "The people" represent a "fragmentary multiplicity of needy and excluded bodies."[35] "The People" have failed to encompass "the people."

Agamben asserts that the French Revolution was founded upon the inalienable rights of man and driven by the ideal of including all citizens in the sovereign body of "the People." Subsequently, the persistence of "the people"—citizens excluded from politics—becomes "an embarrassing presence, and misery and exclusion appear for the first time as an altogether intolerable scandal."[36] The failure to integrate all people into the new politi-

34. Ibid., 171.
35. Ibid., 177.
36. Ibid., 179.

cal order appears as scandal because it begs the question: if the nation-state is founded upon the inalienable rights of man, how can one explain the numerous exclusions integral to its political machinations? On precisely what basis have "the people" been excluded from "the People?"

Agamben asserts that the urge of National Socialists to purify the German state is exemplary of the urge to seal this split between "the people" who have been excluded and "the People" of a nation by permanently and radically eliminating "the people that is excluded." Jews in Nazi Germany represent for Agamben "the living symbol of the people and of the bare life that modernity necessarily creates within itself, but whose *presence* it can no longer tolerate in any way."[37] Such efforts, he insists, are doomed to failure as every instantiation of the People as unified body immediately conjures the manifestation of bare life.

I would suggest that efforts toward a global economy driven by the unholy union between democracy and neoliberal capitalism will find itself in a similar position. While Agamben might find the nation-state to be lapsing toward totalitarianism at present, I find myself at least equally concerned with the dissolution of the nation-state into an even more totalizing transnational corporatocracy, *especially* in light of Agamben's critique of the nation-state and its legal fictions.[38] For if the nation-state cannot integrate everyone into its system despite its territorial and cultural circumscription, how much more likely is the process of economic globalization to fail given the grand scope of its project—particularly if this project is not so much the result of organic sociality as it is the result of enactments of economic renditions of supra-national sovereignty? And if the allergy of the nation-state to what it cannot integrate leads to the death camp, how much more likely is a death camp to arise when the process of globalization fails to integrate everyone into its economic vision? The peasant farmers who resist the imposition of high-input corporate agricultural practices and protest trade agreements that dispossess them of their land constitute, if nothing else, "the people" who cannot be integrated into the global neoliberal economic system. As such, much like the Jews in Nazi Germany, they become *homines sacri*—the bare life created by the transnational corporatocracy that gives the lie to its pretentions at universalism and therefore cannot be tolerated in any way.

37. Ibid.

38. Yet I must also insist that retreating into a staunchly nationalist position does not necessarily provide shelter from a transnational corporatocracy, especially if nationalist rhetoric is leveraged in the service of neoliberal capitalism. Furthermore, my concerns about abusive "supersovereignty" do not diminish my concerns about absolute sovereignty enacted at the level of the nation-state.

"The People," "the people," and Global Food Politics

Although I have already touched upon the relevance of *homo sacer* to contemporary food politics I would like to circle back to some of these points as the explanatory power of Agamben's *homo sacer* in food politics is further illuminated by Agamben's distinction between "the People" and "the people." I would like to deepen the analysis of how the concept of *homo sacer* clarifies the ways in which exclusion from politics legitimates the withholding of nutritious food, and how nutritional deprivation in turn legitimates further exclusion from politics. Further, I would like to provide a brief description of how Agamben helps us to understand how the killing of Brazilian food activists can be of such little consequence that over a thousand of these assassinations have gone uninvestigated.

When over seven million people die of starvation every year on a planet that produces sufficient calories to feed everyone, we must ask ourselves the same question of our food system that Agamben asks of the camp: how have political, economic, and agricultural laws been structured so as to render inflicting death by starvation anything other than criminal? When upwards of 35 percent of Americans suffer from metabolic syndrome, how is the contribution of the food system to this public health problem not legible as a scandal?[39] In the context of food politics, these needy and excluded bodies, politically excluded in practice if not by law, correspond to the bodies of the malnourished, both starving and obese. Because they have been excluded from politics, they become people from whom nutritious food can be withheld without consequence.

If they are obese, they are presumed to be deficient decision-makers; we we need not concern ourselves with the systemic causes of their obesity. If they are starving to death, they signify a degree of abjection and hopelessness that obscures the actors involved in their suffering such that it is unclear who should be punished for what everyone already knows is not a crime.[40] As I will argue at length in chapter 4, the physical habitus that develops from the withholding of nutritious food—whether that habitus be obese or emaciated—further legitimates their exclusion from politics.

These malnourished bodies, both starving and obese, can be read as members of what Agamben has already defined as "the people," the suffering masses perpetually excluded from politics—or at the very least excluded from high-level decisions regarding what sorts of food, if any, should be accessible to them. Many of these people are rural smallholders and peasants

39. Aguilar et al., "Prevalence of the Metabolic Syndrome in the United States 2003–2012."

40. Walker, *Moral Understandings*, 200.

from developing nations who are suffering precisely because they have not been integrated into the international political body and also because the efforts to integrate them into the global economic system have failed. Others of these people are more or less average citizens of developed nations whose access to nutritional food has been restricted by the near-monopoly that transnational agribusiness holds over the global food system as previously described. If failure to integrate "the people" drives the march toward a totalitarian regime because the excluded nations and classes pose a threat to the systems that have excluded them, might we instead prefer to work toward agricultural policies that do not have such integration as their driving force—as do the current policies of the corporate food regime?

But indirect death through nutritional deprivation is not the only way in which *homo sacer* can be killed with impunity within the global food system. The killing can take a more direct approach. This is exemplified in food politics by the killing of food activists in particular but also by the killing of environmental activists in general. The two are connected because environmental activists are in part motivated by the desire to preserve access to arable land and traditional food sources. These activists are, by and large, peasants ("the people"), unassimilable into the global economy and the corporate food regime ("the People"). Any meaningful activism on transnational food politics must grapple with the harsh realities of the failure of the global economy to integrate these activists, and the very real risks such failure poses to the activists themselves.

Economist and food activist Raj Patel notes that "in taking a stand against the illegal appropriation of their land, or even in merely raising their voices against the injustices they face, peasant groups across the world are targeted, often with impunity, by local and national forces, both public and private."[41] He provides specific examples, such as the Korean farmer who died after being bludgeoned by police during a protest and the persistent potential violence faced by Brazilian peasants from both public- and private-sector sources. Despite the astounding numbers of peasant farmers and activists assassinated in Brazil, Patel reports that "only 79 recorded cases have ever been brought to trial."[42] Does the fact that so few of these assassinations are brought to trial imply that they are not regarded as crimes worthy of prosecution?

When describing the assassination of food activists in Chiapas, Jonathan Fox notes that "the use of repression against peasant movements in Mexico has long been justified by the accusation of a revolutionary political

41. Patel, *Stuffed and Starved*, 41.
42. Ibid., 42.

challenge to the state."[43] There were indeed revolution-minded political organizations in the region, but food councils were careful to steer clear of involvement with their activities. The farmers were not interested in overthrowing the government, nor were they seeking handouts or subsidies, only fair prices that include the cost of land, labor, and growing. Yet despite their resistance to politicization, "any networking at all among food councils was perceived by higher-level managers as a threat." Subsequently, higher-level officials conducted "purges" dismantling "most of the autonomous regional consumer mobilization" in the region.[44]

In the case of Chiapas, farmers and consumers alike were perceived as threatening to the "free-market" system when they formed effective food councils. Their refusal to integrate into the global economy was perceived as a threat to the abslute sovereignty enacted on the part of those in the corporate food regime. Since their demands undermine the sovereignty enacted by multilaterals and agribusiness, their protest results in their being cast out from protection of the law—they are rendered (albeit informally) *homo sacer*. Subsequently, they can be killed but not murdered; these deaths are seldom investigated and, as the numbers show, even less often prosecuted. We should not mistakenly believe that this situation is restricted to Mexico or to the 1990s. The similarity of oppressive processes in various locations throughout the world is the central experience uniting the various landless peasant movements into a global Food Sovereignty Movement.[45] And these murders continue to this day: Berta Caceres, Nelson Garcia, and most pointedly, Jose Angel Flores, president of the Unified Campesinos Movement of the Aguan Valley are three such examples in Honduras in 2016 alone.[46]

The State of Exception in Food Politics

Along with the concept of *homo sacer* and his distinction between "the People" and "the people," Agamben has also written about another theory that informs this political theology of food given the context of climate change: that of the state of exception. Agamben quotes Walter Benjamin as saying that, "The tradition of the oppressed teaches us that the 'state of exception' in which we live is the rule. We must arrive at a concept of history that

43. Fox, *Politics of Food in Mexico*, 179

44. Ibid., 180.

45. Patel, *Stuffed and Starved*, 47.

46. Lakhani, "Fellow Honduran activist Nelson García murdered days after Berta Cáceres"; Knight, "Leader of Honduran Campesino Movement Assassinated."

corresponds to this fact. Then we will have the production of the real state of exception before us as a task."[47] While the aforementioned quote on the state of exception appears in the book *Homo Sacer*, this political phenomenon receives fuller attention in a volume of its own: *State of Exception*.

Agamben attempts to set forth a theory of the state of exception since he believes that the suspension of the law is the means by which bare life is captured in the juridico-political order. Subsequently, "a theory of the state of exception is the preliminary condition for any definition of the relation that binds and, at the same time, abandons the living to law."[48] This becomes particularly important since in his view the "voluntary creation of a permanent state of emergency has become one of the essential practices of contemporary states, including so-called democratic ones" since the Third Reich.[49] As already alluded to, this state of exception has similarly been operative in food politics, legitimating the usurpation of a developing nation's sovereignty by multilateral organizations such as the World Bank, IMF, and WTO, although in the case of food politics the emergency has been economic rather than military.

Agamben is concerned here with modern totalitarianism, which he defines as "the establishment, by means of the state of exception, of a legal civil war that allows for the physical elimination not only of political adversaries but of entire categories of citizens who for some reason cannot be integrated into the political system."[50] The trajectory from democracy to totalitarian regime follows a predictable pattern: the state of exception begins as a constitutional dictatorship and over time becomes an unconstitutional dictatorship. He notes that some theorists attempt to defend the state of exception, but cannot "overcome the forces" that transform the constitutional dictatorship into an unconstitutional dictatorship. Problematically, all theories of the state of exception "remain prisoner in the vicious circle in which the emergency measures they seek to justify in the name of defending the democratic constitution are the same ones that lead to its ruin."[51] Democracy, it would seem, suffers from an autoimmune disorder.[52]

Agamben provides an exhaustive history of the state of exception, most of which is outside the scope of the present study. However, one paragraph deserves our attention. He notes that most of the countries at war in

---

47. Walter Benjamin as quoted in Agamen, *Homo Sacer*, 54–55.
48. Agamben, *State of Exception*, 1.
49. Ibid., 2.
50. Ibid.
51. Ibid., 8.
52. Derrida, *Rogues*, 37.

World War I enacted a state of exception that lasted the duration of the war. During this state of exception:

> Many of the laws passed were, in truth, pure and simple delegations of legislative power to the executive, such as the [French] law of February 10, 1918, which granted the government an *all but absolute power to regulate by decree the production and trade of foodstuffs* . . . Predictably, the expansion of the executive's powers into the legislative sphere continued after the end of hostilities, and it is significant that military emergency now ceded its place to economic emergency.[53]

I wish to call attention to the use of the state of exception to usurp power over agricultural production and distribution. On the one hand this mention of food could call into question my earlier contention that the concept of sovereignty remains undertheorized in food politics and that the politics of food remains undertheorized in political theology. Tellingly, this brief mention of food is all that Agamben has to say on the matter.

Nonetheless, as evidenced by Agamben's quote, the state of exception legitimates the usurpation of power over agricultural production and distribution during war time. And as further supported by this quote, Agamben contends that over time *economic* necessity eventually comes to legitimate the state of exception in lieu of military necessity. While one might argue that the enactments of sovereignty in the food system on the part of multilateral agencies such as the World Bank, IMF and WTO do not occur in the context of the state of exception in any particular nation, and further that they profess to circumvent violent conflict, the fact remains that they impose a state of exception upon developing nations that suspends the agricultural and social welfare policies of these nations, in effect usurping their national sovereignty in the process. Such a suspension of law is, I argue, an enactment of Schmittian sovereignty par excellence, even or especially if it is enacted by an external entity.[54]

53. Agamben, *State of Exception,* 13; emphasis mine.

54. What I am calling an "economic rendition of Schmittian sovereignty" others might refer to as a hijacking. In order to understand these agencies' behaviors as enactments of "sovereignty" it is necessary to disarticulate "the sovereign" from "the nation-state." In other words, it is not necessary that "the sovereign" be a state actor. My argument rests upon Schmitt's definition of "the sovereign" as "he who decides upon the exception," and per Agamben that the sovereign is himself outside the law. Similarly, the multilateral agencies are also "outside the law" of these developing nations, and despite their lack of "official" position within the legal structure of the nations have nonetheless "decided upon the exception." Harkening back to Schmitt's assertion that all secular concepts of the state are secularized theological concepts, this further remove of multilateral agencies from any official state role is not at all problematic. In fact, from a "secularized

Perhaps none of this would be so concerning if these enactments of sovereignty in fact resulted in the security and quality of life they claim to provide. Instead, Agamben argues, "today's democratico-capitalist project of eliminating the poor classes through development not only reproduces within itself the people that is excluded but also transforms the entire population of the Third World into bare life."[55] Agamben's argument can be dismissed as purely theoretical and abstract. However, Raj Patel's historical review of the food system enfleshes Agamben's theoretical argument with concrete examples that are less easily ignored. For instance, Patel shows that recently, because of the massive debt incurred due to forced transition to technological farming, many farmers across the globe lose their land and ultimately become laborers on land they used to own.[56]

Patel dates the onset of the modern world food system to the onset of enclosure in England in the fifteenth century, a process that resulted in massive dispossession and migration.[57] This in turn drove colonization as "agricultural commercialization in Europe [drove] smallholders off the land."[58] These smallholders subsequently relocated to colonized territories in order to attempt to regain their landed status. However, none of this re-sulted in food security for "the people." Patel cites an "1878 study published in the prestigious *Journal of the Statistical Society* that contrasted thirty-one serious famines in 120 years of British rule against only seventeen recorded famines in the entire previous two millennia" as evidence of the lack of ef-ficacy of these highly technological farming methods.[59]

There is widespread belief that technological farming reduces famine, and incorporating developing nations into the capitalist economy will im-prove their access to food. Indeed, by some estimates nearly 40 percent of the people on Earth would not be alive today had petrochemical fertilizers not been invented. And while the raw number of hungry people has been fairly steady, global population has grown tremendously, decreasing the proportion of hungry people relative to the total population. Many behave as if a central-ized sovereign authority acting in the guise of multilateral agencies and trans-national corporations can most effectively assure just distribution of food.

---

theological" perspective multilaterals are more thoroughly "transcendent" to the state order than would be a sovereign who at other times fulfills functions within the state. Thus "multilaterals as sovereign" more closely resembles the figure of a transcendent God than does the powerful nation-state leader Schmitt envisioned.

55. Agamben, *Homo Sacer*, 180.

56. Patel, *Stuffed and Starved*, 62.

57. Ibid., 76.

58. Ibid., 81.

59. Ibid., 82.

The booming international trade in agricultural products would testify to the integrity of the infrastructure involved, if not the efficacy of the economics. Yet these beliefs are not unequivocally supported by the facts.

For example, on the one hand the share of calorie-deprived people has decreased from 23 percent in 1990 to just under 13 percent in 2015.[60] Yet, as I will argue in the following chapter, the corporate food regime also drives the obesity epidemic—currently affecting 39 percent of adults worldwide, or 2.1 billion people—in part because the food produced is deficient in micronutrients.[61] So in terms of overall morbidity due to nutrition-related illnesses, clearly the reduction in malnourishment has been more than offset by other metabolic disorders.[62] Even in the face of overall progress at reducing hunger, "natural and human-induced disasters or political instability have resulted in protracted crises with increased vulnerability and food insecurity of larger parts of the population."[63] Quite relevant to the later chapter on climate change, these countries are largely in middle Africa, a region hard hit by climate change–induced drought, likely a contributory factor in the eruption of the violent conflicts that produce famine.[64]

Contrary to the claims of those using the political frame of food security to legitimate their actions, further instantiations of sovereignty on the part of multilateral trade agencies and transnational agricultural corporations in our global food system are more likely to result in food *insecurity* than food security. This is in part because, as Agamben demonstrates, every enactment of Schmittian sovereignty makes a cut that excludes someone as *homo sacer*. Even more compelling, these enactments of sovereignty compel the burning of fossil fuels and the implementation of high-carbon

60. Food and Agriculture Organization, *The State of Food Security of the World.*

61. Based on World Health Organization's "Obesity and Overweight Fact Sheet," updated June 2016. This resource notes that obesity has more than doubled since 1980, http://www.who.int/mediacentre/factsheets/fs311/en/.

62. In particular, by "metabolic syndrome," which is the constellation of obesity, high blood pressure, and diabetes that currently affects nearly 25 percent of adults worldwide, according to the International Diabetes Foundation. http://www.idf.org/metabolic-syndrome.

63. FAO, "State of Food Security of the World 2015." This report also strongly advocates for increased support of smallholders as a means of improving agricultural productivity and reducing hunger in developing nations.

64. Black, "Climate 'Is a Major Cause' of Conflict in Africa," and Bellio, "Can Climate Change Cause Conflict? Recent History Suggests So" make a solid case for the connection, while Westervelt, "Does Climate Change Really Cause Conflict?" makes a careful distinction that climate change exacerbates conflict, and cannot be said to be the root cause. Thus, as the State Department announced some time ago, climate change might best be regarded as a threat multiplier rather than singular cause. Yet its role should not be minimized.

output agriculture, both of which are driving climate change.[65] In turn, climate instability is already beginning to threaten geopolitical stability in general, and food production in particular. As Agamben insists is inevitable, the states of exception posed by climate change and starvation do indeed threaten to become the norm.

Critiques and Limitations of Agamben's Theories

I have argued that Giorgio Agamben's figure of *homo sacer* provides a powerful theoretical model of bodily vulnerability produced within and by transnational food politics. Because the enactments of sovereignty on the part of multilaterals are largely obscured from view, and because food decisions are largely considered "private" matters, it is easy to miss the causative connections between the decisions made by the agencies and the impact on individual human bodies. Agamben's *homo sacer* (and other theories) facilitates the identification of the motions of power in the food system that result in both oppression of peasant farmers and widespread malnutrition globally. I perceive Agamben's theories to be immensely helpful, however the concept of *homo sacer* or the state of exception cannot be applied seamlessly to the situation we face in food politics.

For example, critics of Agamben, such as Derrida, contend that in theorizing how *homo sacer* appears as a consequence of sovereignty Agamben proclaims his own sovereignty. Derrida rebukes Agamben for attributing the theme of the werewolf to Hobbes, overlooking prior mentions of wolves by "Plautus and a few other precedents." The claim that "he is the first to know who came first" is, for Derrida, the hallmark of "the sovereign, if there is such a thing."[66] Agamben's claim to be first, and hence his declaration of sovereignty, draws Derrida's ire.

Derrida also rails against Agamben, and Foucault before him, for claiming some originary and lasting distinction between *zoë* and *bios*. According to Derrida, "all of Agamben's demonstrative strategy, here and elsewhere, puts its money on a distinction on a radical, clear, univocal exclusion, among the Greeks and in Aristotle in particular, between bare life (*zoë*), common to all living beings . . . and life qualified as individual or group life (*bios*)."[67] Agamben, remember, seeks to distinguish bare life from qualified life in

65. Donald Trump's promotion of fossil fuels is widely known. Less widely known is his support for industrial agriculture. See Dayen, "Trump Sides With Big Agriculture Over Family Farmers."

66. Derrida, *Beast and the Sovereign*, 92.

67. Ibid., 316.

order to argue that in the modern era "the species and the individual as a simple living body become what is at stake in a society's political strategies."[68] Agamben argues that in the days of the ancient Greeks "simple natural life," or *zoë* was "excluded from the *polis*," whereas now bare life (*zoë*) has become the focal point of the political in the modern era.[69]

For Derrida, Agamben's insistence that some original distinction between *zoë* and *bios* has subsequently been rendered ambiguous undermines the integrity of Agamben's theory, because "this distinction is never so clear and secure."[70] According to Derrida, there is nothing "modern or new" about the zone of indistinction between *zoë* and *bios* that Agamben, and Foucault before him, claim has been introduced in the modern period.[71] Derrida quotes Agamben's own acknowledgment that the inclusion of *zoë* in the *polis* is nothing new in order to support this critique, in fact quotes it twice in the span of two pages. Agamben writes: "What characterizes modern politics is not so much the inclusion of *zoë* in the *polis*—which is, in itself, absolutely ancient."[72] It would seem even Agamben realizes that the phenomenon he will describe is nothing new, even if he *will* describe it in a new way.

I do not perceive the novelty of these concepts to be crucial to the explanation of the production of starving, vulnerable bodies in our contemporary food politics. As I have spilled much ink to articulate, Agamben's *homo sacer* illuminates the linkage between deployments of sovereignty and profound vulnerability in global food politics. However, I am unconvinced that what *homo sacer* represents is a zone of indistinction, whether old or new. Instead, I perceive *homo sacer* to represent the person who does not enjoy legal protections offered in the context of a legal system. *Homo sacer* possesses little extrinsic, social value in the context of that legal system. Because little social value is attributed to *homo sacer*, the life of *homo sacer* is also considered to be of little if any *intrinsic* value. It would almost be better not to live at all than to live as *homo sacer*.[73] What is more essential to my thesis than proving or disproving any "zone of indistinction" is the sense in which *homo sacer* clarifies what is at stake when unilateral sovereignty is invoked or implemented.

68. Agamben, *Homo Sacer*, 3.

69. Ibid., 2–3.

70. Derrida, *Beast and the Sovereign*, 316.

71. Ibid.

72. Agamben, *Homo Sacer*, 9, quoted in its entirety in Derrida, *Beast and Sovereign*, 316; portions also quoted on page 315.

73. Agamben, *Homo Sacer*, 136–44.

While Derrida argues that "bio-power or zoo-power are not new" he concedes that "there are incredible novelties in bio-power."[74] And to be sure, Derrida is dismissive of neither Agamben nor Foucault, despite his arguments against their claims that biopower is a specifically modern development. He argues that the questions they raise "compel us . . . to reconsider . . . a way . . . of articulating a logic and a rhetoric onto a thinking of history or the event."[75] Derrida calls for the relinquishment of the "idea of a decisive and founding event."[76] Against this founding event, Derrida argues:

> There is neither simple diachronic succession nor simple synchronic simultaneity here (or that there is both at once), that there is neither continuity of passage nor interruption or mere caesura, that the motifs of the passage of what passes and comes to pass in history belong neither to a solid foundation nor to a founding decision.[77]

Derrida concludes that there is no single founding decision, no originary ground, and no lack of ground, but a multiplicity of decisions, and passages.[78]

Correspondingly, while my own argument here emphasizes the sovereign decisions of multilateral agencies as the major contributing factor to problematic food politics at present, this is not to suggest that the formation of these agencies was *the founding event* in our problematic food system. Derrida is correct: there is no single founding decision and no single founding decision-maker. Yet this lack of foundational event or singular threshold need not thwart efforts to shift motions of power toward more socially just and ecologically sustainable trajectories. Instead, the multiplicity of causative factors pries open myriad viable passages to more sustainable, just, and abundant political theologies of food (as I will discuss in further detail in the final chapter).

Criticisms of Agamben's *homo sacer* notwithstanding, his theory of *homo sacer* calls attention to the effects of sovereign power in a way that facilitates inquiry into the food system as a site for the implementation of biopower. For example, whereas the bodies of the starving would appear to

74. Derrida, *Beast and the Sovereign*, 330.

75. Ibid., 332.

76. Ibid., 333.

77. Ibid.

78. Ibid. Certainly, this lack of diachronic succession or clear threshold is evident when reading Harriet Friedmann and Philip McMichael's theories of food regimes as described in the previous chapter. Occasionally their writing is characterized by a lack of clarity that I believe reflects this lack of clear threshold between regimes to which Derrida can be seen as gesturing.

indicate that our agricultural system does not produce enough food, on a planet that produces sufficient calories to feed every single person a 2,100 kcal/day diet, we must reach for some other explanation for the seven and a half million deaths per year by starvation since clearly food is available.[79] I propose that, with the assistance of Agamben, the bodies of the starving—and perhaps even the bodies of landless peasants and the obese—can be read as versions of *homo sacer* insofar as these bodies are formed as a consequence of enactments of an economic rendition of absolute sovereignty.

This is not to suggest that these models of sovereignty were not enacted with similar disastrous (for some) results prior to the development of multilaterals. Certainly famine and starvation have been experienced for millennia and it is the human desire to avoid such circumstances that in part leads us to view the policies enacted by multilaterals as vitally important. My task here is rather to call attention—perhaps not in an entirely new way, but merely in another way—to the manner in which the sovereign decisions of multilaterals perpetuate and potentially increase precarity in the food system such that people starve to death on a planet with plenty of food to feed them, and with, ostensibly, sufficient distribution pathways to ensure that food produced elsewhere could in fact reach those who need it. I am further suggesting that Agamben's *homo sacer* helps to at least partially explain this problematic outcome in a way that might facilitate a new kind of political approach to these problems.

Nonetheless, I find his vision of a new potential political approach troubling. He concludes *State of Exception* by declaring that:

> To show law in its nonrelation to life and life in its nonrelation to law means to open a space between them for human action, which once claimed for itself the name of "politics." . . . the only truly political action, however, is that which severs the nexus between violence and law. And only beginning from the space thus opened will it be possible to pose the question of a possible use of law after the deactivation of the device that, in the state of exception, tied it to life.[80]

The opening of this space would not deliver us to "a lost original state" but one that would permit the alignment of word and "human praxis that the powers of law and myth had sought to capture in the state of exception."[81] Something about this vision does not square with my reading of the conversation between Walter Benjamin and Carl Schmitt—a conversation to

79. Hunger Notes, *2013 World Hunger and Poverty Facts.*
80. Agamben, *State of Exception,* 88.
81. Ibid.

which Agamben devotes an entire chapter. To begin with, the notion that there would be only *one* "truly political action" or *one* space that could be opened within which uses of law could be rendered nontoxic is problematic. Suggestions such as this seem to play right into Schmitt's hand, which it seems elsewhere Agamben would prefer to avoid.

But more importantly, it seems to me that Benjamin would disagree that it was *only* the state of exception that tied the law to life and therefore violence. He might also disagree that there is a way to sever the nexus between violence and law in such a way that would preserve law. Benjamin perceived law to be violent in its establishment and application, and not merely violent in its suspension. This is because for Benjamin, law is an attempt to decide universally, once and for all, what can only be decided upon in its singularity.[82] Even if Benjamin *were* to agree that the "nexus" between law and violence could be severed, he would certainly insist that we could never be certain that such a feat has been accomplished.

The difference between Agamben's perspective and my own view likely hinges on different understandings of the dispute between Benjamin and Schmitt. Agamben argues that "the aim of Benjamin's essay is to ensure the possibility of a violence . . . that lies absolutely 'outside' and 'beyond' the law and that, as such, could shatter the dialectic between lawmaking violence and law-preserving violence. Benjamin calls this other figure of violence 'pure' or 'divine,' and, in the human sphere, 'revolutionary.'"[83] Agamben goes on to say that that "while Schmitt attempts every time to reinscribe violence within a juridical context, Benjamin responds to this gesture by seeking every time to assure it—as pure violence—an existence outside of the law."[84] The potential for extralegal violence is important, in Agamben's view, in order to protect the revolutionary's right to violent overthrow of a violent order.

I would agree with Agamben that Benjamin sought the shattering of the "dialectic between lawmaking violence and law-preserving violence," but I would disagree that Benjamin wanted to assure the existence of a pure violence outside the law in such a way as to validate violent means for the purposes of revolutionary ends. Benjamin is clear: "All violence as a

---

82. Benjamin, *Critique of Violence*, 294. Benjamin decries the "stubborn prevailing habit of conceiving those just ends as ends of a possible law, that is, not only as generally valid . . . but also as capable of generalization, which, as could be shown, contradicts the nature of justice. For ends that for one situation are just, universally acceptable and valid, are so for no other situation no matter how similar it may be in other respects."

83. Agamben, *State of Exception*, 53.

84. Ibid., 59.

means is either lawmaking or law-preserving."[85] This applies to revolutionary movements in pursuit of justice just as certainly as it applies to unjust
legal systems. Any revolution that perceives itself as righteously pursuing
justice through violent means will only result in the renewed instantiation
of a violent law. True enough, Benjamin was trying to defend the so-called
violence of a general strike, an action that is often undertaken as a nonviolent endeavor.

Benjamin's insistence that any violence that can be inscribed within a
juridical context is mythological, then, is not merely an assurance that some
form of violence exists outside the law. It is, rather, a claim that all laws
are founded on myth rather than reality. As such can they never be said to
be divinely ordained, regardless of how closely our "political organization"
corresponds to our "metaphysical image."[86] And here Derrida's reading on
Benjamin will clarify an important reason to resist the law, or *droit,* when it
threatens to make *homo sacer* of us all:

> Blood is the symbol of life, he says. In making blood flow, the
> mythological violence of *droit* is exercised in its own favor
> against life pure and simple, biological life. In contrast, purely
> divine violence is exercised on all life, but to the profit or in fa-
> vor of the living.[87]

But even here Derrida cautions us: "to think at this point that we have . . .
correctly interpreted the meaning, the *vouloir-dire* of Benjamin's text, by
opposing in a decidable way the decidability of divine, revolutionary, historical, anti-state, anti-juridical violence on the one side and on the other
the undecidability of the mythic violence of state *droit,* would still be to
decide too quickly and not to understand the power of this text."[88] The text
simultaneously provokes and resists efforts at its interpretation.

At this point Derrida calls our attention to the fact that at the conclusion of *Critique of Violence,* Benjamin speaks of the existence of violence
outside the law only in the conditional: "but *if* the existence of violence
outside the law . . . is assured."[89] Such a fact is far from certain, even at the
conclusion of the essay. Derrida goes on to reinforce Benjamin's conclusion
by insisting that "the *decision* on this subject, the determinant decision, the

85. Benjamin, *Critique of Violence,* 287.

86. "The metaphysical image that a definite epoch forges of the world has the same
structure as what the world immediately understands to be appropriate as a form of
political organization." Schmitt, *Political Theology,* 46.

87. Derrida, "Force of Law."

88. Ibid., 1033.

89. Benjamin, *Critique of Violence,* 300; emphasis mine.

one that permits us to know or to recognize such a pure and revolutionary violence *as such,* is a *decision not accessible to man.* Here we must deal with a whole other undecidability."[90] A theologian might recognize this "whole other undecidability" as an apophatic allusion.

It would seem that Benjamin calls not so much for a violence unalloyed to law, or the disruption of the lawmaking/law-preserving dialectic but instead cautions that the quest for justice must proceed with humility, must not rely upon violence as its means, and above all must not promote bloodshed—the hallmark of mythological violence. So where Agamben insists that "the only truly political action, however, is that which severs the nexus between violence and law,"[91] I would argue—alongside Benjamin and Derrida—that the only truly political action is that which acknowledges the irreducibility of justice to law. The living call of justice often demands the formulation, activation, and application of just laws—laws that restrain unilateral sovereignty, eliminate systemic iniquities, and multiply the beneficiaries of inalienable rights. This is in large part what we seek in a sustainable food politics.

But because the call toward justice *is* living and therefore dynamic, justice cannot be regarded as a condition achieved but rather as actions taken on an ongoing basis. Consequently, justice cannot finally be assured *solely* by legal formulations. Principles of equity, integrity and decency—and this is what I mean by justice—cannot be reduced to the law itself. Subsequently, the truly political act will express those principles even if—or especially if—they are deemed "illegal" under the auspices of a tyrannical sovereign.[92] This

90. Derrida, "Force of Law," 1033.

91. Agamben, *State of Exception,* 88.

92. Such as, for example, the many people who concealed Jews from Nazi persecution, or people who feed the homeless in any one of the 71 municipalities that have passed laws criminalizing the feeding of homeless people. And here I am reminded of the eschatological vision depicted in Jeremiah 31:33 "I will put my law within them, and I will write it on their hearts." Previously, in Jeremiah 7:5–6: God has accused the Israelites of behaving unjustly toward one another, oppressing the widow, orphan, and alien and shedding innocent blood. Redemption transforms the emotional nature such that external, fixed, written, law will be unnecessary. Each person will "do justice" (Micah, this time!)—immediately enacting equity in each moment. Justice appears here as an action verb, rather than static condition. The transformation will not do away with Torah, or Jewish instruction. Rather, it permits the expression of Torah's creative aim without the need for punitive restriction, because the emotional nature has been transformed in such a way as to always support the creative aim of Torah, especially if Torah is read in the manner of the ancients and mystics in Jewish tradition who perceived it as the blueprint for creation that preexisted creation itself. What we have of written and oral Torah represents but a portion of divine intentions for creation. A fuller explication of this vision is far beyond the scope of a political theology of food, but yet it is worth mentioning in conjunction with the severing of justice and law.

would require some forfeiture of the charade that security can be achieved in any lasting measure, especially by unjust means.

Judith Butler: Beginning with Vulnerability

What would a political theology of food look like if it forfeited the goal of lasting security? Could the concept of sovereignty, let alone food sovereignty or the nation-state, play any role in such a political theology? Judith Butler ponders a similar set of questions in *Precarious Lives*, in which she takes "injurability and aggression as two points of departure for political life" in general, and for a Jewish ethics of nonviolence in particular.[93] While her inquiry was prompted by the nationalist response to the terrorist attack on 9/11, I find her reflections applicable to a political theology of food. Her sense of vulnerability was heightened by those attacks because they exposed her "fundamental dependency on anonymous others" that "no security measures will foreclose."[94] Similar concerns prompted me to write this political theology of food: we are fundamentally dependent on food in a way that no security measures will foreclose.

Generally speaking, it is commonly asserted that prioritizing sustainable agriculture (and ecological sustainability in general) is bad for the economy. It is commonly overlooked that to identify our current way of life as *un*sustainable is to declare that it has an expiration date. We will be forced to adopt new practices, whether we like it or not. The degree to which one "cannot afford" the sustainable choice now seems likely to correlate with how quickly one is likely to become *homo sacer* when the unsustainability of our lifestyle stops being a theoretical consideration and begins to be a lived experience. This might in fact be what the current geopolitical upheaval in Africa and the Middle East represents.

My point is, we cannot possibly achieve sustainable food security through unsustainable agricultural approaches. What I am arguing for in this chapter is that we directly and unswervingly address food politics through the twin lenses of injurability and aggression, in full recognition of our own radical contingency upon and situatedness within food systems. Perhaps then we can conjure the political will to induce substantive policy change toward sustainable practices.

A political theology of food finds resonances with Butler's concerns about corporeal vulnerability: we are *because* we eat, and the fact that we eat renders us both vulnerable to and connected with myriad unseen others

93. Butler, *Precarious Life*, xii.
94. Ibid.

around the planet. Butler argues that "each of us is constituted politically in part by virtue of the social vulnerability of our bodies—as a site of desire and physical vulnerability, as a site of publicity at once assertive and exposed."[95] As I have been arguing in this chapter, part of the way in which we are "constituted politically" is precisely in relation to our "social vulnerability." In the following chapter I will argue that we are also constituted corporeally in part by this same vulnerability, a vulnerability that is communicated by the text—and sociality—of our bodies.

At the same time we must accept our fleshy vulnerability, it seems important to recognize that the abjection represented by *homo sacer* is something we all wish to avoid. The promise of aligning ourselves with (Schmittian) sovereign power is that we can avoid that fate, especially for those of us who are well-fed. However, such invulnerability is an illusion: the sovereign may be the lord of creatures, but he remains a creature himself and therefore vulnerable, right along with the rest of us. Agamben's concept of *homo sacer* demonstrates the risks inherent in reliance upon strong sovereignty to assure our welfare. What we are all fundamentally and irrevocably dependent upon is healthy ecosystems that will provide us with food, for which no human sovereign can substitute.

The dominant methods of food production currently being promoted by the multilaterals who operate under the "food security" frame—which, remember, implicitly function as a Schmittian-type, absolute sovereign—are responsible for up to 30 percent of greenhouse gas emissions,[96] put control over seeds in the hands of transnational corporations, and rely heavily upon monoculture crops that are inherently vulnerable for their lack of diversity. Multilateral agencies promise security, meanwhile concentrating vast amounts of wealth and power in the hands of a few, while exposing the many to overwhelming long-term risk.

Empty promises of multilaterals and agribusinesses notwithstanding, absolute security cannot be achieved. We must source our food politics not from a fear of vulnerability or a desire to erase it, but from an acceptance that to be alive is to be at risk of death.[97] Although vulnerability is an inevitable

95. Butler, *Precarious Life*, 21.

96. The precise percentage of greenhouse gases accounted for by agricultural production and distribution are hotly contested. Estimates range from 9 percent by the EPA to approximately 33 percent by the Consultative Group on International Agricultural Research, reported on in *Nature* by Natasha Gilbert. The EPA figure does not include any factors external to the farm, such as transportation of food across vast distances or storage and packaging of food, in its calculations of the agricultural contribution to greenhouse gas emissions. The CGIAR includes some of those collateral sources of greenhouse gas emission.

97. Butler, *Precarious Life*, 31.

condition, it is unnecessary to consign those who suffer a disproportionate share of it to their fate. Butler proposes the goal of seeking a "world in which bodily vulnerability is protected without therefore being eradicated." [98] Given that some amount of "impingement is inevitable" it is necessary to distinguish between inevitable vulnerability, which we all face to some degree, and that which results from reversible social conditions.[99]

We may be thousands of miles away from those who produce our food, but because we are mutually entangled in the global food system, we are bound by a common fate. As Butler says, "If my fate is not originally or finally separable from yours, then the 'we' is traversed by a relationality that we cannot easily argue against; or rather, we can argue against it, but we would be denying something fundamental about the social condition of our very formation"[100] We are not isolated from those landless peasants crying out for justice, pleading for a patch of land and the right to farm it in such a way as to protect and restore a fragile ecosystem. They are on the front lines of a struggle we will all face eventually if we do not wrestle with the problems in our food system now. Butler asks, "is this not another way of imagining community, one in which we are alike only in having this condition separately and so having in common a condition that cannot be thought without difference?"[101] The differences are myriad: different languages, different vocations, different social classes and relations to power, different countries, and different hemispheres. Plethora of differences notwithstanding, we share in common a profound dependence upon viable ecosystems capable of producing food.

Butler asserts that such a relational community imaginary is "an ongoing normative dimension of our social and political lives, one in which we are compelled to take stock of our interdependence."[102] In a country in which fewer than 2 percent of the population farms, we must acknowledge our interdependence with those who produce food; we could not live without them. Or at least, could not live as we do. By virtue of this interdependence, Butler asserts, it is "incumbent on us to consider the place of violence in any such relation, for violence is always an exploitation of that primary tie, that primary way in which we are, as bodies, outside ourselves

98. Ibid., 42.
99. Butler, *Giving and Account of Oneself*, 107.
100. Butler, *Precarious Life*, 23.
101. Ibid., 27.
102. Ibid.

and for one another."[103] Violence adds to the weight felt as our shared humanity is disrupted.

Butler begins her ethic of nonviolence by asserting that "what binds us morally has to do with how we are addressed by others in ways that we cannot avert or avoid; this impingement by the other's address constitutes us first and foremost against our will or, perhaps put more appropriately, prior to the formation of our will."[104] According to Butler, moral authority arises in the context of "the demand that comes from elsewhere, sometimes a nameless elsewhere, by which our obligations are articulated and pressed upon us."[105] This moral demand is conveyed by the face. Responding to this face requires recognizing the vulnerability inherent in being alive.

The face communicates, wordlessly, prelinguistically, that we not let the Other die alone, "as if to do so were to become an accomplice in his death. Thus, the face says to me: you shall not kill."[106] Aside from this simple plea, the face does not communicate a prescribed formula for responding to the moral demand it conveys.[107] In the absence of a prescription for enacting our moral obligation, it is our responsibility to determine what actions we must take to prevent the unnecessary death of the Other.

Butler's ethic of nonviolence begins with the war between the impulse for one's own survival and the ethical prohibition against killing the Other. In the context of food politics, the ethic of nonviolence comes about as we demand for our own access to nutritious food while simultaneously protecting the welfare of those who produce it, Others who also need to eat, and the ecosystems that make its production possible. The transnational corporate food system treats this as an either/or proposition—either we have access to nutritional food at the expense of migrant workers and landless peasants and the very earth itself, or we will not have access to nutritional food. To the contrary, I argue the reverse: either we figure out how to gain access to nutritional food while protecting migrant workers, landless peasants, and the very earth itself, or we will lose access to nutritional food. Indeed, we are already losing it.

It is not so easy, however, to simply "copy and paste" Butler's ethic of nonviolence onto our contemporary food politics. The challenge results from Butler's entry-point for ethical concern. Butler's essay grapples with

103. Ibid.
104. Ibid., 130.
105. Ibid.
106. Ibid.
107. Ibid., 131.

humanization as approached "through the figure of the face."[108] The address that morally obligates us comes, we are told, through the face itself. Yet we seldom, if ever, are face to face with the Others who produce our food. Or the nonhuman Others who become our food. And even more problematically, some animate and inanimate others that nurture our food—such as pollinators, earthworms, soil microbes, sunlight, and water—have no face at all. How then can they address us? And even if they were to address us, can we really be held morally accountable to this multitude?

To at least the first of these questions, Butler provides a partial answer. She describes how the face can also be "found in the back and the neck," in the way that "these bodily parts . . . are said to cry and to sob and to scream, as if they were a face."[109] It is the agony communicated by the face, and not the face per se that makes the address. It is what is communicated by the face, what the face represents that makes the moral demands, rather than the face per se. This potential for joy and suffering cannot ever be adequately represented, can never be reduced to the face that speaks on its behalf. About this Butler is clear: "there is something unrepresentable that we nevertheless seek to represent, and that paradox must be retained in the representation we give."[110] Might we seek another representation in lieu of the face?

The irreducibility of the potential for joy and suffering, of the moral demand posed by the Other, leaves open the possibility that another representation of suffering could be the "face" through which the ethical claim is conveyed. We may never encounter our food growers or the animals we consume "face to face," but we may encounter images of their suffering faces. We may never meet a Guatemalan coffee grower personally, but we may meet someone who has and who can affirm for us that Fair Trade certification is meaningful—and in particular means fair wages and better working conditions for those who grow our coffee. These images and intermediaries can effectively convey the moral demands and ethical claims inherent within, yet typically obscured by, the global food system.

Or perhaps another object or practice could come to "represent," as it were, the ethical demand that is represented by the face itself: graphic representations of increasing temperatures, decreasing rainfall and reduced crop yields could communicate the suffering of the earth, for example. The sight of my hand reaching for a bright red tomato could hold me morally accountable to the migrant farm worker who picked it. The suffering animal represented by the meat on my plate could call forth moral outrage at the

108. Ibid., 140.
109. Ibid., 133.
110. Ibid., 144.

inhumanity of industrial farming.[111] Maybe the mere fact that I did not grow the food on my plate can serve as a reminder that I cannot live without food, and so neither can I live without the innumerable people, creatures, ecosystems, and conditions who conspired to bring the food to my plate.

The face remains a condition for humanization, in Butler's reading, despite merely being representative of moral accountability. Are we then free of moral accountability within the global food system if we are never "face to face" with the suffering produced, or if the suffering body is not a human body? Not necessarily. Suffering occurs even to those whom we have not humanized. We are always morally accountable, even if we fail to recognize the representation for what it is: a demand that we respond to the suffering of the Other.

Not only is the face a condition for humanization, the face can also be used to dehumanize.[112] The dehumanization to which Butler refers occurs through "the media's evacuation of the human through the image." She insists that we understand media manipulation of the image within the context of the process through which "normative schemes of intelligibility establish what will and will not be human, what will be a livable life what will be a grievable death."[113] One tactic through which the normative scheme operates is "precisely through providing no image, no name, no narrative, so that there never was a life, and there never was a death."[114] This method Butler refers to as "radical effacement," and her description of the results of radical effacement call to mind Agamben's *homo sacer*. Radical effacement establishes conditions through which the radically effaced are rendered killable, because in the absence of an image "no murder has, therefore, ever taken place."[115] No crime has been committed, no one sacrificed.

The radical effacement of pollinators, earthworms, waterways, refugees, migrant workers, landless peasants, the rural poor and inner city slum dwellers, and farm animals is not accidental. Butler declares that "politics—and power—work in part through regulating what can appear, what can

111. In a 2009 interview, Butler states "If humans actually share a condition of precariousness, not only just with one another, but also with animals, and with the environment, then this constitutive feature of who we "are" undoes the very conceit of anthropocentrism. In this sense, I want to propose 'precarious life' as a non-anthropocentric framework for considering what makes life valuable." See Antonello and Farneti, "Antigone's Claim." Based on her statement, raising the issue of animal suffering does not seem to be beyond the scope of her concerns.

112. Butler, *Precarious Life*, 141

113. Ibid., 146.

114. Ibid., 147.

115. Ibid.

be heard." [116] She insists that "these schemas of intelligibility are tacitly and forcefully mandated by those corporations that monopolize control over the mainstream media with strong interests in maintaining US military power."[117] Maintaining control over the global food system is a similarly strong interest they hold, and largely inspires the radical effacement—or what Margaret Urban Walker might call privatization—of these bodies. Nonetheless, we remain profoundly dependent upon and therefore morally accountable to those who suffer as a result of the global food system in which we participate. We permit their effacement at our peril.

But that only begs the question: can we really be held morally accountable to or responsible—that is "able to respond"—to this multitude? The transnational character of the contemporary food system flings far and wide this interdependence, brings the lives of faceless, nameless others to bear in the very cells of our bodies. Our lives are profoundly intertwined with people whose faces we will never see. Some of these people endure abusive labor practices in order to produce our food; still others are murdered for their efforts to preserve the land upon which it is produced. Seldom, if ever, do we see their faces or hear their names. And there are so many, even if we are to restrict our moral accountability to the human. To add the potential ethical claims of the nonhuman to this equation results in an incalculable demand to which we are incapable of responding.

To try to respond to every other, according to Butler, "can only result in a situation of radical irresponsibility."[118] We simply cannot respond to every single entity with whom—with which?—we are entangled without becoming radically irresponsible. So to which others do we respond? I will wrestle with this dilemma in greater detail in the final chapter. For now let me simply say that the limited ability to meet a seemingly unlimited demand does not, in itself, excuse complete inaction. Some form of responsible action is required, and that form will vary based upon one's situatedness within the global food system. For now it is enough to know that the transnational global food system can be characterized as violent. This system may lead us to a sort of zero sum thinking that promotes the idea that we can be safe while others suffer, but in truth the violence of this system will ultimately affect all of us if unchecked. A political theology of food insists that the recognition of mutual vulnerability is a more just starting point for a nonviolent food politics.

116. Ibid.

117. Ibid.

118. Ibid., 170.

Conclusion

Agamben's theories of *homo sacer*, "the people" and "the People," and state of exception shed light on risks inherent in the deployments of sovereignty on the part of multilateral trade organizations and transnational corporations. The figure of one who has been expelled from under the protective auspices of the law is referred to by Agamben as *homo sacer*, he who can be killed with impunity, but not sacrificed. Agamben refers to Jews in Hitler's Germany to illustrate the profound vulnerability, and extra-legal status, of *homo sacer*. Should the sovereign transform into a dictator, everyone is at risk of becoming *homo sacer*. Clearly, Schmittian sovereignty fails to provide the security it promises.

Enactments of absolute sovereignty are legitimated on the condition of existential threat. "The people," as those who cannot be successfully integrated into "the People" pose a persistent threat. Since absolute homogeneity among any population is impossible, the effort to eliminate "the people" will of necessity devolve into one or another version of totalitarianism—and still "the people" will remain. The desire for a unification—whether of a "People" or of an agricultural method—could itself be seen as counterproductive. It is quite possible that a radical embrace of multiplicity might better serve.

If vulnerability is a feature of our very existence, as Butler asserts, then existential threats cannot be eliminated, merely postponed. We might, then, read absolute sovereignty as one political response to the fact of human vulnerability, albeit one with serious potential to increase rather than decrease vulnerability over time. Butler's ethic of nonviolence informs a political theology of food that seeks to minimize vulnerability in full awareness that it cannot be eliminated. This approach derives the strength of its commitment from the recognition of interdependence and contingency.

A political theology of food informed by Butler's approach opens the possibility of severing the nexus between justice and law. Liberated from the conceit that any political structure is capable of eradicating vulnerability, it does not promise absolutely secure or just *ends* for which violent *means* might be used. This political theology of food is not predicated upon integration into a unified "People," but is instead invested in a process of elaborating differences. This political theology recognizes a personal, situation-specific moral accountability to one who suffers rather than the clumsy application of a general statute to a specific situation. This sidesteps the concern of both Schmitt and Benjamin that laws are excessively general whereas their application is specific. The mismatch between general legal ends and specific situations was what bound law to violence, according to Benjamin.

This political theology of food begins to respond to the living dynamism of the urge toward justice by calling for a situation-specific justice that settled law on its own cannot obtain. Following in the footsteps of Butler's ethic of nonviolence, this political theology of food does not demand unification into a People, but rather invokes the elaboration of differences. The fact that "the people" will remain distinct—and that there are likely to be many "peoples"—enriches a radically democratic political theology of food rather than threatening it.

Vulnerability is a fact of human existence, exacerbated in some regards by the global food system. But the consequences of vulnerability are differentially experienced, based at least in part upon social location. In the Global South, vulnerability appears as malnourishment, death by starvation, or the killing of food activists. In the Global North, vulnerability appears as metabolic syndrome and the obesity epidemic. How can the corporate food regime produce such disparate forms of vulnerability? The explanation will be sought in the next chapter, as new materialisms are integrated into the analysis of the materialization of human bodies.

Chapter 5

Deciding What to Eat

Producing the Bodies of the Body Politic

IN THE CONTEXT OF the global food system and the neoliberal economics that drives it, vulnerabilities are not experienced the same way by people in different social locations. In the Global South, this vulnerability appears as malnourishment, death by starvation, or the killing of food activists.[1] In the Global North, vulnerability more often appears as the obesity epidemic, although to be sure hunger is an increasing problem even in affluent nations. Echoes of Agamben's *homo sacer* resonate through both descriptions, provided the ban is not read as a binary either/or situation. For most people living within the regime of a strong, Schmittian-type sovereignty, exposure to the sovereign ban occurs in a gradient fashion.

I recognize that my reading requires integrating greater elasticity into the concept of *homo sacer* than Agamben intended. Agamben, and Schmitt before him, sought to interrogate the limit case as paradigmatic of the norm. Schmitt insisted that the exception—and in particular the state of exception brought about due to existential threat to the state—illustrated the profoundest truths of the state itself. And for Agamben, the exceptional limit case of the death camps reveal "the biopolitical paradigm of the modern."[2] Having vocalized their intention to illuminate more moderate realities by virtue of their theoretical wrestling with the extremes, they have extended invitation to stretch their insights regarding the extreme case into an examination of moderate realities.

1. Please see footnote 7 in chapter 2 for information on the usage of Global South/Global North.

2. In fact, the title of Part III of Agamben's *Homo Sacer*, 119–79.

Homo sacer will be seen to have at least two appearances in our global food system. The emaciated/abjectly poor, found mostly although again not exclusively in developing nations.[3] The obese/relatively poor, concentrated primarily although not exclusively in affluent nations. Certainly, there are more than just these two; *homo sacer* can indeed take on various appearances, some of which obscure the precarity of the one so marked.

Both first-world obesity and developing-world hunger result from the concentration of agricultural decision-making power into very few hands.[4] These power-brokers are the transnational corporations that have benefited from the economic deployments of sovereignty on the part of multilaterals, previously described. A new materialist approach to the body will demonstrate how a single power, concentrated in the agricultural sector, ripples out again, undulating within and around other flows of power, creating manifold differences in material conditions within which bodies become. The results can be as diametrically opposed as the habitus of the Global North obese/relatively poor and that of the Global South emaciated/abjectly poor.[5] Materialized bodies are in turn intercalated into social structures in ways that legitimate asymmetrical flows of power.

A new materialist account of the social production of bodies discloses subtle gradations of *homo sacer* through an integration of Jane Bennett's "vibrant materiality," Karen Barad's agential realism, and science studies. Revealing that bodies materialize as classed, at least in part, by virtue of their intra-actions with food in the context of unjust social structures, will be the task of the first section of this chapter. In the second section, Margaret Urban Walker's feminist ethics will facilitate an analysis of how bodies produced as classed due to differential access to food are subsequently (and simultaneously) intercalated into systems of power in ways that further legitimate

3. Numerous studies and articles support the notion that hunger is becoming a significant problem in the United States, for example. Again, it cannot be stressed enough that Global North and Global South serve more as markers of socioeconomic status than geographic location, especially in a transnational context.

4. Patel, *Stuffed and Starved*, 12–13.

5. The distinction between affluent and developing nations is occasionally referred to as a Global North/Global South distinction. This distinction is drawn upon an overgeneralization. One must always keep in the line of sight the reality that a range of socioeconomic situations exists in every nation. And the mass migration accompanying globalization has brought the Global South into the Global North, and visa versa. Nonetheless, in undertaking the application of new materialisms to food politics, I will align the obese/relatively poor with the Global North and the emaciated/abjectly poor with the Global South. I take this approach because typically obesity is a problem in affluent nations rather than developing nations.

asymmetries of power. Combined, these analyses will deepen our understanding of the social production of subtle gradations of *homo sacer*.

The Materialization of Human Bodies in the Global Food System

The vibrant materiality of food

At the outset, Jane Bennett announces that the political intentions inspiring her publication of *Vibrant Matter: A Political Ecology of Things* is to "encourage more intelligent and sustainable engagements with vibrant matter and lively things."[6] Bennett wonders aloud, "How would political responses to public problems change were we to take seriously the vitality of (nonhuman) bodies?"[7] She goes on to argue for a politics "devoted to . . . a cultivated discernment of the web of agentic capacities."[8] Bennett intends her political ecologies to cultivate a politics that take a fuller account of the interconnected networks of complex systems that condition our shared humanity.

Food is among the lively things whose agency Bennett hopes to elucidate. It is in part through increased awareness of edible matter as actant that Bennett hopes to infuse public life with greater concern for sustainability. Bennett devotes a chapter of *Vibrant Matter* to food, building a "case for food as a participant" in the assemblage she refers to as "American consumption," of which the obesity epidemic is symptomatic. She is convinced that "an image of inert matter helps animate our current practice of aggressively wasteful and planet-endangering consumption."[9] She wagers that were we to experience materiality "as a lively force with agentic capacity"

---

6. Bennett, *Vibrant Matter*, vii.

7. Ibid., viii.

8. Ibid., 38. Political solutions are envisioned as necessary because our food system problems are political problems insofar as the arrangement of the *polis* exerts tremendous influence on and through systems of food production and distribution. Contemporary political systems favor the "economy" at the expense of "ecology." We live in a house divided: the *nomos*/law by which the *polis* is arranged within our *oikos* (earth home) is incongruent with the *logos*/wisdom by which the *oikos* perpetually recreates itself. This *oikos* is comprised of multitudes of nonhuman and even inorganic (subjects and) agencies involved in complexly interacting systems. To live unsustainably is to dismiss the *logos* of the material world, a world with which we are engaged in "mutual transformations" (ibid., 49) through intimate daily interactions that privilege economic laws (*oikos nomos*) over ecological processes (*oikos logos*). Here I am thinking of *logos* as wisdom in the first-century *logos* theology of Philo, as described by Boyarin, in "The Jewish Life of the Logos." In particular, see 113–14 where Boyarin states that God's Word "was the same as his wisdom" and through wisdom/word, God created the world.

9. Bennett, *Vibrant Matter*, 51.

then a greater passion for ecological sustainability might animate public life. She begins her chapter on food in the following way:

> It is not controversial to say that trash, gadgets, electricity, and fire are relevant to politics, or to say that though such things do not qualify as political stakeholders, they form the milieu of human action or serve as means or impediments to it. But do the categories of context, tool, and constraint capture the full range of powers possessed by nonhuman bodies?[10]

The final question in this passage seems to suggest that she is about to sketch a version of food as more than mere backdrop. Will she go so far as to suggest that food is a "political stakeholder"? Or will she mark a third path, between stakeholder and mere context within which stakes are determined?

She goes on to say that she "will treat food as conative bodies vying alongside and within another complex body."[11] This choice of verb—"vying"—conveys the sense of contestation over superiority between us and our food. This contestation for superiority, then, suggests that food might after all be considered a political stakeholder, with interests it pursues. She notes the way that "some foods, say potato chips" seem to trigger a mindless hand-to-mouth motion, seeming "to call forth, or provoke and stoke, the manual labor."[12] At the very least, "the I is not necessarily the most decisive operator" in our engagements with food. If the vibrant materiality of food elicits human behavior, the sovereign self upon which any claim to sovereignty is based is called into question.

Bennett's case for food as participant in the assemblage she has named "American consumption" rests on two foundations. One is the scientific study of "the effects of dietary fat on human moods and cognitive dispositions," and the other is "the robust nineteenth century discussions of the moral and political efficacy of diet."[13] She cites scientific studies which have shown omega-3 fatty acids to decrease violence, increase attention span, and improve mood.[14] She emphasizes that this effect "ought not to be imagined as a mechanical causality," but is rather more likely the result of "an emergent causality" that she stresses is nonlinear in character.[15] For Bennett, the problem of obesity would subsequently require an analysis of:

10. Ibid., 39.
11. Ibid.
12. Ibid., 40.
13. Ibid., 39–40.
14. Ibid., 41.
15. Ibid., 41–42.

not only the large humans and their economic-cultural prosthesis (agribusiness, snack-food vending machines, insulin injec-
tions, bariatric surgery, serving sizes, systems of food marketing
and distribution, microwave ovens) but also the strivings and
trajectories of fats as they weaken or enhance the power of human wills, habits, and ideas.[16]

Here again, her choice of verb—"strivings"—subtly insinuates that fats desire
to be consumed, or that their strivings for inclusion in the human corpus has
some role to play in how we have structured our food system.

The second major source of support for Bennett's assertions about the
agency of food comes from the writings of Thoreau and Nietzsche on the
"moral and political efficacy of diet."[17] That is to say, Thoreau and Nietzsche
concern themselves with the ways in which the foods we ingest form our
moral character. These writers, similar to the authors of recent studies of
psychological effects of dietary fats, "discern a productive power intrinsic to
foodstuff, which enables edible matter to coarsen or refine the imagination
or render a disposition more or less liable to ressentiment, depression, hy-
peractivity, dull-wittedness or violence."[18] Bennett mobilizes both Nietzsche
and Thoreau to support her contention that the food we eat has the "power
to resist or obstruct human projects, but it also includes the more active
power to affect and create effects."[19] Subsequently, "eating appears as a series
of mutual transformations in which the border between inside and outside
becomes blurry: my meal both is and is not mine; you both are and are not
what you eat."[20] The food you eat *becomes* you, but you become a different
"you" in your interaction with the food you eat.

Bennett argues that food is an actant, "operative in the moods, cognitive dispositions, and moral sensibilities that we bring to bear as we engage
the questions of what to eat, how to get it, and when to stop."[21] She sets up
her argument by first noting that "the assemblage in which persons and fats
are participants is perhaps better figured as a nonlinear system."[22] This then,
leads her to "focus one's attention away from individuals and onto actants in
assemblages," with a particular emphasis upon food as an actant.

16. Ibid., 43.
17. Ibid., 43–47.
18. Ibid., 49.
19. Ibid.
20. Ibid.
21. Ibid., 51.
22. Ibid., 42.

In order to better understand at least some of the actants involved in the "nonlinear system" within which "persons and fats are participants" I would like in this chapter to take the line of inquiry Bennett initiates, and curve it in precisely the direction she does not wish to go: toward the economic-cultural prosthetic. In bracketing the economic-cultural prosthesis, Bennett mutes attention to the political dimension of food, which seems counter to her desires to "animate a more ecologically sustainable public." Aside from her introduction to the Slow Food movement, Bennett confines herself to describing the impact of food upon an individual with only a hint, via Nietzsche, that the action of food upon an individual may be altered by other features of the individual's socio-political milieu.

Perhaps the "economic-cultural prosthesis" within which the *polis* produces and consumes food—in other words, politics of food—already diminishes the general awareness of the material agency of food that Bennett is trying to help us see. Could it be that nineteenth-century writers Bennett cited were more likely to acknowledge the materiality of food than contemporary authors because in the nineteenth century farmers constituted approximately 70 percent of the American labor force, compared to only 2 percent today?[23]

I suspect that there is a correlation, and that the lack of recognition of the material reality of food is itself symptomatic of our "economic-cultural prosthesis"—material practices that paradoxically correlate with the divorce of the conceptual from the material. Most of us do not grow our own food, we seldom encounter our food in the form of vibrant, living beings; instead we encounter it as dead matter on a store shelf. We imagine that food comes from the grocery store not from fertile soil; bacon comes in a tidy rectangular plastic package, not from the bloody, once-living flesh of a pig. It is possible that the corporate agribusinesses endemic to this economic-cultural prosthesis drives the eating of low-nutrient, high-calorie food by manipulating the "strivings and trajectories of fats," although the rewarding neurological response of the brain to the fat in the chips doubtless assists the prosthesis. Yet, harkening back to my earlier concern about carving a space for political agency, between the political and economic forces of transnational global capitalism and the material influences of food upon the brain, the average consumer might rightly perceive their individual agency to be eclipsed by these very powerful decision-makers.

And I know that this is precisely the conclusion Bennett is trying to avoid: the conclusion that the "economic-cultural prosthesis" has total

23. See Roser, "Agricultural Employment"; Spielmaker and Lacy, "Growing a Nation"; and Ferdman, "The Decline of the American Family Farm in One Chart."

control in our food systems. She is trying to get us to acknowledge the effect of food upon our individual bodies and so also on our politics with the intention of empowering us to actively shape a more ecological politics. What I would like to do is to drive her point home through sustained attention to the economic-cultural prosthesis as a field of bodily becoming. I want to pick up more explicitly the thread of the economic-cultural, and illustrate how it always already shapes the relationship between the eater and the eaten, and is in turn shaped by the iterative performances of the economic-cultural prosthesis.

The thing is, as food activist Raj Patel writes, "food always exists *somewhere*, in space and time . . . *Where* we live and work shapes *what* and *how* we eat and drink."[24] Patel goes on to note that poor neighborhoods are "likely to have four times fewer supermarkets than rich ones."[25] He cites studies demonstrating that poor people, given the opportunity to choose fresh fruits and vegetables do in fact choose them over their unhealthy rivals, lipid strivings notwithstanding. The obese/relatively poor are not merely at the mercy of the agency of food, but also at the mercy of a complex food system (economic-cultural prosthesis, in Bennett's terms) that does not have their best interest in mind.

Without an approach to food that accounts for the contributions of its social context to the nonlinearity of the systems in which food is consumed—in other words, without accounting for its economic-cultural dimensions—I fear a collapse in individualist engagements with food. After all, what could seem more a matter of personal choice than the food we consume?[26] I would therefore like to supplement Bennett's work by reading her vibrant materialism through Karen Barad's agential realism in a way that accounts for the nonlinearity of the relationship between food and body.

An agential realist accounting of food

In applying Karen Barad's agential realism to the topic of global food politics, I must confess that I do so despite the fact that Barad does not address

24. Patel, *Stuffed and Starved*, 266.

25. Ibid., 269.

26. Vibrating in the periphery of my awareness are psychological/psychiatric engagements with eating as a control issue, as for example in the case of anorexics and infants. Contestations over what, if any, food gets into "my" mouth are very much about autonomy and control. I am hoping to straddle the edge here between on the one hand recognizing the social dimension of food, in the face of which we could perceive ourselves to be powerless, and on the other hand recognizing and reclaiming our collective power to shift the social dimension—shifts that are always happening and perhaps could happen in a way that brings about greater flourishing for all.

her concept of agential realism on quite the same scale that Bennett engages her concept of vibrant materialism. After all, Barad derives her theoretical approach from the quantum theory. But, as Barad herself notes, "quantum mechanics is thought to be the correct theory of nature that applies at all scales."[27] Additionally, the eighth chapter of *Meeting the Universe Halfway* consists of an application of her methodology to the configuration of power in a jute mill. So there is some justification for reading Barad on a larger socio-political scale despite the derivation of her theory from quantum physics. Admittedly, however, this scale does to some degree bypass the level of the individual, which is where Bennett's engagement with food lingers.

Nonetheless, Bennett intends a politics to arise from her engagement; it is on this point that I find Barad's methodology helpful in demonstrating how political decisions about foodways shape the materialization of bodies. Barad's methodology provides sophisticated tools with which to examine what Bennet refers to as the "economic-cultural prosthesis," provided that phrase be recast in Baradian parlance. In the terminology of Barad's theoretical system, the "economic cultural prosthesis" of the global food system might be better described as the "material-discursive practices" through which humans and food reiteratively "intra-act." The phrase "intra-active material-discursive practices" as descriptor for "economic cultural prosthesis" gestures toward the nonlinear, mutually constitutive relations between eaters and foodways.

To make greater sense of this substitution in terms, further acquaintance with a new vocabulary is necessary. As alluded to previously, Barad's agential realism is theoretically moored in her knowledge of experimental quantum physics. Among the questions quantum physicists attempt to answer regards the nature of light: is light wave or particle? Physicists have attempted to answer this question by passing a single photon through what is referred to as a diffraction grating. After passing through the diffraction grating, the photon hits a detection screen, leaving behind a mark of its presence on the screen. Physicists read the detection screen for clues regarding the nature of light.

Although we commonly take light to be a wave, the answer to the question regarding the nature of light depends on the circumstances under which light is studied. The determination of the light's behavior is made in the intra-action between light and the apparatus itself. Construct the apparatus in one way, light behaves as a wave; construct the apparatus differently and it behaves as a particle. The apparatus enacts what Barad refers to as an "agential cut" that shapes the behavior of light such that

27. Karen Barad, *Meeting the Universe Halfway*, 85.

it materializes differently. Barad notes that the same is true of what we take to be solid, particulate matter: "under some circumstances, matter . . . exhibits wavelike behavior."[28] The difference is visible as patterns of marks on the detection screen known as diffraction patterns.

Succinctly, diffraction patterns are the result of overlapping waves such as, for example, the pattern that would emerge on the surface of a pond if two stones were dropped into it from slightly different locations. The intra-action between the waves creates a diffraction pattern:

> When the crest of one wave overlaps with the crest of another, the resultant waveform is larger than the individual component waves. On the other hand, if the crest of one wave overlaps with the trough of another, the disturbances partly or in some cases completely cancel one another out, resulting in an area of relative calm . . . this way of combining effects is called *superposition*.[29]

Superposition might be one way to conceptualize the nonlinearity Bennett observes in the effects of food upon the human body in *Vibrant Matter*.

Because materialization at the quantum level is influenced by the apparatus in which it occurs, and because quantum theory "applies at all scales,"[30] Barad's agential realism attends to diffraction patterns. The aim of Barad's agential realism is to make a difference by "taking responsibility for the fact that our practices matter; the world is materialized differently though different practices."[31] For Barad, "Realism, then, is not about representations of an independent reality but about the real consequences, interventions, creative possibilities, and responsibilities of intra-acting within and as part of the world."[32] She, too, gestures toward the political in her theoretical approach.

According to the relational ontology of agential realism, "things" do not preexist their intra-active becoming in the context of apparatuses. Agential realism holds that "the primary ontological unit is not independent objects with inherent boundaries and properties but rather *phenomena*."[33] These phenomena, similar to diffraction patterns, are "produced through complex agential intra-actions of multiple material-discursive practices or apparatuses of bodily production, where *apparatuses are not mere observing instruments but boundary-drawing practices—spe-*

28. Ibid., 83.
29. Ibid., 76.
30. Ibid., 84.
31. Ibid., 89.
32. Ibid., 37.
33. Ibid., 139.

cific material (re)configurings of the world—which come to matter."[34] The practices in which we engage, whether directed by informal social custom or formal legislation, constitute the material-discursive practices that shape the materiality of our bodies. Simultaneously, we shape the customs and legal systems within which we interact.

Barad's argument is directed toward social constructivists who ignore the materiality of the body, and even to some degree against Butler (although not a social constructivist) whom she says "fails to recognize matter's dynamism."[35] She asks the important question: "If biological forces are in some sense always already historical ones, could it be that there is also some important sense in which historical forces are always already biological?"[36] She seeks an "account of the body's historicity in which its very materiality plays an *active* role in the workings of power," without which matter's passivity is merely reinscribed. Barad insists that "Any robust theory of the materialization of bodies would necessarily take account of *how the body's materiality* (including, for example, its anatomy and physiology) and *other material forces as well* (including nonhuman ones) *actively matter to the processes of materialization.*"[37] It is hoped that this chapter is a beginning gesture toward a theory of the materialization of bodies that accounts for not only the body's materiality, but also the materiality of the global food system in the context of other social structures.

Barad describes materialization as "*an iteratively intra-active process of mattering whereby phenomena (bodies) are sedimented out and actively re(con)figured through the intra-action of multiple material-discursive apparatuses. Matter is a stabilizing and destabilizing process of iterative intra-activity.*"[38] According to agential realism, "apparatuses provide the conditions for the possibility of determinate boundaries and properties of 'objects' within phenomena, where '*phenomena*' *are the ontological inseparability of objects and apparatuses.*"[39] Neither apparatuses nor phenomena can be thought of as merely intellectual propositions or theoretical abstractions. Apparatuses constitute the material arrangements of our daily lives, and phenomena are "real physical entities or beings (though not fixed and

34. Ibid., 139. Barad uses italics frequently. All italicized quotes are replicated as they appear in the original text.

35. Ibid., 64.

36. Ibid., 65.

37. Ibid.

38. Ibid., 210. It is important to note that throughout the text, Barad will use the terms "material-discursive practices" and "apparatuses" interchangeably, and I continue that pattern.

39. Ibid., 128.

separately delineated things)."[40] Material-discursive practices literally shape material reality at a very fundamental level, and material reality itself would be different in the context of different practices.

Barad makes clear that apparatuses are not to be understood as merely pieces of laboratory equipment with determinate boundaries, but instead constitute "a dynamic set of open-ended practices, iteratively refined and reconfigured."[41] Furthermore, they are "material-discursive practices that are inextricable from the bodies that are produced and through which power works its productive effects."[42] The dynamic quality of apparatuses applies not only to laboratory setups, but also to the human social and political landscape, appearances of calcification notwithstanding. Apparatuses, that is to say material-discursive practices, are iteratively reconfigured. Change is possible. In fact, it is inevitable.

One must be mindful that Barad includes matter itself as something that is iteratively reconfigured. She insists that:

> Matter is neither fixed and given nor the mere end result of different processes. Matter is produced and productive, generated and generative. Matter is agentive, not a fixed essence or property of things. Mattering is differentiating and which differences come to matter, matter in the iterative production of different differences.[43]

This passage, in short, nicely summarizes what I hope to demonstrate in this chapter. Bodies materialize differently based upon the social location—the material-discursive apparatus—in which they become. The different differences that materialize significantly shape the iterative becoming of bodies.

The materialization of all bodies, including human bodies, occurs by virtue of "the world's iterative intra-activity—its performativity," which is "true not only of the surface or contours of the body but also of the body in the fullness of its physicality, including the very 'atoms' of its beings."[44] Bodies are not objects with inherent boundaries and properties. They are material-discursive phenomena, ontologically inseparable from the apparatuses within which they materialize. Although Barad does not engage the food system or nutritional studies, she does note that:

40. Ibid., 129.
41. Ibid., 167.
42. Ibid., 230.
43. Ibid., 137.
44. Ibid., 153.

> Surely it is the case—even when the focus is restricted to the materiality of "human" bodies . . . that there are "natural," not merely "social," forces that matter. Indeed there is a host of material-discursive forces—including ones that get labeled "social," "cultural," "psychic," "economic," "natural," "physical," "biological," "geopolitical," and "geological"—that may be important to particular (entangled) processes of materialization[45]

Bodies and the food they consume intra-act in the context of apparatuses—material-discursive practices—which iteratively materialize the body. These intra-actions are causal, although not in a deterministic sense. In agential realism, both "absolute freedom and strict determinism" are rejected.[46] Having rejected absolutism, a political theology of food traffics in possibilities and probabilities, rather than one-to-one correspondences between nutrition or food and a particular bodily materialization, reflective of the nonlinearity in food's agentic capacity noted earlier by Bennett.

Despite the social, cultural, and psychic nature of these material-discursive forces, Barad emphasizes that agential realism is not about how linguistics mysteriously affects bodies. Rather agential-realism describes "the dynamics of intra-activity in its materiality . . . where 'material' is always already material-discursive—*that is what it means to matter*."[47] Engagement with nutritional studies emphasizes the materialization of human bodies, even though Barad argues that an exclusive focus on human bodies overlooks "the crucial point that the very practices by which the boundaries of the human and nonhuman are drawn are always already implicated in particular materializations."[48] Yet eating, by its very nature undoes boundaries between human and nonhuman, and is unquestioningly "implicated in particular materializations." Subsequently, some of these "particular materializations" will also receive scrutiny in this chapter and the next.

My analysis of the intra-actions between human bodies and food takes an anthropocentric approach in order to map the effects of different material-discursive practices upon the materialization of the human body. The apparatuses involved go well beyond individual eaters and their particular meals. Although Patel can describe a "global food system" that connects these various material-discursive practices, we will see that this global food system appears more montage than monolith.

---

45. Ibid., 66.
46. Ibid., 129.
47. Ibid., 153.
48. Ibid.

Different diffraction patterns arise in the context of different apparatuses "through which power works its productive effects. Subsequently, the materialization of raced, classed, and gendered bodies marks "the effects of difference"—differences in power and privilege that result in dissimilar access to and metabolism of food. Hopefully this Baradian engagement with nutritional studies will "highlight, exhibit, and make evident the entangled structure of the changing and contingent ontology of the world" in a way that further elucidates what is at stake in the global food system.[49]

The assumption here is that the intra-actions between human and food do not happen in a vacuum divorced from broader cultural practices—even the chip Bennett observed stoking the hand-to-mouth gesture will only do so in the context of certain cultural practices. It is these practices that perpetuate unsustainable engagements with planetary systems. The chip, and indeed all food, bears some similarities to Barad's description of a cigar, which she insisted was a "'nodal point' . . . of the workings of other apparatuses, including class, nationalism, economics, and gender."[50] Encounters with food are always already shaped by apparatuses—material-discursive practices—which exert tremendous influence over what type and how much food is available to choose from in the first place. Our bodies become detection screens recording the differential intra-actions between these apparatuses and the food we eat. Apparatuses leave marks on bodies.

When we begin to examine the "phenomenon" of the differential materialization of bodies resulting from complex intra-actions with foodways and social structures, we will be faced with an almost impossible task. The human body is profoundly dynamic, as is our rapidly shifting global food system. Distinguishing the effects of one material-discursive apparatus from another is indeed daunting. They intersect and overlap. At the level of dynamism that characterizes the materialization of bodies, materialdiscursive apparatuses themselves are characterized by a type of superposition. Subsequently, some apparatuses may amplify the effect of others, while attenuating the effects of still others.[51]

The superposition of various material-discursive apparatuses creates undulating gradients, neither clearly demarcated distinctions nor linear gradients. Impossible though the task of parsing these diffraction patterns might be, it is nonetheless important. Barad herself notes that "Significantly, taking full account of the nature of material-discursive constraints and

49. Ibid., 73.

50. Ibid.

51. This may relate to what is signified in feminist scholarship by the term "intersectionality."

exclusions is important for understanding the materialization of bodies as well as the nature of abjection."[52] An exhaustive account of the constraints and exclusions in the global food system is well beyond the scope of this or any other single volume, in light of its complexity. Yet the nature of abjection in the context of the global food system nonetheless becomes more readily visible as a consequence of absolute sovereignty as even a partial accounting of constraints and exclusions in the global food system is undertaken.

From an agential realist perspective, "*apparatuses are the material conditions of possibility and impossibility of mattering*; they enact what matters and what is excluded from mattering."[53] In this intra-active process of becoming, "'marks are left on bodies': bodies differentially materialize as particular patterns of the world as a result of the specific cuts and reconfigurings that are enacted."[54] Abjection is no mere theoretical concern. The bodies of the emaciated/abjectly poor are decidedly marked, and all the more so for having intra-acted with an apparatus that has excluded their bodies from mattering.

But what about the bodies of the obese/relatively poor? In what way can they be said to have been excluded from mattering? They have clearly not been altogether excluded from the global food system in the same tragic sense as have been the abjectly poor. Their exclusion is harder to identify. I would suggest that they have been excluded from mattering not by virtue of having been altogether banned, as it were, from the global food system. Rather, motions of sovereign power have unduly attenuated the possibilities and probabilities of mattering from which to choose.

So the issue might not be first of all that the average consumer does not understand the agency of *food*, as Bennett fears, but that the average consumer is alienated from his or her *own* agency in shaping the food system:

> If the quality of food we eat is shaped by work and play, by the neighbourhoods we live in, the jobs we can get and the time we spend travelling between them, then we might want to consider poor diets as a symptom of a systemic lack of control over our space and lives.[55]

I am concerned about the lack of control based upon material conditions of daily life *because* I agree with Bennett that food is "operative in the moods, cognitive dispositions, and moral sensibilities that we bring to bear as we

52. Ibid., 212.
53. Ibid., 148.
54. Ibid., 176.
55. Ibid., 273.

engage the questions of what to eat, how to get it, and when to stop."[56] As a former physician, access to nutritional food is a matter of public health.

How can a person possibly be expected to make good food choices if bad food is their only choice? Then, having already ingested the bad food that is the only choice, how can that food not affect their "moods, cognitive dispositions, and moral sensibilities?" And it is with this in mind that I would proceed to apply Barad's agential realism in a way that closes the gap between the agency of food and contemporary food politics in a gesture that maintains a sense of agency for human individuals while elucidating the collective, political dimension of the food system as a set of material-discursive practices through which the bodies of the body politic iteratively materialize.

Nutrition science

In response to Bennett's assertion that the science of diet would subsequently require an analysis of "not only the large humans and their economic-cultural prosthesis . . . but also the strivings and trajectories of fats as they weaken or enhance the power of human wills, habits, and ideas"[57] and Barad's call for a more "robust theory of the materialization of bodies,"[58] I turn to the science of nutrition. Fortunately, the science of diet is beginning to tell us something about the trajectories of fats and other nutrients (although perhaps not the strivings), and even something about how fats intra-act with the brain in the context of material-discursive practices.

In particular, the science of diet illuminates the social production of the "obese/relatively poor" bodies of the Global North. An examination of "obese/relatively poor" appearance is useful insofar as it describes a phenomenon encountered with increasing regularity in the Global North. It provides a fascinating glimpse into both the vibrant materiality of food as well as an agential realist accounting of the materialization of bodies.[59] It is

56. Bennett, *Vibrant Matter,* 51.

57. Ibid., 43.

58. Barad, *Meeting the Universe Halfway,* 65.

59. At this juncture I must remark again that Global South and Global North fail as geographic markers, since wealth is unevenly distributed in both affluent and developing countries. Thus, there are those in affluent nations who are calorie-deprived and those in developing nations who are obese. The primary reason for using Global South/ Global North terminology is two-fold. The first reason is straightforward: because it is the most common descriptor used in food studies to distinguish between affluent and developing nations. The second reason is more complicated and related to the first. In the literature that refers to Global North and Global South, the implication is that

also a phenomenon that tends to elicit victim-blaming rather than a search for root causes in our food system. Resituating obesity as an intra-active materialization shaped by material discursive practices illuminates the degree to which food choice is a matter of public concern, one to which a political theology of food endeavors to respond.

Bennett notes that food affects behavior—in the case of chips, the chips themselves seem to call forth their own eating. And the romanticists she cites both link food consumption to morality, although in different ways. In order to have any direct effect upon the brain, where I am presuming impetus for physical movement, the seat of morality, and experience of affect all reside, the molecules ingested must impact one or more neurotransmitter pathways. And in fact, research has demonstrated that the dopamine system is particularly responsive to food. This is significant, because the neurotransmitter dopamine is highly implicated in addictive disorders. Dopamine is the uplifting neurotransmitter associated with the brain's reward circuits. As "the principal neurotransmitter of *motivated action,* in the sense of physical and psychological movement toward 'pleasure' or away from 'pain,'" [60] its release tends to increase the likelihood that any behavior triggering its release will be repeated. Say, as in Bennett's example, eating a potato chip.

Dopamine stimulates especially powerful feelings associated with pleasure and reward, which in turn render the brain more likely to repeat the pleasurable behavior. Any behavior that stimulates the dopamine system is likely to be repeated, sometimes against one's better judgment—as in the case of addictions. While all people experience dopamine release when they eat palatable, non-nutritious foods—say potato chips for example—obese people experience a pattern of dopamine release more akin to the pattern characteristic in other addictive disorders.[61] Much as is the case in someone who becomes addicted to methamphetamine—also a potent stimulator of the dopamine system—someone who has eaten a potato chip is highly likely to eat at least one more under the influence of the dopamine system. So Bennett is right in saying that the eating of chips calls forth its own manual

the Global North holds all the power and is oppressive. However, even those in the admittedly privileged "Global North" are not alike in the degree to which they benefit. Over one third of adults in the United States are suffering from the machinations of the corporate food regime, as I am about to demonstrate. It is my hope that recognition of our shared vulnerability might shift our investment, resituate our assessment of what is at stake in our food system, and facilitate solidarity with those in the food sovereignty movement who, as it turns out, live in both the Global North and the Global South.

60. Pani, Porcella, and Gessa, "The role of stress in the pathophysiology of the dopaminergic system," 14; emphasis theirs.

61. Gearhardt et al., "Neural Correlates of Food Addiction."

labor—by virtue of its intra-action with the dopamine system. Potato chips are so damn *rewarding*!

Complicating this even further, merely *anticipating* eating the potato chips also stimulates dopamine response.[62] Whether the anticipation of the chip is a thought ("I will soon eat a chip") or an emotion (somatic sense of desire about to be fulfilled) is debatable, but the fact remains: something as ephemeral as anticipation is nonetheless associated with material effects in the brain. The fact that the *thought itself* creates an observable material effect on the brain, no actual potato chip required, supports my contention that any discussion of the vibrant materiality of food that intends to affect food politics must include the material-discursive practices within which food consumption occurs. This is not because these practices are discursive or intellectual in nature such that thought itself is the key to this materialization, but rather because "'material' is always already material-discursive—*that is what it means to matter,*"[63] as Barad insists.

The finding that eating non-nutritive food (i.e., junk food) provokes dopamine release raises multiple questions. What if non-nutritious food is more likely to initiate an addictive disorder in the already marginalized *because* they are marginalized? For example, perhaps their lives entail greater hardships and fewer rewards, and so fewer competing triggers of dopamine release? Or, if thoughts alone can result in material changes in the brain, can the advertising gimmicks deployed by the "economic-cultural prosthesis" already be shaping brains in such a way as to render them more likely to cooperate with the "strivings of fats?" In short, what if one contributing factor to the nonlinearity of dietary effects that Bennett notes is one's exposure to and position within the "economic-cultural prosthesis?"

Again, the science of diet provides a cluster of clues that allow us to begin to sketch answers to these questions. These answers suggest that a variety of social and economic material-discursive practices inflect the intra-actions between humans and their food—strengthening the argument that food is both a political issue and a political actant. First, let us dispense with one easily answered question: does advertising render our brains more susceptible to the strivings of fats? Well, advertising certainly shapes our taste buds. A 2007 double-blind study of school-aged children demonstrated that they preferred the taste of food that came wrapped in packaging of familiar brands over the taste of the exact same food in generic packaging. So, yes, in a way the advertising gimmicks are working—and so early in our lives that we can scarcely notice.[64] Or, in Baradian terms, the material-discursive

---

62. Ibid.

63. Barad, *Meeting the Universe Halfway,* 153.

64. Robinson, Borzekowski, Matheson, and Kraemer, "Effects of Fast Food Branding on Young Children's Taste Preferences," 792.

practices of the food system iteratively shape intra-actions between humans and the food we eat by creating affective resonances that amplify wave patterns trending toward the increased eating of particular foods, impacting the materialization of the human body.

Next, let us engage the demographics of obesity, because this is where the science of nutrition bears heavily upon Bennett's assertion that food has a nonlinear effect upon the body, and perhaps illustrates how Barad's "superposition" of socio-economic factors impinges upon the materialization of bodies. A 2010 report by the Center for Disease Control (CDC) found that over one third of Americans were obese. Of particular importance is the demographic breakdown of this obesity epidemic based on race, gender, education and income.[65] Mexican-American and non-Hispanic black males experienced the highest obesity at the highest income levels. Non-Hispanic white males, by contrast, exhibited the highest obesity rates in the middle income group. Women in the lowest income groups exhibited obesity at a rate ranging from 40 to 54 percent, as compared to 27 to 34 percent for those in the highest income levels.[66] For white males and all females, there was an inverse correlation between education level and obesity.[67] This was not the case for non-white males, who experienced increasing rates of obesity with increasing academic achievement.

Attempts to explain the relationship of obesity to demographic details by means of "linear" explanations are confounded. For example, one might conjecture that affluence directly correlates with obesity due to increased availability of calories. But that doesn't explain why the wealthiest group of white males has a *lower* rate of obesity than the middle income group, nor does it explain why the wealthiest women are *least* likely to be obese. One might surmise that increasing educational levels provides greater opportunity to learn about proper nutrition, and so therefore higher education leads to *less* obesity. That might explain why, for white men and all women, increasing academic achievement decreases obesity levels. But it doesn't explain why African-American men and Hispanic-American men with college degrees experience the highest rates of obesity among their racial and ethnic counterparts. Linear explanations do not fully account for the data.

I would like to account for the non-linearity of the data by using the study in a fashion similar to the function Barad assigns to diffraction apparatuses: "diffraction apparatuses measure the effects of difference, even more profoundly they highlight, exhibit, and make evident the entangled structure

65. Center for Disease Control, *Obesity and Socioeconomic Status* (2010), 1.

66. Ibid., 4

67. Ibid.

of the changing and contingent ontology of the world."[68] When viewed as a diffraction apparatus, the results of the demographic study cited above could be read as illustrating that income and education intra-act with race and gender in ways that significantly impact the materialization of bodies. These factors do not deterministically cause obesity, to be sure. But the apparatuses that mark social differences such as income, education, race, and gender also contribute to differential materialization of the human body—including the foods it calls forth and how it metabolizes them.

The demographic study of obesity constitutes what could be understood in Baradian terms as an effort to distinguish one apparatus from another, to enact, as it were, an agential cut that will permit examination of a portion of the sociocultural food apparatus within which bodies are materialized. In addition to the agential cuts previously made regarding race, gender, and class, none of which alone explain the findings, I would like to explore one additional possibility. Perhaps the influence of a less easily observed factor is superimposed upon the influence of race, gender, education and income. I would like to explore the possibility that stress influences metabolism in ways that differentially affect the intra-action between particular groups of people and the food they eat. The diffraction patterns resulting from the superposition of stress with the other more readily identifiable markers may reveal something about the nature of the apparatuses within which bodies are materialized.

It turns out that stress affects the dopamine system in some intriguing ways. Pani et al. conducted a thorough review of research on the effect of stress on the dopamine system.[69] These studies, conducted primarily on rats, found that stress alters dopaminergic systems in a way that renders stressed rats more susceptible to addictive disorders.[70] Remembering that a study previously mentioned concluded that food functioned addictively in the obese, it is at least plausible to suggest that stress may play some role in shaping the intra-action between race, gender, class, and food in the ongoing process of materialization of bodies by way of its impact on the dopamine system.

68. Barad, *Meeting the Universe Halfway*, 73.

69. Pani, Porcella, and Gessa, "The Role of Stress."

70. Ibid., 18–19. These particular types of studies are conducted on rats instead of humans for ethical reasons (one would not "intentionally" stress a human in this way, and even if one did, one would not then dissect the human's brain for further analysis) and also for scientific reasons (human exposure to stress cannot be "controlled" in the same way as rat stress can be controlled). The results are considered to be, although not directly translatable to humans, at least informative of likely processes occurring in the human brain.

In keeping with Bennett's nonlinearity and Barad's intra-activity, Pani et al. also found that not all stressors are created equal. Some stressors are relatively easy for the rat to shrug off without a dopamine-hitch, and others significantly impact the rat—sometimes permanently. Furthermore, not all of the stressors had to be directly applied—merely being in the presence of a stressed rat could trigger similar responses in a non-stressed rat. In other words, some stressors can be viewed as apparatuses that leave permanent marks on bodies, marks that in turn create ripple effects on other bodies, influencing both bodies' intra-actions with food.

This begins to sketch food as intra-active within extremely complex, material-discursive practices. It is not just that food can co-opt decision-making around food and create addictive patterns of neurological firing and subsequent behavior. Some brains in some situations are more susceptible to these effects because they are encountering stressful situations, either directly or vicariously through their social entanglements with others. There is little room for deterministic explanations in the face of such profound complexity.

In a review article, Peek and Chrousos note that stress results in increased cortisol levels, which in turn results in increased fat storage, excessive production of insulin, and ultimately insulin resistance and diabetes.[71] Of additional concern, increased cortisol also results in abdominal obesity, the most likely type of obesity to result in cardiovascular events.[72] Reviewing the literature on stress, cortisol and obesity leads them to conclude that "The complex interactions of the stress axis upon . . . the adipose tissue, suggest that chronic stress, whether psychological and/or physical, exerts an intense effect upon body composition, which, in turn, significantly affects the longevity and survival of the organism."[73] So whereas stress can render the brain more susceptible to the addictive potential of food through the interaction of stress with the dopamine system, it tends to simultaneously interact with the cortisol system in a way that slows metabolism of the calories ingested.

How might stress relate to the above material-discursive apparatuses of race, gender and education? A more recent review article facilitates the connection between race, class, gender and stress: "Studies examining the relationship between social position, psychological stress, dietary behaviors, and obesity risk present extensive evidence that lower social position is associated with higher stress, poorer diet quality, and higher body

71. Ibid.
72. Peeke and Chrousos, "Hypercortisolism and Obesity," 771.
73. Ibid., 665.

weight."[74] Mindful that *homo sacer* names the lowest of all possible social positions, this last bit seems to suggest that, provided sufficient calories are available, the closer one's social position is to *homo sacer*, as opposed to "the sovereign," the more likely one is to become obese. The contribution of material-discursive apparatuses to materializations of human bodies becomes increasingly apparent.

What about food that has been stripped of actants? Could "missing agents" in food contribute to the obesity epidemic in the United States? Could it be that we cannot "regulate" our own weight and that we rely upon nutrients in food to regulate it with us? What I'm getting at here is the potential that the nutrient content of food consumed in the United States may have a material effect on our body not only by the nutrients present in the food, but also by the *absence of nutrients*. Dr. Donald Davis at University of Texas conducted a nutritional analysis of food produced at the end of the 1990s, and compared the results to archived records of the nutritional content of food established in the 1950's. What he found was that, taken as a whole (rather than on a food-by-food basis), "six out of thirteen nutrients showed apparently reliable declines between 1999 and 1950."[75] He attributes this decline to the selection of cultivars that are higher yield, pest resistant, and/or adaptable to a wide variety of climates, based upon the "emerging evidence [that] suggests that when you select for yield, crops grow bigger and faster, but they don't necessarily have the ability to make or uptake nutrients at the same, faster rate."[76] While conventional agriculture has excelled at producing adequate calories, the nutritional content of those calories has not kept pace.

Compounding the troublesome selection of cultivars is the untoward effects of phosphorous-containing fertilizers. As it turns out, phosphorous competes with other micronutrients for its spot in the plant matter, resulting in a decrease of 20 to 55 percent in other minerals.[77] According to Martin Poole, writing for *Scientific American,* soil depletion can be added to the list of reasons our food is less nutritious than it used to be. Last, but probably not least, nutrients, as it turns out, are typically fragile creatures. They cannot withstand the multiple processes involved in the global food system. Extensive processing in conjunction with the natural aging process that occurs in the time it takes to ship our apples from Chile deplete our food of its already-

74. Moore and Cunningham, "Social Position, Psychological Stress, and Obesity: a Systematic Review," 525.

75. University of Texas, *University of Texas News.*

76. Ibid.

77. Long, "Industrial Farming is Giving Us Less Nutritious Food."

diminished nutritional content.[78] It is not only *we* who are intra-actively becoming in the context of our global food system, but our food is also intra-actively becoming—and it is becoming less nutritious.

But how does the intra-active becoming of (less nutritious) food link to obesity? A review article by Michael Via suggests that at the very least, micronutrient deficiency worsens the medical complications caused by obesity. In particular, deficiencies in vitamin D, chromium, vitamin C, biotin, and thiamine all "have the potential to impair glucose metabolism and cause insulin resistance."[79] Some of this, to be sure, is the result of choosing fewer fruits and vegetables—so it is the result of "poor dietary choices," or perhaps the result of food addiction triggered by the eating of non-nutritive foods, which in turn might be facilitated by food advertising.

According to physician Mark Hyman, personal choice is not singularly responsible. Our nutrient-depleted foods leave our bodies craving more nutrients—which is precisely what our food lacks.[80] The World Health Organization refers to the co-occurrence of nutrient deficiency and obesity as the "double burden of malnutrition."[81] We continue to eat an abundance of food because our material flesh in its wisdom knows that food is the best place to seek nutrients. Unfortunately, those nutrients are no longer in our food because of the material-discursive practices of the corporate food regime. Could it be that one of the stressors to which many bodies—obese and otherwise—are currently responding is chronic low grade malnutrition as a result of their participation in these material-discursive practices (to which I here collectively refer as transnational corporate agriculture)?

The effects of material-discursive practices on the materialization of bodies are not restricted to easily observable physical metrics, but extend to the materialization of the nervous system in a way that subtly (yet durably) impacts cognitive development. Ruth Morley and Alan Lucas undertake a review of research into the effects of early childhood nutrition on cognitive development, including their own research. They begin with animal studies, by far easier to "control" because it is less ethically disturbing to restrict variables such as food and affection from a developing rat pup than it is from

78. Martin Poole, "Dirt Poor." This article also highlights that the difference between one apple and another is not necessarily visibly perceptible. One reason "food" intra-acts with human bodies differently at different times is that the meals differ quite significantly in their molecular composition, even when by all accounts the ingredients are the same.

79. Via, "The Malnutrition of Obesity," 4.

80. Hyman, "How Malnutrition Causes Obesity."

81. See World Health Organization, "Double Burden." http://www.who.int/nutrition/double-burden-malnutrition/en/.

a human infant. Morley and Lucas note that the effects of poor nutrition on later performance measures have been well documented. Cumulatively, these studies show that "disadvantage for undernourished animals was significantly more likely if the period of undernutrition included gestation. Interestingly, the advantage was most often seen in male animals."[82] Their results raise particular concerns about prenatal nutrition.

As an illustration of the many components of a potential apparatus within which food is eaten, Morley and Lucas found that if the undernourished rats are patted, the "later behavioural deficits" are "ameliorated." Diminished performance was found to correlate with "a permanent reduction in brain iron and dopamine D_2 receptor site concentration."[83] Taken as a whole, the results of this study demonstrate that the materialization of malnourished brains was *different* in different social circumstances, such as being patted or the timing of deprivation. These differences were in turn associated with permanent alteration in neurobiological markers and consequently different behavioral outcomes. These findings account for the nonlinearity of food noted by Bennett, and in Baradian terms reflect the ways that differences in material-discursive practices leave different marks on bodies.

Studying nutritional deprivation in humans is confounded by the many "variables" that cannot be accounted for in the experimental apparatus. Although one can never be certain that it is nutrition per se that causes the effect one observes in these studies, "in many, though not all studies, poor nutritional status has been associated with lower cognitive or attainment scores."[84] In one study in Guatemala, nutritional supplementation during pregnancy was shown to have a beneficial effect lasting into adolescence, based on measures of school achievement. Numerous studies have also used sibling controls, and about half of the time these studies demonstrate benefits of improved nutrition on children's cognitive abilities.[85] The marks left on the bodies of these developing children affected their minds in lasting ways. Lasting impairment in cognitive abilities doubtless poses a significant obstacle to gainful employment.

Bennett's concept of vibrant materiality in conjunction with Barad's concepts of superposition and material-discursive practices help us to understand our participation in the global food system and its diffractive

82. Morley and Lucas, "Nutrition and Cognitive Development," 124.

83. Ibid., 125–26.

84. Ibid., 125.

85. This study, in fact, gets precisely at the concerns that nagged at me during my medical training: how can we collectively and conscionably fail to assure that all children receive truly adequate nutrition and simultaneously expect these children to work their way out of poverty?

materialization in and as our flesh. Careful reflection upon the demographic data reveals that there is not a simple linear correlation between sex and obesity, or race and obesity, or income and obesity. Each time, the linearity of the correlation is disrupted by some "exception." I propose that these different social contexts can be read as Baradian apparatuses within which food intra-acts with human bodies, sometimes in ways that attenuate nutrient waves, and—less often—in ways that amplify them. The demographic data regarding the obesity epidemic could be read as a diffraction pattern marking the agential cuts enacted by social apparatuses. These demographic diffraction patterns tell us how the socially constructed concepts like class, race, and gender become materialized in and as human bodies.

The superposition of the stress-induced dopaminergic drive to consume more food with the metabolic effects of stress—its stimulation of the cortisol system—serve to amplify the impact of the calories consumed. The material-discursive practices through which we iteratively become— many of which are not directly related to food—materialize bodies in nonlinear and indeterminate ways. The body does not precede its engagement in these apparatuses or its engagement with food; it materializes through iterative intra-actions with food in the context of myriad material-discursive practices. That Moore and Cunningham specifically name social position as a contributing factor to obesity highlights Barad's wisdom in insisting that: "Crucial to understanding the workings of power is an understanding of the nature of power in the fullness of its materiality."[86] The apparatuses of power within which humans are intercalated participate intra-actively in the materialization of human bodies marked by social position—Moore and Cunningham's term—or, in the terms of this political theology of food, marked by proximity to sovereign power, and perhaps even marked as *homo sacer*.

These material-discursive practices, as Barad says of all apparatuses, leave marks on bodies. They do so in indeterminate, intra-active ways, to be certain. While I would certainly not argue that the bodies of the poor are immediately distinguishable from those of the wealthy completely independently of other factors such as grooming, fashion, geographic location and other markers, what I hope I have at least accomplished is to account for the differential materialization of human bodies in relation to the apparatuses of race, gender and class in which those bodies are situated.

Above all, reading nutritional studies through Barad's agential realism reveals the extent to which the social apparatuses of power do not measure pre-existing human beings, whether fit, obese or malnourished. These

86. Ibid., 66.

apparatuses *materialize* them. In the following section I will argue that material-discursive apparatuses rely upon the physical appearance of the bodies they have created to further reinforce the social status, using physical appearance to prop up what would otherwise be evident as unjust systems of power operating in the politics of food.

Socially Produced Necessary Identities

I hope to demonstrate that the "obese/relatively poor" and the "emaciated/ abjectly poor" are identities that are the products *of* a particular social order, and in turn are necessary *to* that order. I will establish this through application of Margaret Urban Walker's concept of necessary identities. Walker's "necessary identities" bears resonances to Agamben's *homo sacer*. Unlike *homo sacer*, one with a "necessary identity" is not subject to the sovereign ban. Nonetheless a necessary identity signifies a socially subordinate role, and a profound degree of bodily vulnerability stopping just short of banishment. Walker's theory lends credence to Agamben's assertion that within the modern city *homo sacer* has become *"more internal than every interiority and more external than every extraneousness."*[87] Walker accomplishes this by aptly articulating the manner in which machinations of oppressive power regimes numb our awareness to the injustices they commit.

Walker's theory is also worth elaborating upon because it reveals something about the "motions of power" in a given social system—in the present case, the global food system—and about how those "motions of power" inflect the materialization of bodies. The "motions of power" are shown to operate via four primary mechanisms, to be discussed below. This exposition will clarify the iterative process whereby, in Baradian terms, the marks that a material-discursive apparatus leaves on bodies are retroactively utilized to legitimate not only the marks on the bodies, but also to legitimate the material-discursive apparatus that marked the bodies to begin with.

I will first need to argue that (malnourished) bodies mark social class in such a way as to produce "obese/relatively poor" and "emaciated/abjectly poor" as two interrelated "necessary identities." Walker defines "necessary identity" as:

> A social role or status that is inevitably or comfortably well fitted
> to the people whose social position it is, because of some natu-
> rally occurring feature of those people. The idea that there are
> necessary identities is the view that some are born for (rather

---

87. Agamben, *Homo Sacer*, 111.

born to) and naturally suited (rather than more or less forcibly fitted) to certain social roles or stations.[88]

In what way can an identity be said to be necessary, and to whom? Necessary identities "are not necessary for the ones who bear them, but for others who need to legitimate the ways they treat the bearers or to foreclose examination of those ways."[89] These identities are necessary to a kind of social order, and serve to maintain that order more or less without question.

Walker asserts that the idea that someone in particular is born for, rather than to, a social role is perpetuated "by inducing in or requiring of people certain physical or behavioral traits as marks of a social role, and then using those marks in turn to justify those people's assignment to it."[90] By way of example, Walker points to ancient observations that a slave's stooped posture demonstrates their natural fit for the role of slave to demonstrate the way in which coercing someone into a social role produces bodily effects that are then used to retroactively legitimate having forced them into that role in the first place. This retroactive legitimation occludes examination of the social structures that define the context for the body's becoming.

These identities are not "naturally" occurring. No one is "born for" the necessary identity (of slave, woman, or, as I will argue, "poor") into which they have been pressed; some degree of coercion is required. Walker stresses that there is a difference between "evidence of coercion into and within a social role, and the coercers having to acknowledge that evidence and admit what it is evidence for."[91] When we overlook the role of coercion in establishment and maintenance of roles we overlook the constructed and necessary nature of those roles in maintenance of a system of power. Subsequently a secondary goal of unjust structures is to conceal the violence required to coerce people into necessary identities. The more obvious the coercion, the more obvious is the injustice of the social structures necessitating such coercion. The appearance of injustice delegitimizes the coercive system. Consequently, the more *necessary* a social role is in the maintenance of a social structure, the greater the effort must be to *conceal* the violence needed to fit someone into that role.

There is "no one fact" that explains a given society's inability to tell that an identity is socially constructed, Walker says. Instead, "the relevant facts are about relations of power and resistance, address and response,

88. Walker, *Moral Understandings*, 162.

89. Ibid., 165.

90. Ibid., 163

91. Ibid., 165.

expression and recognition *between* people or groups."[92] Social identities represent "interpersonally significant positions, standings, or roles characterized by powers and prerogatives, responsibilities, and exposure to expectations and claims." Because of the social power (or lack thereof) encoded into these bodily markers, Walker urges us to "look for the apparent necessity of identities, then, in many facts about who has recognized power over whom, how the power is expected to be exercised."[93] Who has power over whom in the global food system? Whose claims are regarded as authoritative? Who is marginalized? How is power expected to be exercised?

Walker states that necessary identities "are roles necessitated by institutions taken as given, but these institutions are constituents of one among possible ways of life."[94] She articulates artfully that these identities "identify people for certain activities or treatments," and determine moral relationships and power dynamics between people based on easily (usually visibly) recognizable signifiers.[95] In a move resonant with Barad's agential realism, Walker declares that "marks of identity are only, as it were, the signifiers of possible modes of interaction, responsibilities, and treatments."[96] To render her assertion more "Baradian," perhaps we could rephrase this as "marks of identity are materializations of possible modes of intra-actions within apparatuses of bodily production."

What is it that precludes our immediate recognition of coercion into social roles in the first place? Walker cites four mechanisms through which this violence is concealed:

> These identities need to be *naturalized, privatized, or normalized,* in some combination. Those who bear the identities must be *epistemically marginalized* or *unauthorized,* so that the setup in which identities are naturalized, privatized, and normalized cannot be contradicted or contested by them. In the "ideal" case, it cannot even be pointed out.[97]

To be certain, as Walker herself notes, there is no ideal case in which the coercion required to maintain necessary identities can remain completely hidden indefinitely. For Walker this is because of the ongoing and participatory nature of social orders.[98] From an agential realist perspective, one might say

92. Ibid., 177.
93. Ibid., 178.
94. Ibid., 169.
95. Ibid., 180.
96. Ibid., 181.
97. Ibid., 177.
98. Ibid.

that everything is involved in intra-active processes of becoming—including identities and apparatuses themselves.[99] It is the iterative nature of all materializations that allow us to glimpse the apparatus, and it is this iterative nature of becoming that opens the potential for real change.

The social dynamics of naturalization, privatization, normalization, and marginalization merit closer attention in the context of a political theology of food. Emphasis will be placed on "obese/relatively poor" because the data to support this analysis is more plentiful than data regarding the emaciated/abjectly poor. Nonetheless, as should by now be clear, the "obese/relatively poor" and the "emaciated/abjectly poor" are socially produced by the same global food system, and parallel processes are presumed to be operative in both cases.

According to Walker, naturalization of identities:

> involves producing and sustaining appearances of the spontaneous inevitability of certain places for certain people . . . Since nothing denaturalizes a situation quicker than evidence of coercion into [identities], the most effective implementation of naturalized identities is making them conditions of birth, ceasing at death.[100]

The "appearance of spontaneous inevitability" serves to distract us from any thoughts that it could have been otherwise for this group of people. In the case of obesity, numerous factors create the appearance of inevitability. For one thing, there is a degree to which bodily habitus is heritable. Transgenerational poverty also shapes the food choices available in similar ways throughout one's life. Add to this the fact that food traditions are also taught within the family, and it can appear that certain types of people simply make poorer choices than others.

Privatization occurs when coercive interactions between the ruler and the ruled are shielded either literally behind closed doors, or when "customs, moral understandings, or laws . . . declare certain interactions outside legitimate or acceptable scrutiny, reaction, or public comment by others, even if those interactions take place in plain sight, or in places not private in the former sense."[101] The new customs of the transnational global food trade shield numerous abuses of people, ecosystems, and farm animals from scrutiny. Industrial food processing adds proprietary, unpronounceable, and non-nutritious ingredients to our food, such that we are often unaware

99. Barad herself makes this point regarding experimental apparatuses; *Meeting the Universe Halfway*, 146.

100. Walker, *Moral Understandings*, 180.

101. Ibid., 181.

of what we are eating. The recent legislative refusal to label GMOs is yet
another instance of this privatization. Furthermore, Americans are inclined
to value individual liberties over public welfare, such that former Major Michael Bloomberg's attempt to ban super-sized sodas from New York City in
the interest of public health was met with legal challenges.

Naturalizing and privatizing pose effective barriers to identification
of coercive practices, minimizing the protest that such coercion might
otherwise arouse. According to Walker, naturalizing and privatizing "aim
to keep some people and what happens to them outside the view of some
authoritative community of mutual moral accounting."[102] Practices that
naturalize and privatize coercive dominance can be shored up by practices
that *normalize* coercive dominance. "Certain patterns of behavior and relations are normalized when there are effective norms pertaining to them,
but the norms *presume* these relations and patterns to exist as a threshold
of application for the norms."[103] For example, at one time it was "normal"
to beat a slave; "normal" for a man to beat a "disobedient" wife. The norms
supporting coercive violence in these instances presuppose hierarchical
relations of domination.

Walker is not arguing that social norms per se are bad; she recognizes
their inevitability. Norms become problematic, she insists, "when what
norms tell us to do given the assumed conditions tends to deflect attention
from why these conditions are assumed to obtain and whether they need or
should obtain."[104] This is everywhere operative in food politics. Subsequently, Walker's remarks about feminist protest apply to food politics as well:
"Those who rebel against what 'everyone' accepts appear as irrational freaks,
malcontents, complainers, unstable deviants, or dangerous elements out of
control."[105] Food movement activists are regarded as dangerous, people who
can be killed with little consequence. And how many people roll their eyes
when obese people dare to hold McDonald's accountable for the fact that
their food drives obesity?

Marginalization entails the assignment to certain identities a "reduced, circumscribed, or discredited status as knowers and claimers."[106]
Before they can begin to protest their mistreatment they are discredited:
"Some people are 'known' going in to be liable to irrational discontents,
manipulative complaints, incompetent assessments, childish exaggera-

102. Ibid.
103. Ibid.
104. Ibid., 182
105. Ibid.
106. Ibid., 183.

tions, dangerous willfulness, malicious ingratitude, wily deceit, or plain stupidity."[107] Walker refers to this as being *epistemically unauthorized*. Stripping someone of epistemic authority is a particularly effective means of enforcing necessary identity, because the process of epistemically marginalizing someone also removes their ability to authoritatively comment on their own experience. Walker states:

> It is not just that their views don't count; given what those people are, their views can't count. Women cry, manipulate, and complain. Slaves lie and run. Servants loaf and steal. Laborers are stupid. Natives are childish. No identity is so necessary as one that successfully precludes its bearer's confuting it. *All the better if the means of enforcement of the identity actually induce or require in its bearers behavior that makes it impossible to deny.*[108]

And what behaviors would the poor and/or obese need to deny in a capitalist economy? Stupidity, sloth, infirmity, and impulsivity to name but a few.[109]

In researching discrimination against the obese, Deborah Carr and Michael Friedman note that "Research conducted over the past forty years shows that obese persons are viewed as . . . responsible for their weight due to some character flaw or 'blemish,' such as laziness, gluttony, or a lack of self-control."[110] Their study controlled for the discriminatory effects of other apparatuses of social power such as gender, race, and class yet still found that very obese persons were 40 to 50 percent more likely to experience "daily discrimination . . . major discrimination, work-related discrimination [and] health-care related discrimination" when compared to normal-weight individuals.[111] Carr and Friedman use language resonant with Walker's in noting that obesity is a "'discredited' personal attribute."[112] This suggests that the reason for the discrimination is that obese people have been in some sense epistemically unauthorized. Indeed, beginning in childhood, overweight children are perceived as being mean and stupid by their peers.[113]

---

107. Ibid.

108. Walker, *Moral Understandings*, 183; emphasis mine.

109. And in the case of the obese/relatively poor, gluttony would be added to this list. As demonstrated earlier in this chapter, however, our food system drives gluttony through its impact on neural dopamine systems and its poor nutritional content. These are the direct effects on the body; this says nothing about the situation of many people working multiple jobs who pick up fast food at a drive-thru between jobs.

110. Carr and Friedman, "Is Obesity Stimatizing?," 245.

111. Ibid., 249–52.

112. Ibid., 253.

113. Obesity Society, "Obesity, Bias, and Stigmatization."

Major discrimination in the study by Carr and Friedman is defined as having been discouraged by a teacher or advisor from pursuing aspirations for higher education, denied a scholarship, or denied an apartment rental; workplace discrimination included being passed over for promotions. Carr and Friedman found that obesity is "inversely related to socioeconomic status"—a much stronger support for my claim that "obese/relatively poor" is a necessary identity than the demographic data from the CDC cited earlier—and that obese persons were less likely than normal weight persons to work at professional occupations.[114] They further found that those who *do* work in professional occupations encounter even more workplace discrimination than obese *non*professionals. Could it be that they are perceived as somehow "out of place" because their physical appearance identifies them as "obese/relatively poor," automatically disqualifying them from professional employment with its middle-to-upper class connotations?

Obese people are perceived as less intelligent, and that perception leads people to advise them *not* to pursue further education, increasing the likelihood that they will achieve less academically. This lack of encouragement has the effect of *creating* the obese as less credible "knowers" rather than finding them to be that way in the first place. Workplace discrimination—being passed over for jobs and promotions—perpetuates the association of obese with lower social class, welding together, at least in the US, obesity and relative poverty through social processes resonant with Walker's descriptions of necessary identities. Fat people become viewed as inevitably stupid and poor.

The workplace discrimination encountered by the obese on the basis of this necessary identity is an example of the privatization of the coercion of fat people into subordinate roles so as to obscure both the fact that they are *not* naturally fitted to the role of obese/relatively poor *as well as* the unjust social order requiring someone to be fitted to the role in the first place. For example, in the case of obesity, Carr and Friedman note that the perception of obese people as lacking self-control is a cause of workplace discrimination. Certainly, people with extremely poor self-control should not be permitted to mismanage businesses and the like. And some researchers, such as Stephen O'Rahilly and I. Sadaf Farooqi, *have* suggested that the obese suffer from a neurobehavioral disorder that diminishes their self-control regarding food intake.[115]

But in the case of obesity, the "regulative function" of the norm prohibiting people with impulse-control problems from assuming leadership

---

114. Carr and Friedmann, "Is Obesity Stigmatizing?," 251.

115. O'Rahilly and Farooqi, "Human Obesity," 2905–10.

roles "deflect(s) attention from why these conditions are assumed to obtain and whether they need or should obtain" as regards obese people.[116] What *are* the conditions under which this lack of control over food intake obtains? O'Rahilly and Farooqi, while arguing that obesity is a neurobehavioral disorder, *also* argue that not only is this genetically inherited as a dysregulation of satiety and appetite, this genetic inheritance itself is only problematic in a socio-political context in which food is excessively plentiful, cheap and aggressively commercially promoted.[117]

O'Rahilly and Farooqi cite several longitudinal studies of obesity and socioeconomic status, establishing a case for the assertion that "in highly developed societies, obesity may be a *cause* of economic disadvantage rather than simply a consequence."[118] The economic disadvantage creates obese *as* relatively poor (although clearly not abjectly poor), binding the two together almost seamlessly. The obese body materializes as an effect of class, gender, and race structures such that obesity itself becomes a marker for social status. O'Rahilly and Farooqi go on to note the obese are subjected to "a reaction that might be more understandable if directed at people parking inappropriately in disabled parking spaces or serially cheating on their spouses," illustrating the way that epistemic marginalization compounds normalization in the case of obese/relatively poor people. The body thus marked intercalates with systems of social power such that physical habitus becomes justification *for* perpetuating the social system that produces it: it becomes acceptable to discriminate against fat people.

Unfortunately, O'Rahilly and Farooqi, in arguing for the genetic heritability of obesity would seem to undermine my contention that social factors contextualize the materialization of obesity. They do not address fabricated desire or diminishing nutritional content of food or the way in which low social status (already a problem for the obese) can lead to obesity, instead focusing on the heritability of obesity. But heritability of obesity *does* describe how obesity becomes naturalized. Naturalization is the process of creating the appearance of "spontaneous inevitability of certain places for certain people," the purpose of which is to conceal the force involved in fitting them to their identity. And, "since nothing denaturalizes a situation quicker than evidence of coercion into [identities], the most effective implementation of naturalized identities is making them conditions of birth, ceasing at death."[119] Walker's concept of naturalization explains

116. Walker, *Moral Understandings*, 182.

117. O'Rahilly and Farooqi, "Human Obesity," 2907.

118. Ibid., 2908; emphasis mine.

119. Walker, *Moral Understandings*, 180.

the utility of discrimination based upon readily observable genetic markers for propping up unjust systems.

The genetic heritability of a tendency toward obesity obscures the factors in the food system that drive the production of obese bodies in much the same way that, for example, genetic heritability of African ancestry obscures the socioeconomic factors driving much of the cycle of poverty experienced by African Americans. In the case of poverty among African Americans, racial discrimination in employment results in inadequate access to health care and increased incidence in chronic illness, which in turn results in decreased capacity for productive work. This is read as "laziness" and used to retroactively justify racist hiring practices. In the case of obesity, factors such as extreme amounts of commercial advertising of unhealthy foods directed toward young children, food deserts in low-income areas, and diminishing nutritional content of food—drive the body toward addictive eating patterns and obesity, which are read as poor self-control. For both African-American and obese children, the lack of academic encouragement can lead to diminished school performance, later read as inferior intellect.

Obscuring the workings of power is *precisely* the point of naturalization of a necessary identity. If we can blame obese people for their own obesity we never have to look at the abuses of power rampant within the food system itself.[120]

While I've been focused on obesity as both product and determinant of socioeconomic class, it must be remembered that it is but one of at least two class markers in a transnational global food system characterized by inequity—the other significant marker addressed in this chapter being emaciation, of which I have until now said little. My contention is that both are class markers insofar as they signal class-based malnourishment in a transnational food system that provides empty calories to those in the Global North, and inadequate calories to those in the Global South. An examination of "obese/relatively poor" as a necessary identity is useful insofar as it describes a phenomenon encountered with increasing regularity in the Global North, a phenomenon which obscures motions of power within the global food system. Viewing obese/relatively poor as a necessary identity illuminates the faults in the food system in the Global North in a way that may mobilize a more robust response to the situation.

One might conjecture that images of emaciated/abjectly poor people of the Global South would have long ago led to identification of our food system as problematic. Or one might anticipate that images of starving

---

120. And in light of the vitriol directed at the obese, it seems we may *also* be (unconsciously) blaming them for eating all of the calories of which the "emaciated/abjectly poor" have been deprived.

children would outrage decent people, compelling them to hold those in power accountable for their decisions. However, images of abjection can have precisely the opposite effect. Walker asserts that visual depictions of the abjectly poor instead serve to conceal the machinations of power structures responsible for their starvation in much the same way that I've argued regarding obese/relatively poor people in the Global North. Their lack of control over their hunger is obvious; the parties responsible, less so.

In words reminiscent of Agamben's *homo sacer*, Walker likens the images of "starving Africa" to those of the Jewish victims of Nazi atrocities. Of the camp inmates, Walker declares their emaciated form to be "the production of a body signifying one 'already dead,' beyond hope, care or relief, and yet frightening, even repellent, in its not-quite-deadness."[121] She sees a connection between these victims of Nazi horror and those seven million who starve to death annually, albeit with a twist:

> While images of starvation have evoked outpourings of concern and money, the effects of the repetitive imagery occlude the actors, African, European, and American, and the histories and political complicities that figure in the explanations of why these particular actual people are starving or dying at this particular place and time. At least the concentration camp imagery unambiguously signals a specifically moral monstrosity, not only the obscene fate of victims but the culpability of a particular set of perpetrators.[122]

By implication, the mass of emaciated Africans obscures the culpability and the identities of the perpetrators.

What both the obese/relatively poor and emaciated/abjectly poor necessary identities achieve is a distraction from the (systemic) actors and actions involved in coercing *these* particular people into states of malnutrition in the first place. And this, I argue, is the most convincing reason, based on Walker's definition, for viewing "poor person" as a necessary identity in both its "obese/relatively poor" and its "emaciated/abjectly poor" incarnations: necessary identities serve to obscure the lines of power propping up unjust social arrangements, making these arrangements appear natural and inevitable.

Walker states that "identities are necessary to make treatments of some people look 'matter of course' where those treatments would be extraordinary

121. Ibid., 200.

122. Ibid. Even in the case of Nazi Germany, as Agamben noted, the horrific travesty visited upon Jews and others in Nazi death camps was entirely legal according to German law, and therefore necessary.

for some other people, especially for those delivering the treatment."[123] Imagine a member of the World Trade Organization subjected to starvation conditions, or steered (by a combination of marketing campaigns and limited access to fresh food) toward high calorie, nutrient-deficient food. It is unthinkable. Yet decisions made by the WTO, IMF, and World Bank impose "austerity measures" on those in developing nations, measures that assure that many people in those nations will suffer extreme malnutrition and even starve to death. These policies further protect agribusinesses in their growing and marketing of nutrient-deficient food to children in industrialized nations. Meanwhile these decisions appear nothing if not "matter of course."

The bodies of those upon whom this treatment is imposed materialize in the context of various social apparatuses to produce various, recognizable physical forms that are subsequently coerced into particular social roles on the combined basis of appearance and social class, a phenomenon that Walker has defined as "necessary identities." In Walker's scheme, "necessary identities" always refers to the identities given to the marginalized, corresponding to some degree to Agamben's *homo sacer*. *Homo sacer*, in the global food system, is always a member of the poorer class. The poor, whether relatively or abjectly poor, are not consulted about structural adjustment programs, agricultural policies, or the legitimacy of perceiving nutritious food as a commodity rather than a necessity or right. Having been epistemically and in some cases morally discredited, they can hardly be permitted to make such important decisions. They are simply consigned to continued obesity or starvation due to their position within a rather sharply stratified global economy.

Conversely, those seated on the International Monetary Fund board are the well-fed elite of the elite. Thus, it appears that whether or not one gets a seat at the decision-making table depends upon whether or not one has had a seat at the dining table. The reverse is also true: whether or not one has had a seat at a dining table replete with the right amount of nutritious calories depends upon whether or not one has already had a seat at the decision-making table.

Conclusion

No essential quality legitimates why some people suffer obesity or starvation. No essential quality legitimates the sovereignty of those seated on boards of multinationals and agribusinesses. The bodies and brains of the elite and the abject alike are equally vulnerable to the vibrant materiality

123. Ibid., 178.

of food; both wealthy and poor intra-actively materialize in the context of social apparatuses of power. Malnutrition and starvation are regarded as "bad luck" within a social system that has accepted "bad luck" as inevitable. Obesity is considered a personal failure.

A political theology of food questions the inevitability of such "bad luck." Instead, a political theology of food insists that the "luck" involved in being born privileged versus disenfranchised should not be confused with "random chance." A political theology of food recognizes a relational ontology all the way down and all the way up, consonant with a new materialist philosophy. In this context, the obesity surfaces as a collective failure, rather than the product of individual character deficits. Access to food is anything but random; it is contingent upon a variety material-discursive practices that amplify waves of privilege or deprivation present as a condition of birth. A political theology of food challenges us to transform material-discursive practices with each iteration, shifting them toward more equitable practices of inclusion.

Each cell of the body is socially constructed within sets of material-discursive practices. *All* human bodies are subject to radical contingency and dynamic flux of material flows of power and privilege—especially as power and privilege flow in and as the transnational global food system. Yet only a privileged few have so far been permitted to make agricultural decisions that impact the rest of us. The traditional sovereign, being creaturely, is subject to the vibrant materiality of food and is therefore no less socially produced than are those subject to his decisions. How, then, can his credibility as sovereign be maintained?

Chapter 6

Deciding upon the Exception in an Exceptional Climate

Political Ecology and the "Metaphysical Image of [Our] Epoch"

A POLITICAL THEOLOGY OF food asserts that the vibrantly material, itera-tively intra-active relationship between food and human body is character-ized by mutuality. On the one hand, different foods materialize different human bodies. And on the other, different human practices materialize different food. Among other things, food changes along with ecological changes wrought by human action, a noteworthy cause of environmental change being the agricultural practices. Intra-actions between food, human practices, and ecology signal the need to analyze yet another layer of en-tanglement in considering a political theology of food: the entanglement of nature and politics. Conceptually, "nature" and "the natural" are the subjects of political debate, alternately leveraged to liberate or deployed to curtail public debate. Rather than attempting to separate them, they are best viewed as a single issue.[1]

The inseparability of "nature" and "politics" takes on added significance in a political theology of food. The intra-action between human systems and nonhuman ecological systems jeopardizes agricultural production—which in turn jeopardizes all of us. Additionally, this intra-action calls into ques-tion the capacity of the sovereign to fulfill the promise of protecting the public from existential threats. Especially when the sovereign dismisses the

---

1. Latour, *Politics of Nature*, 1.

relevance of particular threats in the course of short-circuiting public life—such as when climate science is dismissed at very high levels of government.

What I hope to accomplish in this chapter is to call into question the legitimacy of claims to and enactments of Schmittian-type sovereignty, and also the wisdom of permitting such claims to proceed unchallenged, in the context of food politics on a planet in peril. A review of intra-actions between agricultural practices and planetary climate change will contextualize the ecological challenges to absolute sovereignty and transnational global capitalism. These challenges will involve, among other things, the high potential for shocking blows to agricultural production. These are the existential threats to which a political theology of food must respond. Facilitating this response, Latour's political ecology will be brought to bear upon the question of any absolute sovereignty, demonstrating the utility of more inclusive decision-making regarding production and distribution of food in the context of climate change.

The Intra-Active Becoming of Agriculture and Climate

The Effect of Agriculture on the Climate Change

The question of how to produce and distribute food becomes critically important, because, as one would expect in light of Barad's agential realism, food and ecosystems intra-actively materialize one another. Agricultural methods exert a tremendous influence on ecological systems. As described in the last chapter, the nutritional content of food has diminished over the past fifty years as industrial agricultural methods reliant upon monocultures and heavy inputs of pesticides, herbicides and synthetic fertilizers deplete the soil of nutrients and cause plants to mature faster than they can absorb nutrients. The impact of material-discursive practices of the corporate food regime ripple outward, far beyond soil depletion in a given field or nutritional deprivation of human bodies.

The impact of industrial agriculture on waterways and aquatic animals illustrates the far-reaching and unintended effect of agricultural methods on ecosystems. Confined animal feeding operations (CAFOs), where most livestock are now raised, produce high concentrations of nitrogenous waste in the form of manure and urine. This waste seeps into groundwater and streams. Fertilizers from crops and residual nutrients in animal waste entering waterways promote the flourishing of algae, known as algal bloom. When algal blooms die off, they sink to the bottom and decompose. Decomposition of the algae consumes all of the oxygen in the water immediately over the decaying algae. The lack of oxygen, in conjunction with other toxins emitted in the decomposition process, can kill marine life unfortunate enough to swim into the area. The result is referred to as an oceanic dead zone.[2]

Runoff from cattle farms in the central region of the United States resulted in a dead zone in the Gulf of Mexico measuring "eight thousand five hundred square miles, the size of New Jersey" and causing the extinction of several species native to that area.[3] While some dead zones have decreased in size thanks to environmental regulations, the dead zone in the Gulf of Mexico has been worsened by increased corn production in the Midwest, spurred on by a shift in federal government policies.[4] Although a plethora of other industrial chemicals are also poisoning marine life, agricultural runoff proves itself a significantly destructive force.[5]

Not only does waste runoff from high-intensity monoculture crops and CAFOs result in oceanic dead zones, but cattle farming and irrigation are draining our watersheds, as "farm animals alone consume 2.3 billion gallons of water daily."[6] In the Punjab region of India, the use of GMO seeds—largely touted as drought-resistant—required such extensive irrigation that groundwater levels dropped "at over a foot a year in some areas" and the resulting salt deposits in the soil rendered vast swaths of land unusable.[7]

Not only do agricultural methods release harmful nutrients into waterways and deplete aquifers, but "food production and distribution contribute dramatically to greenhouse gases."[8] In turn, "climate change has negatively impacted wheat and maize yields for many regions."[9] The precise percentage of greenhouse gases accounted for by agricultural production and distribution are hotly contested. Estimates range from 9 percent reported by the Environmental Protection Agency (EPA), to approximately 33 percent by the Consultative Group on International Agricultural Research (CGIAR).[10]

---

2. UUA, *Ethical Eating Study Guide*, 16. See also: Food and Agriculture Organization, *Livestock's Long Shadow*.

3. UUA, *Ethical Eating*, 16.

4. Scheer and Moss, "What Causes Ocean 'Dead Zones'?"

5. Sielen, "The Devolution of the Seas."

6. UUA, *Ethical Eating*, 17.

7. Patel, *Stuffed and Starved*, 125.

8. UUA, *Ethical Eating*, 16.

9. Field et al., "2014: Summary for Policy Makers," 5.

10. EPA, "Draft Inventory of U.S. Greenhouse Gas Emissions and Sinks: 1990–2015," and Natasha Gilbert, "One-Third of Our Greenhouse Gas Emissions Come from Agriculture."

What accounts for this vast discrepancy? For one thing, the EPA figure does not include any factors external to the territorial boundary of the farm, such as transportation of food across vast distances, refrigerated storage, or processing and packaging of food in its calculations of the agricultural contribution to greenhouse gas emissions. Nor does it account for emissions of carbon due to land use changes, such as conversion of forest to farm land. Nor does it account for the energy used on-farm. Despite their inextricable entanglement with the global agricultural system, these sources of carbon emissions are all attributed to sectors other than agriculture, such as transportation or industry. The CGIAR, on the other hand, includes some of those collateral sources of greenhouse gas emission in its assessment of the ecological impact of agriculture. The calculation of greenhouse gas emissions attributable to the global food system is complicated by the fact that what happens on an actual farm is but one scene in a larger drama.

Even when we are speaking strictly about what happens directly on farms, agriculture accounts for at least 10 percent of greenhouse gas emissions. That figure rises to a high of 33 percent when associated processes such as transportation, processing and storage are added. Omitted from both calculations is the methane released as nearly one-third of the food in the United States decomposes in landfills, having gone uneaten.[11] Greenhouse gas emissions are challenging to quantify. Impossible to quantify is the suffering experienced by animals confined to the point of near-immobilization, or the emotional and physical distress inflicted on farm workers.

We are told that high-input agricultural methods are necessary in order to produce adequate food for a growing population. The industrial agricultural system churns toward ever greater unification around high input agricultural methods, mowing down peasant farmers daring to stand in its way. They claim it is a matter of warding off the existential threat posed by famine. They fail to account, however, for the fact that climate change poses threats on another register entirely, including threats to food production, and the claims of any sovereign to assure stability in the face of those threats are dubious, if not duplicitous.

The Effect of Climate Change on Agriculture

Findings outlined in the 2014 report from the Intergovernmental Panel on Climate Change (IPCC) call into question the capacity of the sovereign to decide at all, especially when multilateral trade organizations and transnational corporations are acting as sovereign. Predictions are fraught with

11. United States Department of Agriculture, *Foodwaste*.

uncertainty in part because factors influencing the outcome are themselves currently in formation. Risks posed by climate change vary from region to region, shaped by both relatively stable factors such as geography and also by potentially dynamic factors, such as socioeconomic patterns. Heavy hits to food production, distribution, and cost are expected in the face of climatic instability, regardless of what interventions are staged.[12] The sovereign will likely be unable to anticipate the precise existential threats; the threats are likely to call for a more complex and creative response than a state of exception typically engenders; and it is unlikely that a sovereign will be able to restore stability. The sovereign will not be able to decide, and the decision will not be adequate to the situation.

The IPCC's 2014 report notes that "climate change involves complex interactions and changing likelihoods of diverse impacts."[13] The report places great emphasis on risk factors to facilitate planning for resistant communities. Some risks are incalculable, as components that might ultimately influence the outcome are still in creation. And "diverse values and goals" shape risk assessment as much as the sheer facts. In responding to virtually incalculable risks, values *matter*. Whose welfare will be protected, and at what cost?

The IPCC has gained significant knowledge since the previous reports, in part because the effects of climate change are already beginning to appear. Numerous species "have shifted their geographic ranges, seasonal activities, migratory patterns, abundances, and species interactions," and "water quality and quantity have been affected."[14] Alarmingly, significant weather events have led the IPCC to observe a widespread under-preparedness for climate-induced disasters such as droughts, floods, heat waves, wildfires, cyclones, and other storms.

The adaptive response to climate change is proceeding at different levels of government in different locales—in one geographic region responses are at the national level whereas in another region adaptive efforts occur at the municipal level. These regional differences are reflective of specific risks faced due to geographic particularities of the community responding, yet the unevenness of the efforts renders prediction about the impact of climate change fraught with uncertainty. Regional responses to climate catastrophes

12. Field et al., "Summary for Policy Makers," 18. The future economic impact of climate change would seem to provoke some sort of "advance planning" response on the part of transnational corporations. However, they are, at this point, legally mandated to act solely in their shareholders' immediate best interest. The profits of future shareholders—or indeed anyone else—thirty years from now are off-limits in this calculation.

13. Ibid., 3.

14. Ibid.

become increasingly important in the context of numerous simultaneous natural disasters, such as encountered in the United States in 2017 with disaster areas declared in four states due to major hurricanes and repeated, massive wildfires in two others. Food production and/or distribution was negatively impacted in all instances.

Uncertainty results from not knowing which mitigation efforts will be undertaken or precisely where or when a particular climate-related problem will arise. However, even if decisions are made to implement mitigation efforts, uncertainty will persist in the form of "continuing uncertainty about the severity and timing of climate-change impacts and with limits to the effectiveness of adaptation."[15] Thus, we are well past the point at which any sovereign could be relied upon to ward off the existential threat posed by climate change. There is simply no restoring certainty in the present context, and no amount of sovereign decision-making will fix that.

While at one time many were in denial that climate change was real and also human caused, it is increasingly common now to hear that we are "past the point of no return." The IPCC, to some degree, concurs with that dire sentiment. They assert that in the near term we will receive little immediate benefit from reduction of carbon emissions in terms of cooling the planet. In that regard, we are indeed past the point of no return. However, in terms of reducing risk to human and nonhuman communities, the IPCC names the "societal response" as centrally important.[16]

Consequently, although the planet is likely to get hotter over the next thirty years, the risks enumerated below *could* be mitigated if societal factors—in Baradian terms, material-discursive practices—were altered in such a way as to improve resilience. Planetary warming will continue throughout the next three decades regardless what decisions are made. Beyond that point, temperature change is entirely within our current capacity to influence. In fact, the behavioral changes we make right now to curb emissions— or not—are the most significant factor in determining planetary warming beyond 2050. For many of us, the behavioral changes needed to counter the threat of climate change require deep commitment to a future we will not live to see, even if all goes swimmingly.

The plethora of "interacting social, economic, and cultural factors, which have been incompletely considered to date," that is to say material-discursive practices, will all play some role in contributing to or mitigating risk. The IPCC pinpoints these factors as:

15. Ibid., 8.
16. Ibid., 10.

Wealth and its distribution across society, demographics, migration, access to technology and information, employment patterns, the quality of adaptive responses, societal values, governance structures, and institutions to resolve conflicts. International dimensions such as trade and relations among states are also important for understanding the risks of climate change at regional scales.

Decision-making should, they argue, take full account of as much data as possible. They suggest that "forms of evidence include, for example, empirical observations, experimental results, *process-based understanding*, statistical approaches, and simulation and descriptive models." [17] One would hope that "empirical observations" rendered during agricultural experiments conducted by peasant farmers participating in the food sovereignty movement might be included in the data set of these discussions.

In the context of this uncertainty, the IPCC recommends "*Iterative* risk management . . . [as] a useful framework for decision making in complex situations characterized by large potential consequences, persistent uncertainties, long timeframes, potential for learning, and multiple climatic and non-climatic influences changing over time." [18] As opposed to narrowing in on the most likely outcomes, they recommend "assessment of the widest possible range of potential impacts, including low-probability outcomes with large consequences" as central to the capacity to conduct the risk/benefit analysis necessary to ascertain the most advantageous risk management plans. Above all, they caution against thinking we have either understood or addressed the problems once and for all; continued monitoring and learning are essential for effective adaptation to rapidly shifting situations.

Because unpredictability will persist and specific risks remain incalculable, no singular sovereign decision seems likely to offer significant safeguards from the existential threat posed by climate change. Decisions will need to be made and remade as circumstances shift and data is accumulated. No amount of sovereign decision-making can restore predictability to the current or future climate situation. The existential threat cannot, in this case, be removed. Any declaration of a state of exception contingent upon broad resolution of the threats posed by climate change would likely prove to be so long term as to be effectively permanent, as Agamben fears.

Although unencumbered by democratic bureaucracy, it is possible that that the type of centralized decision-making typified by the Schmittian sovereign may amplify vulnerability, for many, because it is less able (or

17. Ibid., 13; emphasis mine.
18. Ibid., 9; emphasis mine.

willing) to adapt to or account for local and regional threats. Some regions and cultures constitute what the IPCC refers to as "unique and threatened systems." Furthermore, risks are differentially distributed in part due to multidimensional inequalities including socioeconomic status and also "because of regionally differentiated climate change impacts on crop production in particular."[19] Material-discursive practices, apparatuses of intra-active becoming, vary from place to place creating a variety of diffraction patterns in the context of climate change.

As has been explicated in previous chapters, decision-making of the unilateral sovereign tends to marshal widespread resources for deployment on behalf of those proximal to the seat of power. This could prove highly deleterious for locales far from decision-making centers. Hurricanes Katrina (2005) and Maria (2017) demonstrate that impoverished areas heavily populated by people of color receive less infrastructure investment over time, so powerful storms leave even more destruction in their wake than they would have otherwise. In the aftermath of the storms, emergency efforts in both cases have been criticized as inadequate, meeting with additional charges of racism leveled at both presidential administrations.

Human security is threatened as climate change is likely to "increase the displacement of people." In light of the argument that refugee (or any other non-citizen) status renders people particularly vulnerable to having no rights at all, the forced migration of sizeable populations is troubling. Although massive dislocations are likely to occur, the "complex, multicausal nature" of migration reduces the ability to predict which countries or regions will be most affected by this trend. The IPCC noted the risk of "violent conflicts in the form of civil war and inter-group violence" will likely increase as arable land and potable water become scarce. Additionally, "some transboundary impacts" to ecosystems "have the potential to increase rivalry among states." Subsequently, "territorial integrity" will be threatened. Indeed, as will be discussed below, such disruptions are already well underway in Africa and the Middle East.

The IPCC concludes that "risks will vary through time across regions and populations, dependent on myriad factors including the extent of adaptation and mitigation." The IPCC appeals to "intergovernmental institutions . . . to . . . manage many of these rivalries." In other words, they call for something akin to a transcendent (intergovernmental) supersovereign figure capable of managing conflict between rival states.[20] While on the one

19. Ibid., 12.

20. While this figure would not be metaphysically "transcendent," because still earthly, it would nonetheless be structurally transcendent as regards the state.

hand it is hard to imagine the survival instinct *not* giving rise to all out warfare in the absence of a mediator, on the other hand this reliance upon a transcendent figure bears resonances with the sovereign as described by Schmitt. Subsequently, such a supersovereign poses its own set of risks, and if the scale of risks corresponds to the scale of sovereignty, these risks would prove perhaps not worth taking.[21]

But what about the present and projected effects of climate change on food in particular? The IPCC is highly confident that extreme weather events such as droughts, floods, unseasonable temperatures, and variable precipitation will contribute to disruptions in food supply, especially for already vulnerable populations.[22] Some of these changes are already occurring. Recent years have witnessed negative impacts on corn and wheat yield both regionally and as global aggregate measures. In fact, 2011 was the first year in decades that crop yields were reduced, a decline attributed to climate change.

Despite the claims of some that warmer temperatures and increased atmospheric carbon will benefit crop yields, numerous studies including results from several geographic locations and crop varieties demonstrate that climate change affects crop yields negatively more often than positively. Additionally, fisheries are threatened due to reductions in marine biodiversity and migration of marine species seeking more suitable habitats, both of which are in part caused by the production and distribution of food, as discussed above. These findings are particularly alarming because despite the fact that farmers produce sufficient food to feed every person over two thousand calories per day, due to political and economic structures over seven million people per year starve to death.[23] As food production decreases, this problem can only be expected to worsen.

How much will food production drop, and when? This is yet another area of tremendous uncertainty. Projections for the near-term (2030

21. Jacques Derrida alludes to the dangers of this approach when he says, "Universal democracy, beyond the nation-state and beyond citizenship, calls in fact for a supersovereignty that cannot but betray it" (*Rogues*, 101).

22. Field, *Statement on Climate Change*, 12–13.

23. The United Nations World Food Programme attests that sufficient calories are produced worldwide to feed everyone, yet 1 in 9 face hunger on a daily basis. One in three is malnourished (see World Food Programme, "Zero Hunger"). Based on data from Oxfam, UNICEF, and the World Food Programme, Poverty.com reports that 21,000 people die every day from hunger, amounting to over 7.6 million people per year. According to a recent Reuters report, famine in four areas of Africa puts twenty million people at risk of starvation within the next six months (Miles, "Four Famines"). Most of this famine is somewhat indirectly related to climate change. The more proximal cause is violent conflict, spurred on by climate change.

through 2049) vary dependent upon which crops, regions, and adaptation scenarios are calculated. About 10 percent of those projections predict yield increases of 10 percent, whereas another 10 percent predict yield losses of over 20 percent when compared with the end of the last century. Long-term predictions are fraught with even greater difficulty, as much is contingent upon our decisions to reduce emissions now. Compounding fears of declining crop yield, violent conflict arising as a consequence of climate change altogether disrupts food supplies, again a phenomenon already prevalent in Africa and the Middle East.

While the specifics remain incalculable, the final conclusion of the IPCC is that crop yields will vary significantly, with a general downward trend. Meanwhile, due to population growth demand will rapidly increase.[24]

> All aspects of food security are potentially affected by climate
> change, including food access, utilization, and price stability.[25]

Climate change promises negative impacts to production and distribution, both near and long term. While currently the emphasis is on integrating rural workers into the global economy in order to increase their purchasing power, in the future there may well be less food for them to purchase. Perhaps their security would be better ensured by supporting smallholders after all? And indeed, the Food and Agriculture Organization is increasingly advocating for this approach.[26]

Persistent uncertainty and existential threats in the face of climate change render sovereignty a risky proposition, calls for a global supersovereign capable of refereeing international conflicts notwithstanding. This is particularly true in light of the fact that the unacknowledged global sovereigns of the multilateral trade agencies and transnational corporations are enforcing agricultural practices that worsen climate change. That this occurs under the political frame of "food security" is all the more ironic when the impact of climate change on food is deliberated. Yet, multilaterals—or at least the International Monetary Fund—seem to be awakening to the threats posed by the imposition of their neoliberal agenda.

The Environmental Fact Sheet published by the International Monetary Fund suggests that "broad-based charges on greenhouse gases, such as a carbon tax, are the most effective instruments for encouraging cleaner fuels and less energy use."[27] This change, if implemented in the short run,

24. Field et al., "Summary for Policy Makers," 18.

25. Ibid., 19.

26. FAO, *The State of Food Insecurity in the World*, 2015.

27. International Monetary Fund, *IMF Factsheet: Climate, Environment, and the IMF*.

could improve the trajectory of climate change in the latter half of the century, even if it does not substantially improve the experience over the coming thirty years. They go on to suggest that such taxation could also "deal much more effectively with broader environmental and related problems that can be a significant drag on economic growth, such as the health and productivity impacts of poor air quality." The authors of this report express the sentiment that post-Paris Climate agreement is an "opportune time" for reform, and need not wait for international agreement.[28] The multilaterals are beginning to feel the economic pinch resulting from decades of ecological irresponsibility, it would seem.

A staff discussion paper published by the IMF in the wake of the Paris agreements advocates the use of fiscal policies to address carbon pollution, based on their economic assessment that:

> At the heart of the climate change problem is an externality: firms and households are not charged for the environmental consequences of their greenhouse gases from fossil fuels and other sources. This means that establishing a proper charge on emissions—that is, removing the implicit subsidy from the failure to charge for environmental costs—has a central role.[29]

Implicit subsidies and externalities have been the concern of environmentalists for quite some time. While the insistence on eliminating these implicit subsidies would seem to cast the IMF on the side of environmentalists who have been calling for such things for years, the discussion paper begins with a disclaimer asserting that this discussion paper does not necessarily reflect the *official* position of the IMF. As a staff discussion paper, then, it implies nothing about the official commitment of the IMF as regards economic policy in the context of climate change.

The authors of this discussion paper further recommend improved practices for assessing and disclosing the carbon footprints of various corporations and bolstering regulatory oversight as beneficial for development of "resilient institutions and well-functioning financial markets."[30] The authors concern themselves with projections of "significant market impacts, with output losses through effects on climate-sensitive sectors (for example, agriculture, forestry, coastal real estate, tourism)."[31] As did the IPCC, these authors note considerable regional variation in vulnerability to climate-change impacts. Areas at greatest risk are "regions with

28. Ibid.
29. Farid et al., "After Paris," 5.
30. Ibid., 6.
31. Ibid., 8.

lower per capita income and higher initial temperatures," which could aptly describe much of the Global South. And perhaps it is concern for "the market" more so than for people or ecosystems that drives these suggestions. Then again, they also argue for "substantial carbon pricing in order to reduce "premature deaths from air pollution"—probably about as "touchy-feely" as it is acceptable to appear in an IMF publication of any kind—so perhaps such a conclusion might be excessively cynical.

But while it may seem excessively cynical to assume that financial motivations are the preoccupation of staff at the IMF, we might be cautioned against extending such generosity to the entire corporate regime. Naomi Klein observes a pattern in which "extreme shocks" such as natural catastrophes and violent conflicts are "exploited" by "corporate interests" in an effort to push a policy agenda that appropriates wealth on behalf of a small elite "by lifting regulations, cutting social spending, and forcing large-scale privatizations of the public sphere." Not only have these crises been leveraged in the service of concentration of wealth, but these crises "have also been the excuse for extreme crackdowns on civil liberties and chilling human rights violations."[32] Klein asserts that this trend will only continue in the context of climate change, with ensuing climate catastrophes again leveraged in the service of further enriching the 1 percent. Recent political events in the United States suggest that even the much milder "shock" of suboptimal economic growth is being leveraged to dismantle environmental protections and all manner of federal regulatory oversight.[33]

Climate "Shocks" and the Sovereign Exception

Building on her earlier work, *Shock Doctrine*, Naomi Klein hopes to prepare groundwork that will enable "People's Shock, a blow from below," that would embolden a "muscular mass movement" with the capacity to transform the status quo and engender more socially and economically just policies on a wide scale.[34] She believes that the threat posed by climate change might promote the dispersion of power rather than its concentration, resulting in a radical expansion of the commons. She favors inclusive societal processes

32. Klein, *This Changes Everything*, 8.

33. For example, despite relatively low unemployment rates, President Trump has declared that "regulatory oversight is killing jobs." Subsequently, he has ordered that a task force be formed in order to recommend regulations for repeal or modification. See Olorunnipa, "Trump Signs Executive Order to Impose Additional Layer of Oversight on Regulations."

34. Klein, *This Changes Everything*, 8, 10.

that might, perhaps, prove more adaptive in the face of climate change than our current social, political, and economic structures are proving to be.

Klein doubts that the daunting nature of the task explains why "tough and binding" legislation on climate change has not been enacted. She cites the creation of the World Trade Organization (WTO) as evidence that broad-scale cooperation has in fact been possible over the past several decades. The WTO is "an intricate global system that regulates the flow of goods and services around the planet, under which the rules are clear and violations are harshly punished."[35] While environmentalists were focused on climate change, the political focus was on economic development that benefitted the few at the expense of the many, while claiming to do precisely the opposite through "trickle down" economics. This set of priorities was recapitulated at the close of 2017 with the passage of the Republican tax bill.

There was a widespread lack of political will to address the looming disaster posed by climate change, whereas heroic effort was exerted on be-half of the neoliberal economic agenda driving greenhouse-gas emissions. Nevertheless, "we need not be spectators in all this: politicians aren't the only ones with the power to declare a crisis. Mass movements of regular people can declare one too."[36] If the declaration of a crisis is read as a "decid-ing on the exception," Schmitt's definition of sovereignty, what she is calling for bears family resemblance to popular sovereignty.

Klein argues against those who insist that human nature is too self-serving to sacrifice for the sake of climate change. The fact that "we sacrifice our pensions, our hard-won labor rights" in order to prop up an economic system that fails us is evidence that we are capable of sacrifice. The prob-lem, she claims, is that "we have not done the things that are necessary to lower emissions because those things fundamentally conflict with deregu-lated capitalism, the reigning ideology for the entire period we have been struggling to find a way out of this crisis."[37] Although these changes would be beneficial to the vast majority of people (as well as planetary systems) they are nonetheless viewed as an existential threat to "an elite minority presently controlling our economy, our political process, and most of our major media outlets." She refers to neoliberal capitalism as "market fun-damentalism," and observes that this attitude is publicly embraced with

35. Ibid., 16.

36. Ibid., 7

37. Ibid., 21. Schmitt might assert that the central domain of our epoch has re-gressed from the technological back to the economic, having subsumed the technologic into its neoliberal methodology, and that the (perhaps up and coming) ecological do-main has yet to consolidate its centrality.

such fervor that suggestions to make "the most direct and obvious climate responses seem politically heretical."[38]

Klein's use of the words "fundamentalism" and "heretical" underscores the value of political theology as it clarifies the manner in which formerly theological concepts traffic in the secular political arena. As has already been discussed, these concepts, in part because they have been secularized, have been adopted in their most orthodox formulations. Furthermore, because they have been sanitized of their theological origins, they are not accessible to critique as religious dogma. Richard Dawkins can write with relative impunity about *The God Delusion*, whereas referring in the same terms to "the invisible hand of the market" renders one's patriotism suspect. Rather, the validity of these orthodox formulations as infused into neoliberal economics is presupposed as fact. It is in part to pry loose the theological concepts and expose them to critique that this political theology has been undertaken.

After observing that reductions in greenhouse-gas emissions have only ever accompanied "economic collapse or deep depressions," Klein goes on to say that "our economy is at war with many forms of life on earth, including human life."[39] What is needed to avoid widespread ecosystem collapses, she insists, is a reduction in consumption of resources. Unfortunately, neoliberal capitalism "demands . . . unfettered expansion." Klein argues, "only one of these sets of rules can be changed, and it's not the laws of nature."[40] If we adhere to our economic doctrine at the expense of planetary ecosystems, we will run afoul of those laws and environmental crises will no doubt result.

Problematically, environmental crises often serve as provocations for enactments of a strong, if not quite Schmittian, sovereignty.[41] Given that hurricanes and superstorms, droughts and failing crops pose an existential threat to numerous individuals—not to mention the state—the legitimacy of these enactments of strong sovereignty appears self-evident in response to catastrophic events. The capacity of the state to maintain, or at least

38. Ibid., 18–19.

39. Ibid. Klein is not alone in naming neoliberal capitalism as the major barrier to effective climate action, incidentally, but a fuller explication of the rationale behind this thought is beyond the scope of the present project.

40. Ibid. The notion that nature has ironclad "laws" is a subject of ongoing debate. Alfred North Whitehead would suggest that nature has "tendencies." See Whitehead, *Process and Reality*. Nonetheless, I do agree that whether we describe these as laws or tendencies, since we are profoundly dependent on the welfare of functioning ecosystems, it behooves us to prioritize the processes that maintain their capacity to maintain us.

41. States of emergency declared in the wake of natural disasters are one example, although these are not always accompanied by a suspension of constitutional rights.

very quickly restore, order and security in the face of these climate-related existential threats may be criticized as woefully inadequate or deplorably racist, but demands that the nation-state "stand down" altogether during these crises are lacking.[42] If anything, in the wake of these crises, what is called for is a more robust, efficient, and socially just response on the part of the nation-state. In other words, environmental crises can serve to consolidate the power of the sovereign state, or at least to curtail resistance to its maneuvers insofar as these crises tend to deepen the desire for a strongly protective nation-state.

Simultaneously, however, climate change promises an ecological instability so profound that no amount of sovereignty seems likely to restore order or ensure security. For example, the inability of some states to provide food to their people has, even as recently as 2008, destabilized nations, in part contributing to the uprisings of the Arab Spring.[43] Some of the difficulties with food production over the past two decades are a direct result of environmental changes secondary to climate change—to which we have already noted high-intensity agricultural methods contribute. Yet, despite the fact that these agricultural methods worsen climate change, we are told that worsening climate demands that these methods be singularly and forcibly pursued.[44] The decisions of these sovereigns, in other words,

42. For example, in the aftermath of Hurricane Katrina and Superstorm Sandy, in our own country. Or, in the case of the Arab Spring, the inability of governments to feed their people resulted in the demand for a regime change.

43. See for example: Mortada, "Let Them Eat Baklava"; PBS, "Did Food Prices Spur the Arab Spring?"; Zurayk, "Use Your Loaf"; and Johnston and Mazo, "Global Warming and the Arab Spring." Incidentally, the ongoing Syrian conflict is related to the lack of arable land in several of these sources.

44. These methods are imposed via the structural adjustment programs, as indicated in chapter 4. Efforts are being made to impose these methods on individual consumers, for example by legislative efforts to ban explicit labeling of GMO products, which would effectively prohibit consumers from choosing non-GMO foods. Furthermore, scientists are being pitted against environmentalists, accusing environmentalists who oppose GMO foods of depriving the poor in developing nations of adequate nutrition on the basis of their opposition to GMO foods. See Chokshi, "Stop Bashing G.M.O. Foods, More Than 100 Nobel Laureates Say." However, despite being declared "safe" and environmentally advantageous, as already mentioned, some, such as Raj Patel, argue that GMO crops require inordinate amounts of irrigation, depleting water tables and are thus not altogether environmentally advantageous. Lending substance to Patel's claim, in June of 2012 the Union of Concerned Scientists reported that "USDA analysis of data supplied by Monsanto show that DroughtGard produces only modest results, and only under moderate drought conditions at that." Incidentally, during a recent visit to the Museum of Science and Industry I viewed an exhibit on GMO's. This exhibit asserted that GMO crops were better able to recover after a four- to five-day drought than non-GMO plants. Drought conditions in Sub-Saharan Africa have persisted much longer than four to five days; it is altogether unclear what advantage drought-resistant GMOs provide in cases of extreme and prolonged drought.

are driving us toward ever greater existential threats, rather than away from them. These existential threats subsequently induce greater necessity for strong sovereignty.

I am certainly not suggesting that the nation-state abdicate its role in emergency responses. Nor am I suggesting that any entity whatsoever is intentionally driving climate change in order to consolidate power. I am merely demonstrating that climate-related catastrophes provoke demand for—and enactments of—strong sovereignty. Simultaneously I am calling awareness to the fact that economic renditions of absolute sovereignty on the part of the corporate regime (multilaterals, transnational corporations) contribute significantly to the worsening climate situation. In other words, we are increasingly reliant upon the sovereignty of the nation-state to protect us from the sovereignty of the corporate regime.[45] Perhaps in this regard, we in the Global North can find some common ground with peasant farmers of the Global South, whose recognition of this dynamic gave rise to the food sovereignty movement over two decades ago.

What Is Really at Stake in This Conversation?

Taken as a whole, the previous section casts doubt on the ability of the sovereign to make sound decisions upon the exception in the exceptional climate that has become the new planetary norm. Based on the widespread prioritization of neoliberal economic agenda over a reasonable response to these threats, it is altogether unlikely that those in power will pursue legislative solutions any time in the near future. Furthermore, extreme weather events, droughts, crop failures, and massive dislocation resulting from climate instability certainly pose existential threats of the sort typically invoking the sovereign to decide upon the exception, thereby suspending the constitution. These events are likely to occur so frequently as to become unexceptional. As already discussed, Agamben contends that an unexceptional state of exception is the fate of the nation-state under the Schmittian sovereign.

45. At one time those of us in the Global North operated under the fiction that these sovereignties were distinct and that the sovereignty of our nation-state could protect us from the corporate regime, while the two have been conflated in the eyes of the Global South for quite some time. The awakening of many Americans to the degree of control exercised over our government by the corporate regime, I would suggest, underlies both the crisis of sovereignty on the left and the calls for nationalism on the right. See Nace, *Gangs of America*, for an exhaustive account of how corporations have undermined democracy beginning in the mid-nineteenth century.

But how pivotal, really, is food to this conversation? Geographer Evan D. G. Fraser and editor Andrew Rimas assert that "just as there is no life without food, so there is no civilization without a food empire."[46] Having researched the rise and fall of various empires (such as Sumer and Rome) in conjunction with their food supply over the last three millennia, they come to some startling conclusions. For a food empire—that is, a civilization—to flourish, farmers must produce more food than they consume and transport or store surplus safely and efficiently. When the food empire surpasses its sustainability, the civilization implodes. To prioritize economics over sustainability is to miss this one vital fact: "while a financial crisis ruins lives, a food crisis ends them."[47] The short-term economic priorities of the sovereign decision makers have little to do with our collective, long term welfare.

Fraser and Rimas identify weaknesses in our contemporary global food system, seeing the potential for collapse secondary to climate change. Nonetheless, they advocate for the retention of transnational global trade. At the same time, they also recommend nesting within it local food hubs, based on small local farms growing a diverse blend of crops and livestock. This is not a suggestion they anticipate will be welcomed with open arms by the corporate food regime. Fraser and Rimas assert that the transnational global corporate food regime is unlikely to cease is potent thrust toward unification in the absence of effective legislation. To permit this unification is, they insist, suicidal. So it is up to us, the eating public, consumers, voters, and hopefully activists (if not yet, in the near future) to demand this transformation.

Jared Diamond also studied civilizational collapse, although his research was not restricted to the study of food.[48] He studied civilizational collapse at Easter Island, among the Anasazi of the American Southwest, and the Mayan Empire. He argues that complex societies have repeatedly collapsed specifically due to a failure to protect their natural resources; failure to anticipate a problem; or failure to perceive a problem that is staring them straight in the face. Occasionally, civilizations collapse because one group pursues its own interests with disregard for another group. At other times, attempts to fulfill certain values blind members of a society to the costs incurred.

Because we are currently so globally interconnected, and interdependent, and because we are engaging in practices that are disrupting ecosystems around the globe, the potential exists that a civilizational collapse could reach global proportions, according to Diamond. Fraser and Rimas perceive the

46. Fraser and Rimas, *Empires of Food*, 7.

47. Ibid., 11.

48. Diamond, *Collapse*.

same possibility about the global food empire: "instead of famine, our tottering food system will first deliver a spike of cheap, nutritionally bankrupt calories . . . and then it will slump."[49] Are we already seeing the spike of cheap, nutritionally bankrupt calories Fraser and Rimas prophesy?

Diamond sees cause for hope in the dissemination of environmental thinking, wiser consumer choices, and an improvement in values. A political theology of food locates hope within eating publics—ordinary folk animated by an ethic of care (whether religiously derived or secularly inspired) and strengthened by spiritual practices or secular "arts of self." Hope is embedded in networks of average people with exceptional courage, participating in grassroots movements to foster local food hubs and garner legislative support for sensible food policies.

Clearly, we do not have "politics" on one side and "nature" on the other. There is no easy distinction between facts and values in a world of intra-active becoming. The values of a society shape the material-discursive practices of that society. Material-discursive practices are the apparatuses within which bodies—bodies of land, water, and sky along with bodies of humans—materialize. The bodies materialized through these processes constitute the "facts" that inflect value formation in a series of iterative becomings. A political theology of food worries over the materialization of all of these bodies, and must therefore grapple with political ecology. Particularly on a planet endangered by climate change in no small measure brought about by agricultural practices.

Bruno Latour's Political Ecology

According to Bruno Latour, politics is so thoroughly entangled with nature that it is impossible to avoid engagement in political ecology. As already mentioned above, Latour argues that in fact the division between nature and politics was established in large part in order to "limit, reform, establish, short-circuit, or enlighten public life."[50] Subsequently we must tackle the questions of political ecology, either "*surreptitiously*, by *distinguishing* between questions of nature and questions of politics, or *explicitly*, by treating those two sets of questions as a single issue that arises for all *collectives*."[51] In other words, both politics and nature must be open for deliberation as we attempt to forge a common life. There can be no appeal to any transcendent entity—whether divine or natural—that

49. Faser and Rimas, *Empires of Food,* 248.

50. Latour, *Politics of Nature,* 1.

51. Ibid.

can "miraculously simplify the problems of common life" in the way that Schmitt had hoped the sovereign could do.

Latour's *Politics and Nature* is a theoretical piece, occasionally dipping into, yet never plumbing, the depths of any particular issue. Its utility for the present work is not that it offers a political ecology of food that can be copied and pasted onto a political theology of food. Rather, its utility lies in its nondualist framework and its explication of multiple concepts that clarify the risks inherent in the problematic maneuvers previously mentioned in the context of food politics. The particular ideas that will be described below include Latour's nondualist metaphysics; the collective as a process of composing a good common world; the role of speech, speech prostheses, and spokespersons; and the externalities that haunt the collective.[52] Finally, Latour reapportions the tasks involved in composing the good common world in such a way that clearly illuminates a potential role for peasant farmers (and religious scholars), creating a theoretical framework that supports their inclusion in global food decision-making.

Nondualist Metaphysics: Neutralizing Agent or Invigorating Force?

Latour denounces a dualistic metaphysics of nature that he claims serves to short-circuit politics. Latour argues that dualistic metaphysics of nature operates basically under a rubric of Cartesian dualism capable of neatly distinguishing subject from objects, facts from values. This division renders "nature" to be both indisputable fact and mute object, fully comprehensible, but only by elite experts who can reliably mediate the relationship between politics and nature. In this way, nature serves as transcendent authority bolstering nefarious political agendas.[53] The ecological crises we now face in the context of climate change are historically important not because they result in "new concern with nature but, on the contrary" because they make evident "the impossibility of continuing to imagine politics on one side and, on the other, a nature that would serve politics simultaneously as a standard, a

---

52. This by no means exhausts its utility; it merely reflects the most salient aspects of his theory for the present study.

53. For example, Latour insists that militant ecology "claims to defend nature for nature's sake—and not as a substitute for human egotism—but in every instance, the mission it has assigned itself is carried out by humans and is justified by the well-being, the pleasure, or the good conscience of a small number of carefully selected humans— usually American, male, rich, educated, and white" (*Politics of Nature*, 20).

foil, a reserve, a resource, and a public dumping ground."[54] We must, in light of climate change, address the nonhuman world as a political issue.

Latour knows, however, that while ecological crises make evident the political entanglements with nature, they have not "immediately undermined [the old] metaphysics of nature. On the contrary, their theorists have tried hard not only to save modernist nature, but also to extend its lease, by offering it a more important role in short-circuiting public life."[55] He contends that in order to overcome these toxic, and some might say archaic, metaphysical constructs, we must engage in metaphysics once again. He encourages experimental metaphysics, described as "an active search for what makes up the common world."[56] Latour's metaphysics does not presume to address matters of fact, but instead addresses matters of concern—a distinction that will be clarified below. This metaphysics concerns itself with procedure, and promotes learning from experience.

As is the case with Schmitt before him, Latour is driven by concerns about the neutralization of the political. However, his concern differs sharply from Schmitt's. Schmitt wanted a *stronger* sovereign supported by a transcendent authority to settle debates in order to invigorate a certain type of politics released from the drudgery of endless conversation. By contrast, Latour worries that the political is neutralized when debate is short-circuited, conversations curtailed, and "nature" is invoked as a source of transcendent (and mysterious) power that props up sovereignty.

The process of collecting ourselves into a common world will inevitably cast some agents outside of the collective—say, for example, cancer cells or flesh-eating bacteria—paralleling the sovereign ban, as it were. Unlike Schmitt, Latour is not content to let the sovereign decide. Neither, he argues, is anyone else: "None of these members of the collective wants to have an 'opinion' that is personal and disputable 'about' an indisputable and universal nature. *They all want to decide about the common world in which they live.*"[57] It is perhaps this desire to decide about the common world that inspires dreams of democracy.

Latour insists that the concept of "nature," as distinct from politics, must be abandoned because it has served as the "transcendent figure" that settles all debate, thereby neutralizing the political. The concept of "nature," when severed from the political, has most often been used "to abort politics," a concern shared by oppressed minorities and people in developing

54. Ibid., 58.
55. Ibid., 128–29.
56. Ibid., 242.
57. Ibid., 130. Emphasis mine.

nations who fear, rightly, that climate catastrophes will rob them of what little capacity for self-determination they currently enjoy. Latour's nondualist metaphysics injects nonhuman nature into the political sphere, a move he insists will prevent the short-circuiting of public life. Latour's experimental metaphysics and his political ecology open a debate—not only between rich and poor, North and South, left and right, but between human and nonhuman—about our common world.

What is particularly interesting about Latour's approach is that it begins to pry loose the tight-fisted grip that the sovereign has on epistemic authority: everyone has a say about the nature of nature, not just the experts. Latour is not content—or perhaps not concerned?—with simply distributing authority to disenfranchised humans. Rather, he seeks to forge an opening through which the nonhuman can actively participate in the political process of composing a good common world. Thus, Latour seeks distribution of decision-making powers that will in some way permit participation of the nonhuman. For this he needs to reconfigure "nature" in order to bring it into the political order. This differs significantly from the employment of the concept of nature in the writing of either Schmitt or Benjamin.

For Schmitt, nature figures primarily as spatial territory, the appropriation of which constitutes the initial stages of formation of a legal and economic order.[58] While this spatial territory was at one time restricted to land, over time the concept of this spatial territory has expanded to included portions of sea and sky as well.[59] Although jurisprudence plays its part, for Schmitt the boundaries of these spaces are to some degree established by "divine providence," as these boundaries are established quite frequently through armed conflict and the vagaries of fate.[60] Again we see that for Schmitt the transcendent God is the template for the human sovereign, capable of standing outside of creation, arranging a hierarchy of value, establishing order.

I must acknowledge that my reading of Schmitt differs significantly from Latour's reading in *Facing Gaia*. He lauds Schmitt for insisting that spatial relations are created by political action, with little mention of Schmitt's reference to divine providence as the decisive factor in territorial conquest. He also finds Schmitt's emphasis on war, and with it the friend/enemy distinction, much more helpful than I do. I am also somewhat uneasy with Latour's embrace of Schmitt's territorializing and deterritorializing vision.

58. Schmitt, *The Nomos of the Earth*, 80.

59. Ibid., 183.

60. Ibid., 329; divine providence is Schmitt's term, not mine. See Latour, *Facing Gaia*, 228–54.

Oddly, Latour does not explicitly connect these priorities of Schmitt with his assertion that Schmitt is—by Latour's own reckoning—toxic.

It must be remembered that Schmitt was something of a darling of Hitler's, at one point fully embracing Nazi ideology. His views on sovereignty were at least compatible with Hitler's if not identical. Hitler's politics, ecological vision, and thirst for territorial domination were intrinsic to one another. Hitler's account of nature dictated that life was, at the bottom, a war of all against all in which might truly does make right.[61] Jews, as Hitler would have it, had conned the gentiles with their ethical monotheism, leading people to view life as potentially something more meaningful. Territorial struggles were, for Hitler, a matter of spatial control whereas the struggle against the Jews was primarily an ecological struggle about the conditions of life on earth.

This struggle was urgent for Hitler because he envisioned the world in its finitude. Science—including agricultural science—would never produce the means by which "more" could be derived from a finite territory. Science would eventually fail to produce fertile soil, whether now or in the future, and belief in limitless progress only deferred our collective grappling with the problem of finite resources. The only hope was to conquer more fertile territory. There was nothing to be done other than name one's enemies (in racial terms) and fight for control of resources. Thinking otherwise was part of the Jewish delusion of progress.[62]

How much Schmitt himself held Jews accountable for this "delusion" is not a question I can answer; but in this Schmitt agreed: without a strong sovereign to safeguard one's territory, life would indeed devolve into a war of all against all. For Schmitt, nature was more or less the stage upon which the drama was enacted. In light of Schmitt's support for Hitler's fascist regime, a political theology of food remains skeptical of all war analogies, even Latour's. We must seek other modes of relation with and within finitude.

These differences aside, both Latour and I read Schmitt as devoid of any true ecology. Having no intrinsic value, nature functions as something of a vacuous space within which the sovereigns of competing legal and economic orders can be said to vie for domination. Thus, neither Schmitt nor the sovereign need concern himself with nature as such. Nature, in Schmitt's *Nomos of the Earth*, figures more as prop than character. There is little need to wrestle with the recalcitrant nature of nature, its surprising capacity to facilitate or thwart human endeavors, its inability to remain within the bounded territories established by the sovereign. Once the boundaries are

61. Snyder, *Black Earth*, 1–10.

62. Ibid.

established through "divine providence," the natural world itself is malleable at the hands of the sovereign.

In contrast to Schmitt, Benjamin *does* address nature as such. Instead of being a source of transcendent authority propping up the sovereign, or even a container over which the sovereign rules, it figures instead as an exteriority that undoes the sovereign. According to Samuel Weber, Benjamin's *Trauerspiel* establishes that:

> The German Baroque theater "flees" wildly to nature . . . only to discover that there is no grace or consolation to be had there, either. The undoing of the sovereign is the fact that in a creation left entirely to its own devices, without any other place to go, the state of exception has become the rule.[63]

Benjamin demonstrates that the Baroque views nature as a locus of profound uncertainty in the context of which the sovereign proves incapable of establishing order. The resulting *dis*order masquerades as a permanent state of exception. For Schmitt, nature appears to be nothing more than context within which the sovereign consolidates his power; for Benjamin nature is the chaos that undoes the sovereign.

Latour's thesis is resonant with Benjamin's illustration of the way that nature undoes Schmitt's version of sovereignty, yet quite dissonant with Schmitt's assertion that loss of sovereignty is equivalent to the loss of politics. In fact, it is precisely uncertainty—including uncertainty about sovereignty itself—that Latour contends bestows upon political ecology its great utility:

> Political ecology has never claimed to serve nature for nature's own good, for it is absolutely incapable of defining the common good of a dehumanized nature. It does much better than defend nature (either for its own sake or for the good of future humans). It *suspends* our certainties concerning the sovereign good of humans and things, ends and means.[64]

In other words, resonant with Benjamin's depiction of the relationship between nature and the sovereign as described above, Latour insists that certainties—including the certainty of sovereignty—must be suspended in the context of political ecology.[65]

This does not mean for Latour, as it does for Schmitt, the end of the political. Nor does it entail a permanent state of exception. Instead, for Latour the abolition of certainty, and sovereignty with it, is the *beginning*

63. Weber, "Taking Exception to Decision," 14.

64. Latour, *Politics of Nature*, 12. Emphasis in the original.

65. Ibid., 121, 133, 164, 200.

of the political order, albeit a very different political order than that envisioned by Schmitt. Any "certainties" are the destination of a political
order, rather than its origin, and all "certainties" serve more as working
hypotheses, remaining open to reformulation in the face of new data. For
Latour, nothing about whatever we might call "nature" is certain enough
to serve as mere backdrop and it certainly is no respecter of territorial
markers on maps. It cannot, in other words, legitimate the sovereign.
However, neither does "nature" necessitate a permanent state of exception, as Benjamin suggests in *Trauerspiel*.

Collectives of Speaking Actors

What is this political order envisioned by Latour? First of all, Latour's political order is no longer founded upon the distinction between experiencing
subject and inert object. It is even less reliant upon "nature" to serve as a
source of stability preventing a war of all against all. And while Latour's
political ecology explicitly names the "progressive composition of the common world" as its task, it does not perceive the open-ended and iterative
nature of this composition to justify a permanent state of exception. It is
simply not the case that all rules must be suspended until security can be
established. Rather, procedural rules must be implemented in order to collectively determine the boundaries of the good common world.

Latour uses the term collective to refer to both the group whose members compose a common world and to the procedure by which this common world is composed.[66] Abiding by due process, the collective establishes
the boundaries of its common world by means of conversation, rather than
combat. The collective is nothing if not "an assembly of beings *capable of
speaking.*" Not only must conversation replace combat, discussion must also
"replace *both* silence and the not discussable." Critically, the nonhuman
must be invited to participate in the conversation:

> To limit the discussion to humans, their interests, their subjec-
> tivities and their rights, will appear as strange a few years from
> now as having denied the right to vote of slaves, poor people,
> or women.[67]

But the question remains: how can the nonhuman be said to participate in
a conversation?

66. Ibid., 38 and 238.
67. Ibid., 69.

The first step Latour takes toward articulating the roles and functions of members of the collective is to dispense with subject-object dualism. Replacing this distinction is the concept of actors, or he says, in order to "rid the word of any trace of anthropomorphism, *actants*." Actors, more so than objects, possess traces of self-organization. Significantly, actants affect one another, iteratively.[68] In Baradian terms, actors are intra-actively entangled with other actors in the context of material-discursive apparatuses, and we know this because marks are left on bodies

Latour goes on to say that "the notion of *recalcitrance* offers the most appropriate approach to defining their action."[69] They are not easily dispensed with. The notion of an actor as interrupting closure, in conjunction with the concept of externalities to the collective will, nicely reframes how we might view the previously identified problems in our current global food system.

Latour describes actors (or actants) acting—affecting one another, thwarting the pretense of mastery and preventing the closure of the collective. How, though, can mute nonhumans be said to speak?[70] Latour resolves the dilemma of mute nonhumans by permitting scientists the role of spokespersons. The fact that they are cast in this role does not, however, grant them either epistemic or moral authority. In fact Latour cautions that we must always *"entertain serious but not definitive doubts"* about the fidelity of their representation. Thus, scientists and policymakers may perform as spokespersons for a variety of others—"landscapes, chemical-industry lobbies, South Sea plankton, Indonesian forests, the United States economy, nongovernmental organizations or elected governments"—but the accuracy and integrity of their performance can never be presumed.

Recalling Margaret Urban Walker, one questions at this point whether Latour has fully eliminated the problem of epistemic authority and the speech it authorizes. For example, Latour might clarify the way in which the nonhuman can "speak" by means of an interpreter who has conducted an experiment that serves as speech prosthesis, but he does not quite clarify why it is that some humans who are physiologically able to speak for themselves nonetheless cannot make themselves heard. More to the point, Latour repeatedly speaks of those able to conduct experiments that serve as "speech prostheses" as "lab coats," rather than "overalls." By referring to "scientists" as "lab coats" he implicitly endorses the notion of authorized, expert scientists. It is not immediately obvious that this includes experiments being

68. Ibid., 73–75. Jane Bennett draws her concept of actants from Latour.

69. Ibid., 80.

70. I can't help but think of Spivak at this juncture.

conducted and results interpreted by innumerable people who are not typically recognized as scientists.

In the context of the Food Sovereignty movement, farmers are the ones conducting experiments, and field test after field test demonstrates higher yield, improved soil conditions, and reduced water consumption when the agroecological methods they promote are utilized.[71] Nonetheless, their results are discredited as agricultural policies are written. For example, the farmers of the *Campesino a Campesino* movement routinely conduct field experiments in order to optimize yields, yet the term "lab coats" does not gesture toward the peasant farmer as contributing substantively to ecological knowledge.

Nonetheless, I do not believe that he intends to further marginalize peasant farmers. Instead, I perceive the concept of spokesperson to provide a necessary opening wedge, permitting the results of their experiments entry as evidence. We can no more presume that they speak for nature (rather than their own interests) than we can presume that the CEO of Monsanto speaks for nature (rather than Monsanto's interest). As Latour insists, we can doubt their fidelity to the natural world, but we cannot immediately discount their input. We must permit the entry of multiple sets of data into our deliberations, which will of course complicate the questions of what food to grow and how to grow it.

This complication, as it turns out, simultaneously signals an ending and a beginning that are entangled with Latour's reading of "facts" as both unification and complication. Latour understands facts to represent on the one hand *unification* of certain actors into "collective life" and on the other hand *complication* or the sudden punctuation of our collective life by surprising actants. These complications, in other words, pose a threat to the political order—the good common world as it has already been composed by the collective.

A Schmittian sovereign may declare an emergent complication to be an enemy of the state, implementing a state of exception intended to fortify the boundaries of the political order and once again banish the complication. From Latour's perspective, however *premature closure* poses an even greater threat to the collective than does the complication that such closure hopes to eliminate. We cannot free ourselves from the *risks* represented by a complication by quickly banishing the *complication* from our midst. In fact, a previous premature closure of the collective likely resulted in the expulsion of the complicating externality that now

71. As reported by Holt-Giminez in *Campesino a Campesino* and by Santos and Lacanilao in "Women Contributing to Food Security."

demands reconsideration. Only by refraining from premature simplifica-
tion and insisting instead upon perplexity can one be assured that "our
interlocutors, by limiting in advance the list of states of the world, do not
hide the risks that put our well-regulated existences in danger."[72] Existential threats to collective well-being cannot necessarily be eliminated by
means of the sovereign ban or the state of exception. Nor, for that matter,
can the risks of climate change be eliminated by removing all reference to
climate change from government websites.

Four New Functions, Two New Powers

To avoid premature closure of the collective, and risking the disruptive
return of externalities, Latour proposes four new political requirements:
perplexity, consultation, hierarchization, and institution. These functions
replace the former dualism between "fact" (presumed to be neutral and
established by a transcendent sovereign) and "values" (presumed to be a
matter of somewhat arbitrary opinion). The purpose formerly fulfilled by
"facts" is distributed to the requirements for perplexity and institution. The
function of values has been distributed to the requirements of consultation
and hierarchization. These four roles have been reassembled into two new
"powers of representation": the "power to take into account" and the "power
to arrange in rank order."

The "power to take into account" consists of the requirements for perplexity and consultation. Perplexity demands that we must admit numerous
propositions for consideration, while consultation demands that we do not
arbitrarily limit the number of participants in the decision-making process.[73] The "power to take into account" bears some resemblance to efforts
made in the previous chapter to define apparatuses and read diffraction patterns, both theoretically as Barad articulates her agential realism and practically in our application of her theory to the question of social production of
classed bodies in the global food system. In its demand for perplexity and
consultation, the power to take into account asks us to read the diffraction
patterns produced by a series of agential cuts so as to have a broader array
of both apparatuses and materializations to study. This avoids premature
closure of the deliberation that might occur if we satisfied ourselves with
examining a restricted data set, and it at least gestures toward consulting the
myriad materializing bodies involved in the collective.

---

72. Latour, *Politics of Nature*, 65.
73. Ibid., 109.

The "power to arrange in rank order" consists of hierarchization and institution.[74] Hierarchization refers to the assignment of the new propositions a legitimate place in the collective, and the function of institution makes that place permanent. It is only once all four requirements are met that the collective is closed, if only temporarily. The "power to arrange in rank order" answers the question "What order must be found for the common world formed by the set of new and old propositions?"[75] This set of processes must meet the requirements of hierarchization and institution. Hierarchization requires us to assign a "legitimate place" to the members of the collective. The requirement of "institution" means that the proposition must come to be regarded as "at the heart of collective life."[76] In other words, the power to arrange in order requires the integration of value in the composition of new facts.

Redistributing those four functions to two new powers highlights the manner in which the corporate food regime has poorly executed the power to take into account. Based on the ecological data provided above alone, one could argue that the industrial agriculturalists have prematurely simplified the "number of propositions to be taken into account in the discussion."[77] They have failed to consider specific and significant threats posed by what they presume to be external to the conversation and have not met the requirement for perplexity.[78] The voices of those in the food sovereignty movement can be perceived as spokespersons or speech prostheses for specific ecosystems that constitute at least some of the externalities banished from consideration by the transnational industrial food system. Not only have the farmers themselves been banished from consideration, but similarly disregarded has been the integrity of ecosystems with which these farmers are well-familiar. In turn, these ecosystems may speak of complications that pose a threat to the global food system as a whole.[79]

Failing to take into account all voices invested in our food system, what Latour might refer to as a failure of publicity, has led the corporate food regime to grave errors in its power to arrange in rank order. We are exposed to inordinate risks by the transnational corporations and

74. Ibid., 109, 243.

75. Ibid., 110.

76. Ibid., 109.

77. Ibid.

78. This is evident even in how the carbon footprint of our food system is officially calculated based upon what happens on the farm in isolation from either the rest of the supply chain or in ecosystems subjected to damaging runoff from farm waste.

79. For example, all of the environmental threats described in the first section of this chapter.

multilaterals who push high-input agricultural methods to the exclusion of all others because they have prematurely closed the debate without due consideration of the risks inherent in doing so. Of these, Latour might say that they have met "in secret to unify prematurely what is."[80] And of the food sovereignty movement and those they represent, Latour might view them as "those who demonstrate publicly that they wish to add their grain of salt to the discussion, in order to compose the Republic."[81] Only by insisting that all voices be brought to the decision-making table can we assure that "the number of voices that participate in the articulation of propositions is not arbitrarily short-circuited."[82] In that way we will meet Latour's requirement for consultation.

Externalities

Even though Latour operates from a nondualist philosophy, he is well aware that some actants transcend the collective insofar as "the collective still has an outside."[83] Externalities take many forms: "humans . . . animal species, research programs, concepts, any of the rejected propositions" for which the human collective has declined to accept responsibility or presumed it can do without. Externalities may have been dismissed by the collective, but they have not been eliminated from existence. Latour cautions that externalities do not necessarily always remain outside of the collective. Not infrequently, they return. When they do, they pose an existential threat to the collective "provided that the power to take into account is sensitive and alert enough. What is excluded by the power to put in order . . . can come back to haunt the power to take into account."[84]

The return of an externality requires another iteration of the collective composition of the good common world. The world beyond the collective cannot be said to be comprised of immutable essences, unfeeling objects, or divine assurances. Instead, it "has been the object of an explicit procedure of externalization."[85] It has been banned, so to speak.

---

80. Ibid., 106.

81. Ibid.

82. Ibid., 109.

83. Ibid., 123.

84. Ibid., 125.

85. Ibid. While it is this outside that still for Latour is the stopgap against a merely arbitrary determination as to who and what can be included in the collective, it is no source of divine authorization of the sovereign decision. It exists, in Baradian terms, not as "absolute exteriority" but rather as "exteriority within phenomena." Agential cuts established by the collective may portray externalities as irrelevant, but nonetheless the

Externalities are of increasing concern in the context of environmentalism in general and climate change in particular. Many problematic features of transnational global agricultural practices could be summarized into this one overarching theme: failure to account for externalities. The term "externalities" refers to any cost not included in the financial accounting process. Some externalized costs are quantifiable, such as the subsidized fossil fuels required to fertilize crops, and farm subsidies to prevent farmers from losing money when prices fall due to overproduction. These items are omitted from the ledger because the entire point of the subsidy is to create the appearance of profitability.

Other externalities are incalculable, such as the carbon emitted in the agricultural process; decimation of pollinators by insecticides; depletion of water tables secondary to excessive irrigation required to sustain these methods; and contamination of waterways with fertilizer runoff and livestock waste.[86] The cost of food produced by conventional methods is artificially reduced by the failure to account for these externalities. As externalities, by Latour's definition of the term, these are components of our "good common world" for which the transnational global food system can be said to have "refused to take responsibility."[87] Political debate regarding issues such as carbon taxes, cap and trade agreements, and so forth represent a growing awareness that what has previously been "externalized" in these sovereign decisions is, as Latour notes, putting the collective in danger. Accounting for these externalities is exactly what the aforementioned IMF staff paper suggested.

Failure on the part of transnational agricultural corporations and multilateral agencies to take responsibility for the well-being of bodies of land, water, and air upon which the bodies of humans depend is increasingly recognized. While the elaboration of this point is beyond the scope of this volume, Latour argues that the "economization of relations" could provide one means of accounting for—of quantifying and thereby assuming responsibility for—the impact to these externalized bodies.

Questions of economics aside, the fact that the damage to these externalized bodies threatens the well-being of many millions of human bodies

---

collective and the agents externalized by it remain perpetually engaged in "iterative intra-activity."

86. In the presence of strict regulations insisting that air, land, and waterways were restored to their original condition, it might be easier to quantify the "non-quantifiable" externalities. Such regulation would force the need to calculate the cost of the damage done: what materials, and how many hours of labor over what period of time would be required to restore the ecosystem?

87. Ibid., 124.

does raise questions as to the security provided by multilateral and transnational corporate entities enacting a Schmittian version of sovereignty within
the context of the Food Security Frame. Revisiting Latour's model of four
requirements (consultation, perplexity, hierarchization, and institutionaliza-
tion) distributed to two powers (the power to take into account, the power
to arrange in rank order), it might be said that the sovereign enactments on
the parts of these agents *instituted* particular agricultural practices into the
global collective without adequately addressing the other three tasks. I would
argue that these enactments of sovereignty rested upon failure to account
for environmental damage caused by high-input agriculture. This failure
arose from an overly simplistic understanding of ecosystem dynamics and
a premature closure of the debate—failures in perplexity and consultation,
respectively. Furthermore, these decisions were generally rendered behind
closed doors, rather than democratically, failing to meet the requirement for
publicity characteristic of Latour's hierarchization.

The reemergence of these externalities in such a widely menacing
form as global climate change does not necessarily indicate that all high-
input methods should be immediately abandoned. That would be disastrous. Nonetheless, the threats posed by high input agricultural practices
do suggest that the institution of these methods should not be further
pursued to the exclusion of other methods such as those promoted by
the food sovereignty movement. Peasant farmers (and others in the food
movement) might be consulted as spokespersons for the soil, plants,
animals, and humans with whom they interact. The results of their small-
scale experiments could be admitted to the conversation as vitally important data that might shed light on how to collect at least some of these
externalities into a good common world.

This would mean, harkening back to Walker's *Moral Understanding*,
granting these landless peasants epistemic authority despite the necessary
identities that have been pressed into their flesh. It also might mean *hearing*
the many spokespersons—environmental scientists, food scientists, theorists, activists, the obese and the starving—as representing members of the
collective who are expressing the simple fact that we cannot create a good
common world by proceeding with business as usual because *business as
usual is not good for them*, or indeed, for any of us.

Beneficial though it may be, Latour's political ecology doesn't quite
sound the depths of the ways in which humans and nonhumans intra-
actively become with each other. Based on Latour's presentation it could
almost appear as if the good common world is a work in progress, but that
nonetheless it is yet composed of fixed entities. The lines between the inside
and outside of the collective may be drawn through due process, and the

drawing of the line may affect the *goodness* of the common life within the collective, but Latour appears unconcerned that closure of the collective fundamentally alters the *materialization of bodies* on either side of the line.

Integrating Latour's political ecology with agential realism adds texture to the concept of "closure of the collective," and sounds a note of caution regarding the alleged need to identify enemies. Read through agential realism, the closure of the collective becomes visible as an agential cut that inevitably shapes the *materialization* of bodies both internal and external to the collective. It is not always the case that mutual entanglement entails mutual dependence. Some entities, while entangled, could possibly do quite nicely without each other. For example, some species of bacteria are harmful to humans but capable of living in another host so we can do without one another.

Nothing is to say that the agential cut will necessarily influence materialization for the better, on either side of the boundary. In some cases, this agential cut may entail the extinction of an agent that has been externalized from the collective. In cases where mutual entanglement signals mutual dependency, such that the entities cannot do without each other whatsoever, the extrusion of an entire class of agents from the collective poses significant risk to the collective. And, as with many other factors related to ecosystems, the complexity of relationships is such that we often cannot know in advance which entities are vital for survival of the collective. The problem is not only that externalities might reappear demanding inclusion in the collective, but that they might disappear altogether. We might create a world in which something that we have externalized from our collective, but upon which we depend, perishes and its extinction jeopardizes our own survival. Bees, for example.[88]

Conclusion

Multilateral trade agencies and transnational corporations have narrowly prioritized the economic concerns of the elite over ecological integrity, staging economic enactments of Schmittian, absolute sovereignty in crafting global food polities. These agencies have demonstrated lackluster efforts to

---

88. Raine and Gill, "Tasteless Pesticides Affect Bees in the Field"; Thompson and Oomen, "Hazards of Pesticides to Bees"; "Pesticides and Bees: EFSA Finalises New Guidance, World Food Regulation Review." In Whiteheadian terms, one might surmise that the problem with pesticide use is the "fallacy of misplaced concreteness." We do not think of pollinators as pests, so have been delayed in realizing that they might be harmed by pesticides.

reduce the causes of climate change as such reductions threaten the financial well-being of the elite.

Climate change is the primary threat to global food supply at present, displaying the degree to which the vast majority of us cannot rely upon the agencies to guard our welfare. Climate change is likely to manifest differently in different regions—floods in one locale, drought in another—calling for a more widely distributed ability to respond in regionally appropriate ways to these catastrophes—or, put another way, a dispersion of (sovereign) decision-making capacity.

Schmitt asserted that "the metaphysical image that a definite epoch forges of the world has the same structure as what the world immediately understands to be appropriate as a form of political organization."[89] The Schmittian sovereign can no longer be said to be compatible with the current metaphysical image of our epoch as disclosed through science studies. It appears that our metaphysical image no longer depicts a static condition in which unilateral control as an assurance of security plays any meaningful role. Influence is multi-directional and iterative, and any semblance of control is at best temporary.

A political theology of food rejects Schmitt's metaphysics, embracing instead a nondualist metaphysics resonant with Latour's. This metaphysics recognizes iterative, intra-active becoming as the process of all materializations. Not only the bodies of humans are socially produced, but indeed all bodies, including bodies of other animals, and bodies of land, sea, and air upon which humans depend for our very lives. The guiding ecological image of a political theology of food is not one of declension, as a "fall from grace" would have it, nor is it an inevitable march toward redemption that will retroactively justify widespread suffering. Instead, material existence is configured as an iterative re-creation, in much the same way as the seven-day cycle of the Jewish Sabbath recapitulates the original seven-day creation narrative. It is a re-creation, or a re-membering of commonly shared earthly experience, with the goal that it should be very good for all.

Subsequently, a political theology of food supports "iterative, process-based" decision-making, as called for by both the Intergovernmental Panel on Climate Change and Latour's political ecology. Must a political theology of food shed the theological dimension of political theology altogether, claiming itself to be "purely" political? Is such a thing even possible, given the extensive history of entanglement between the theological and the political? Or might other theological models less reliant upon transcendance better suit the metaphysical image of our epoch?

89. Schmitt, *Political Theology*, 46.

Part III

A *Tehomic* Political Theology of Food

Chapter 7

Reimagining the
Sovereignty of God

GIVEN THE DIRE PREDICTIONS about climate change, it would seem that time is of the essence. By some accounts we have only a few years left to reduce our carbon emissions before we doom our grandchildren to a horrible fate. Already the consequences of climate change are underway: drought, floods, famine, extreme weather condition and massive forest fires. The state of emergency remains undeclared on the part of a United States presidential administration that prefers to remain in denial. Do we have time, really, to conjure either new theologies, new politics, or new perspectives on the old ones that might serve the interests of this political theology of food? Do we have time *not* to?

Schmitt, Revisited

Noting that "all significant concepts of the modern theory of the state are secularized theological concepts,"[1] Schmitt touted orthodox theological models as the remedy to World War I and its chaotic aftermath. From Schmitt's perspective, it was God's transcendence, more than any other divine quality, that could underwrite his image of a strong human sovereignty capable of assuring order. Furthermore, Schmitt feared secularization because according to his analysis the immanent plane provided no source of valuation, no safeguard against brutality, and therefore no assurance of order.

Yet under the strong sovereignty of Hitler, whom Schmitt himself supported for many years, brutality found unprecedented expression. In fact,

1. Schmitt, *Political Theoloy*, 36.

199

Hitler's death camps are precisely the example to which Agamben turns in order to illustrate the dangers of sovereignty in a liberal democracy. What are we to make of the fact that precisely Schmittian sovereignty can be shown to devolve to a brutal totalitarianism? On the one hand, Schmittian sovereignty could be contested by claims that a *human* sovereign can never achieve that which has been guaranteed by the *divine* sovereign at the closure of time.

And to some degree, Benjamin's critique of Schmitt's sovereign, following along precisely those lines, could be summarized in a single passage: "he is the lord of creatures, but he remains a creature."[2] By this argument, divine sovereignty—however defined—cannot underwrite human sovereignty, effectively severing the analogical relationship between divine and human. But brutal, fascist totalitarianism also flourished in the guise of Stalinism, following close upon the heels of the Bolshevik revolution. So following Benjamin's inclinations toward anarchic Marxism as the necessary or only antidote to Schmittianism does not appear to solve this conundrum.

Schmitt also observed that "the metaphysical image that a definite epoch forges of the world has the same structure as what the world immediately understands to be appropriate as a form of political organization."[3] The metaphysical image of this epoch has been subtly shifting since the inception of quantum physics, although it would be a stretch to say that the full implications of these developments have a solid grip on our collective imagination. Yet the Schmittian model of sovereignty is incompatible with the metaphysical image of the contemporary epoch as disclosed through even the sciences that are more widely regarded as comprehensible than quantum theory. In other words, the model of divine sovereignty upon which Schmitt based his description of sovereignty no longer squares with the world as experienced directly or revealed through scientific exploration.

It has become *de rigueur* for the academic and scientific communities to shun metaphysics. Nonetheless the previous two chapters have argued that a metaphysical image is both implicit within and disclosed by science studies. *The metaphysical image of our epoch as disclosed by science studies is iterative and process-oriented—as the IPCC suggests decision-making in the context of climate change must be. It is also at least to some degree immanent, intra-active, and relational.*

Even Schmitt knew that transcendence was incompatible with the "metaphysical understanding" of the epoch as evident by his own observations that "Conceptions of transcendence will no longer be credible to most

---

2. Benjamin, *Trauerspiel,* 85.
3. Schmitt, *Political Theology,* 46.

educated people, who will settle for either a more or less clear immanence-pantheism or a positivist indifference toward any metaphysics."[4] Yet Schmitt disavowed immanent constructions of the divine—typified best, in his opinion, by Hegel—because, in his opinion, they heralded the death of politics because they constituted an effort to avoid "the exacting moral decision."[5] Thus, in formulating his concept of sovereignty, Schmitt rejected theological models consonant with the immanent metaphysics of the epoch that perhaps it could be said we share with him. Instead, he returned to orthodox theologies relying heavily upon a metaphysics of transcendence.

To be sure, there is a distinction between metaphysics and theology, and there is no universal agreement upon either metaphysical images or theological models. Nonetheless, Schmitt's reliance upon secularized orthodox theological models of God raises a twin set of theological questions regardless of whether one embraces the metaphysical image conjured by science studies. The first is whether orthodox theologies necessarily support models of sovereignty consonant with Schmitt's as their only or most logical response. The second is whether immanent theologies are in fact incapable of guiding moral valuation, as Schmitt feared. If it could be argued *either* that a transcendent sovereign does not, in fact, legitimate the enactment of human sovereignty *or* that an immanent divine can yet provide a framework within which "the exacting moral decision" can be made, the next question would be: what sorts of politics might be enacted that would be resonant with the metaphysical image of our epoch in the absence of a model of divine, Schmittian sovereignty transferable to the human context?

This chapter will examine Schmitt's theological presuppositions more closely. Exploration of Karl Barth's neo-orthodox Christian theology will sever the easy link between divine power and human authority. Revisiting the process theology of Catherine Keller will elucidate the possibility that divine immanence might undergird a more potent moral framework for a political theology of food than Schmitt supposed.[6] The following chapter

4. Ibid., 50.

5. Ibid., 65. See also the following quotes: "Insofar as it retains the concept of God, the immanence philosophy, which found its greatest systematic architect in Hegel, draws God into the world and permits law and the state to emanate from the immanence of the objective. But among the most extreme radicals, a consequent atheism began to prevail" (50); and "Today nothing is more modern than the onslaught against the political. American financiers, industrial technicians, Marxist socialists, and anarchic syndicalist revolutionaries unite in demanding that the biased rule of politics over unbiased economic management be done away with. There must no longer be political problems, only organizational-technical and economic-sociological tasks . . . the core of the political idea, the exacting moral decision, is evaded in both" (65).

6. Panentheism straddles the line between a fully transcendent theology and a fully

will contemplate the compatibility of Paulina Ochoa Espejo's construction of popular sovereignty with an immanent theology.

When applied to the question of food politics and perhaps modified somewhat, Espejo's political theory calls attention to the ways in which all of us as the eating public participate in "people moments" with each forkful of food we eat, and perhaps serves as a practical model for implementation of a political theology of food. Can a political theology of food emanating from process-oriented political theories and theologies avoid the appeals to unification upon which sovereignty, even of the popular variety, is founded? And does it provide ample room for dissenting voices without banishing them to the status of *homo sacer*?

The importance of these questions cannot be underestimated. Climate change is already wreaking geopolitical havoc. The ensuing chaos is already driving political polarization toward the extremes of the absolute, represented by Schmitt, and the dissolute, represented by Benjamin. It is hard to imagine a politics rooted in either extreme being of more benefit now than they were seventy years ago. Clearly, as Catherine Keller insists, some third option must be sought, not as "neutral middle ground" but as resolute commitment to mutual flourishing.[7] Such a commitment is anything but neutral; it takes the side of mutuality over and against the zero-sum thinking that animates much of contemporary politics. A resolute commitment to mutual flourishing is foregrounded in a political theology of food.

A Barthian Critique of Schmittian Sovereignty

Inclusion of an orthodox theology in an analysis of Schmittian sovereignties must be undertaken in part because any "people as process" forming in the context of a political theology of food will necessarily include people endorsing a range of theologies, from orthodox to none at all. Such inclusion is more than a matter of expedience. This political theology of food owes its

---

immanental theology. God is perceived as intimately within all things in material reality, as indicated by the "pan," which gestures toward the "all things" in which God can be found. The "en" distinguishes the panentheist position from the pantheist position, which views God as more or less identical with material reality. Theologian Stephen Bede Scharper's *Redeeming the Time* provides a lovely ecotheological formulation much in keeping with the theme of this present work. For example, he identifies concerns for social justice alongside concerns for the nonhuman world independent from humans as simultaneous concerns, and he draws upon process theology (including Keller's) in his formulation. Because Keller is something of a primary source for Scharper, her work was engaged directly.

7. Keller, *On the Mystery*, 25.

inception to Jewish and Christian texts and traditions on many counts, de-spite its divergence from traditional theological formulations. From within the scriptural cannon of Jewish and Christian traditions spring concerns about the weight of suffering born by the oppressed—the concern Mark Lewis Taylor names as "theological"—inspiring this political theology of food.

For instance, the notion that the value of the nonhuman world is not calculable in human terms but is in some sense of ultimate value. Or that whatever might be referenced by the word God, it operates in and as numerous contingencies that allow life to emerge. Further permeating the scriptural cannon is the idea that we are all tenants of Earth, not owners, and must therefore share its bounty with others. And as the Exodus nar-rative would have it, any political leader arrogant enough to insist he can protect us from the consequences of our collective irresponsibility to free the oppressed will certainly be taught a lesson, and so will we. It is with reverence, then, that Barth's neo-orthodox theology is included, even if not wholeheartedly endorsed, in this political theology of food.

Karl Barth, a theologian and contemporary of Schmitt's, was affected by World War I in much the same manner as Schmitt. Disillusioned with liberal theology, he too sought refuge in (neo)-orthodox theological con-structs that emphasized God's transcendent sovereignty.[8] Barth's "word of divine sovereignty and transcendence" startled theologians of his day with its prohibition against confusing "its own aspirations and achieve-ments," with divine will.[9] Barth's theological emphasis on God's sover-eignty was targeted toward the inclination of mainstream liberalism to efface the boundary between immanence and transcendence, redrawing God in man's image in the process.[10] The calamity that was World War I had eroded "confidence in the essential divineness" of the "aspirations and achievements" of humanity rendered in divine terms for both Schmitt and Barth, and such an elevated anthropology did not ring true. Despite sharing the traumatic disappointment in liberal democracy, Barth's neo-orthodox version of God's transcendent sovereignty did not underwrite human sovereignty as it did for Schmitt.

According to philosopher E. L. Allen, Barth contended that "God never passes over to the human side, he always remains transcendent, ma-jestic, unique." Furthermore, God alone possesses sovereignty, defined as

8. Herberg, "Introduction," 15.
9. Ibid., 15–16.
10. Ibid.

"unfettered self-determination."[11] Barth's assertion of God's transcendence was "a vehement . . . reaction from the tendency to merge him with the evolutionary process."[12] According to Allen, Barth viewed divine authority as no "mere fiat of power to which we perforce submit." Rather, Barth insisted that "God has a claim upon us from which we can never escape, solely because all that we have and are is from him."[13] Thus, all humans are absolutely and inescapably dependent upon a divinity who provides the conditions for our very lives. We see that Barth's concept of God's transcendence is not mobilized in support of human sovereignty, as it was for Schmitt, but rather verges on becoming something of an antidote to it. Barth was adamant that divine sovereignty is not transferable to the human sphere.

But how are humans—particularly the Christians to whom Barth addressed himself—to relate to the state? According to Barth, Christians must be obedient to the government per biblical precepts.[14] However, the Christian attitude "cannot possibly consist of an attitude of abstract and absolute elasticity towards the intentions and undertakings of the State, simply because," according to Barth's reading of Scripture, "the possibility may arise that the power of the State, on its side, may become guilty of Opposition to the Lord of lords."[15] The state cannot be assumed to be acting in a godly manner, let alone on God's behalf, also a notable point of distinction between Barth and Schmitt.

The state cannot be presumed to be godly, but that does not put the church at odds with the state in all cases. Barth insists that the church must support the state so long as it serves the purpose of "the limiting and the preserving of man by the quest for and the establishment of law." The law established by the state would presumably be law supportive of Barth's understanding of divine law. However, "the church will never be found on the side of anarchy or tyranny."[16] When the state fails to establish laws protective of human dignity, or in Barth's words when the state "perverts" its authority (God-given, as suggested by Barth's interpretation of Scripture), the church *must* criticize it.

Not only is the call to obedience limited, in Barth's view, so is the call to critique. He goes on to say that "the Church will not in all circumstances withdraw from and oppose what may be practically a dictatorship, that is,

11. Allen, *Sovereignty of God and the Word of God,*" 17.
12. Ibid.
13. Ibid., 42.
14. Barth, *Community, State, and Church,* 137.
15. Ibid., 130.
16. Ibid., 172.

a partial and temporary limitation of these freedoms, but it will certainly withdraw from and oppose any out-and-out dictatorship such as the totalitarian State."[17] In more Schmittian terms, a Christian is not obliged to protest any and all states of exception, only those that have become permanent, transforming the sovereign into a dictator. It would seem that Barth, much like Schmitt, perceives as necessary something akin to a temporary state of exception and also its propensity to outlast its usefulness, devolving into totalitarianism and tyranny.

Although Barth is aware that "no State can exist without the sanction of power," he nonetheless discerns that "the power of the good State differs from that of the bad State."[18] In particular, according to Barth, the good state aligns itself with the power that "flows and serves the law," rather than the anarchic power that misshapes or breaks the law. On the surface of things it may appear that Barth would side with Schmitt and against Benjamin for the latter's "anarchist" leanings. Closer consideration suggests that he might not align with either of their thinking very well. While on the one hand anarchic power may break the law, on the other, a permanent exception renders law impotent. It seems unlikely, in other words, that a "good state" can endure a "state of exception," in which the law has been suspended, for very long without transforming itself into a bad state that has misshapen or broken the law by suspending it.

Barth strives to stake a nuanced position, encouraging Christians to support international understanding and cooperation. He strives for peace in accordance with his reading of Scripture and Christian tradition. Nonetheless, he is clear: the church "can never stand for absolute peace, for peace at any price."[19] In particular, peace must not be sought at the price of the "abolition of the lawful State and the practical denial of the divine ordinance."[20] Indeed, the state of exception was, for Barth, too high a price to pay for peace, since in the state of exception the law no longer applies. Therefore, a Barthian version of orthodox theology cannot be said to support Schmitt's version of sovereignty.

Initially, Barth did not set out to critique the political order *as* a political order. His intention was to oppose the intrusion of the political order into the workings of the church. Barth stood in opposition to the "'German Christian' ideology, which closely identified 'Germanism' with Christianity and saw in the Nazi revolution an act of divine redemption and a source of divine

17. Ibid., 179.
18. Ibid., 177.
19. Ibid., 178.
20. Ibid.

revelation."[21] These concerns prompted Barth to participate in drafting the Barmen Declaration. Barth also opposed the installation of Nazi church leaders, and eventually, when the church was instructed to expel Jews, Barth rejected the anti-Semitism as a "rejection of the grace of God."[22]

Throughout this early period Barth viewed this essentially as an intra-church struggle. He was not concerned with executive overreach in the secular state, but instead was concerned about the intrusion of the secular state into church affairs. Barth had no "thought of challenging the Nazi state as a legitimate state."[23] When required, as a professor at Bonn, to pledge loyalty to Hitler, Barth wanted to qualify this with a statement of his higher loyalty to God. The government refused to accept second-string position in Barth's loyalties, and dismissed Barth from his post.[24] Transformed by this expulsion, Barth became impatient with a church that remained silent in the face of "the millions of the unjustly persecuted."[25]

Barth, in a letter to American Christians penned after his expulsion to Switzerland, wrote that:

> When [the church preaches] about the sole sovereignty of Jesus Christ . . . [it is] actually preaching, through a simple, strict interpretation of the Biblical texts (and, as a rule, without naming persons and things specifically) against Hitler, Mussolini, and Japan; against anti-Semitism, idolization of the state, oppressive and intimidating methods, militarism, against all the lies and injustice of National-socialism and Fascisim in its European and its Asiatic forms, and thus [it] will naturally (and without "dragging politics into the pulpit") speak on behalf of the righteous state and also for an honestly determined conduct of the war.[26]

Even though Barth falls short of precisely defining the point at which what is "practically a dictatorship" has become an "out-and-out dictatorship," he is nonetheless clear that the sovereignty of God cannot unproblematically be invoked to legitimize a human sovereign. Especially when the definition of "the sovereign" is contingent, as Schmitt's is, upon a suspension of law that transforms that "good" state to a "bad" state. Idolization of the state, or its leadership, constitutes idolatry.

21. Herberg, "Introduction," 38.
22. Ibid., 40.
23. Ibid., 41.
24. Ibid.
25. Ibid., 42.
26. Ibid., 52.

Barth at least gestures toward a relational ontology in which "human freedom is not realized in the solitary detachment of an individual in isolation from his fellow men . . . I am a man only in relation to my fellow men."[27] The understanding of human togetherness is based in part on an *imago Dei* depicting God as being not only for himself but for us: "God's freedom is essentially not freedom from, but freedom to and for."[28] This is because for Barth, "God's freedom is not merely unlimited possibility or formal majesty and omnipotence, that is to say empty, naked sovereignty."[29] Likewise, the freedom of man is similarly limited. To believe otherwise is to endorse "the false freedom of sin, reducing man to a prisoner."[30] These limitations are, to be sure, hardly minor and go a long way toward undermining the pretenses of any human to absolute power.

Barth goes even further than simply denying one human absolute power over another. He also denies humans in general absolute power over nonhumans. This is because Barth did not construe the nonhuman world as inconsequential, as Schmitt seemed to. Rather, Barth insisted that "God was not and is not bound to choose and to decide Himself for man alone and to show His loving-kindness to him alone."[31] Not only does Barth not believe that the nonhuman world is of no importance to God, he is willing to entertain the thought that it might be more important than the human world: "The thought of any insignificant being outside the human cosmos being far more worthy of divine attention than man is deeply edifying and should not be lightly dismissed."[32] The possibility that nonhuman creatures may be of greater importance than humans in the eyes of God certainly humbles anthropocentric arrogance, perhaps Barth's intention here.

So we see that although Schmitt claims to ground his political concept of the sovereign in orthodox theology, this same theology can simultaneously be a source of critique of absolute or top-down sovereignty. This is not surprising if one recalls that what is true of God from a religious perspective is not necessarily therefore true of humans. Secularizing an orthodox theology is a fundamentally flawed maneuver; a person of faith might even consider it idolatry.[33] While this goes a long way toward delegitimizing the Schmittian sovereign, it does not provide a robust theo-

27. Barth, *The Humanity of God*, 77.
28. Ibid., 7.
29. Ibid.
30. Ibid.
31. Ibid., 73.
32. Ibid.
33. Martel, *Divine Violence*, 77.

logical vision to underwrite the alternative political vision we desperately need in the context of climate change.

Naturally we cannot expect Barth to address our contemporary ecological situation given that climate change was not even a topic of conversation in his era. Even if we sought to adapt his theological position to something more ecologically enlightened, however, it would not prove to be a theological model within which Bruno Latour's political ecology could find its theological moorings. If, as Schmitt suggests, all significant theories of the state are secularized theological concepts, we would find that Barth's theology would fail to support this more ecologically inspired politics. This shortcoming arrives in the form of a certain determinism that robs humans of the responsibility for social structures that Barth elsewhere gives them. For Barth, the value of humanity "is a matter of God's sovereign togetherness with man, a togetherness grounded in Him and determined, delimited, and ordered through him alone." Human agency, let alone the agency of the nonhuman, is rather curtailed in this theological vision.

Despite the deterministic tenor of this passage, elsewhere it is clear that Barth does not advocate passivity in the face of social ills. Barth was not alone in vacillating between endorsing God's omnipotence and recognizing human responsibility. Negotiating this Scylla and Charybdis of theodicy is familiar terrain for theologians of the Abrahamic traditions. Ethical monotheism reinforces a strong sense of personal accountability for one's behavior, both ritually and socially. Yet, the images of God frequently portrayed in sacred text and other traditional sources depict a deity ultimately in control of the final outcome.

Nonetheless, this image of God's power as deterministic is at odds with the iterative and intra-active becoming disclosed by science studies. Furthermore, as Will Herberg argues, despite Barth's apparent rejection of the concept of the state as an "order of preservation," nevertheless the state bears this primary resonance in Barth's work. Barth's implicit yet disavowed endorsement of the state as an order of preservation may be due to his perception that chaos is diametrically opposed to God's goodness.[34] Unfortunately, Barth does not lead us far enough away from Schmitt's dangerous version of sovereignty to reject it, nor nearly enough toward something at least akin to a nondeterministic metaphysics to fully embrace it.

Barth's theology *does* raise substantial challenges to Schmitt's version of sovereignty—and indeed to any attempt to legitimate "the sovereign" on a theological basis. Further, it does so from within a framework that endorses a more or less orthodox version of a sovereign God. This, I believe, is rather

34. Keller, *Face of the Deep*, 86.

compelling in the present political climate. President Trump's rhetoric bears certain resemblances to the nationalism implicit within Schmitt's version of sovereignty. His strategic deployment of religious language likely accounts for the fact that Evangelical Christians voted for him in overwhelming numbers.[35] Illuminating the ways in which this version of sovereignty is fundamentally at odds with the Christian framework guiding their decision-making could possibly create some cognitive dissonance between their un-examined faith in Trump and their unshakable faith in God. Those who find orthodox theologies compelling may find their resistance to unjust power fortified by this Barthian critique of top-down sovereignty.

What about those of us for whom the orthodox depiction of God does not capture the whole picture? Must we restrict ourselves to orthodox con-structions of God's sovereignty that are at odds with the metaphysical image of our epoch in order to challenge Schmitt's formulation of sovereignty? Must we embrace his premise of a transcendent God in order to challenge Schmitt on his own terms? Or might other models of divinity more consonant with the metaphysical image of an iterative, process-oriented, intra-active and nondeterministic model of reality be teased from traditional sources? More importantly, if we abandon this orthodox or neo-orthodox doctrine of God, must we jettison morality along with it, as Schmitt implies?

Re-creativity of God as Re-starting Point for Political Theology

Might a panentheist theology be better suited to the metaphysical image of the current epoch? Science studies reveals a more immanental, iterative, and relational metaphysics than an orthodox, highly transcendent theology might support. A panentheistic alternative is a godsend for those of us who weary of the "science vs. religion" debate, finding them both indispensable. Fortuitously, Catherine Keller's panentheist theology, as explicated in *Face of the Deep: A Theology of Becoming*, not only aligns well with the meta-physical image of the current epoch, it also retains a framework for morally sound decision-making.

While not claiming to be an ethicist, process theologian Catherine Keller is driven by ethical concerns mirroring those animating this po-litical theology of food: the suffering that permeates multiple issues such as "ecology, economics, race, gender, sex."[36] Keller suggests that this

---

35. Exit polls reported by Pew research reported that 81 percent of Evangelical Christians voted in favor of Trump; see Smith and Martinez, "How the Faithful Voted."

36. Keller, *Face of the Deep*, xvi.

suffering is integrally linked to the doctrine of *creatio ex nihilo*, by virtue of the corresponding tendency to project "chaos and nothingness onto the non-Christian or sub Christian Others."[37] Ultimately, "the nothingness" intolerable within this theological framework, "invariably returns with the face of the feared chaos—to be nihilated all the more violently." Latour's externalities returning to haunt the collective and Agamben's *homo sacer*—as not only he who cannot be sacrificed, but also as he who cannot be integrated—reverberate in the depths of Keller's "nothingness" that threatens orderly existence—sounding an alarm to which a political theology of food must respond.

Face of the Deep "continues a *deconstruction* of the paradigm and presumption of linear time: the bottom line of origin, the straight line of salvation history, the violent end of the line of time itself" initiated in others of her constructive engagements with Christian tradition.[38] Discarding linear preconceptions, the theme of "re-creation from chaos" emerges from traditional texts.[39] This beginning again will not establish itself as "a unifying order" but will instead instigate "multiple movements of creativity."[40] Replacing the doctrine of *creatio ex nihilo*, Keller conjures a *creatio ex profundis*—a creation from the depths present in the opening lines of Genesis. Her theology becomes "a *tehomic* theology," or a theology of the deep. This is no simple matter of declaring chaos "good," but rather a matter of recognizing chaos to constitute a deep "matrix of possibilities," at least some of which might be good. This requires a disposition she identifies as *tehomophilia*, the ability to embrace the complex, chaotic, messiness of life—even though not necessarily safe, and decidedly frightening—as brimming with creative potencies.

Barth is, coincidentally, one of Keller's interlocutors. Barth, she argues, recognizes that the text of Genesis 1 suggests that *something* was present before creation, although he stops short of embracing the primeval chaos. Neither Keller nor Barth is satisfied with either acceptance of the doctrine of *creatio ex nihilo* on the one hand or endorsement of the *tehom* as existing independently of God on the other. In this they agree: a third option is needed, yet the task of constructing this third possibility is daunting.

Both are committed to relational approaches "in which difference is not swallowed up by the self, but enhanced."[41] Yet despite their mutual in-

37. Ibid., xvii.

38. Ibid.

39. Ibid., xix.

40. Ibid., xvii.

41. Ibid., 87.

vestment in relational theologies, ultimately their constructive maneuvers are diametrically opposed. Keller finds two particular claims of Barth's objectionable. First, she objects to Barth's claim that assertions of God's dominance alone are sufficient to eliminate tyranny. It is simply not enough, in Keller's opinion, that God be declared the *only* dominant figure, particularly because of Barth's own espousal of *analogia relationis*. She argues that "Theologies of analogy have this right: since we will use anthropomorphic God-talk, we should at least use the best possible images. Would this not require of us metaphors arising from non-hierarchical, democratizing visions of sociality, not metaphors of totalizing economic and political order?"[42] Not only are we inclined to talk about man in a loud voice when talking about God, as Barth famously denounced. We are also inclined to talk about God in almost as loud a voice when talking about humans, rhetoric unacceptable to a political theology of food.

If we are to draw analogies between god-like qualities and our own behaviors as creatures made in the image of God, we had better think twice about the portraits of God we render. For Keller, Barth's neo-orthodox construction of God's unidirectional power becomes the model upon which notions of "empowered humans" base their behavior, Barth's objections notwithstanding. Of particular concern, Barth's disavowal of human sovereignty on the basis that it is *human* and not divine vacates the seat of power in earthy, material reality. This vacancy draws in nefarious pretenders to God's throne—as we see with critiques of the Schmittian sovereign.

Keller goes on to argue that Barth's apologetics also suggest "that a violent context justifies the demonization of chaos."[43] This is especially surprising in light of his opposition to National Socialism, which one might assume "would have sharpened his suspicion of the high value of order."[44] Even more problematically, Barth erects "an ineradicable boundary [that] cuts against the possibility of a true interdependence"[45] between God and humanity. According to Keller, Barth envisions a deity who "remains unconditioned" and unidirectionally controlling of the outcome of worldly affairs,"[46] and is unsuitable for her theology of becoming. Keller's unorthodox panentheism promises to cut a trap door under the throne of the Schmittian sovereign as no one, not even God, is above being affected by others.

42. Ibid.
43. Ibid.
44. Ibid.
45. Ibid.
46. Ibid., 99.

The bidirectionality of influence between God and world is tangled up with God's role in creation. Keller's rereading of Genesis, inclusive of rabbinical interpretation such as that by Rashi, reveals that:

> Chaos is neither nothing nor evil; in which to create is not to master the formless but to solicit its virtual forms. Such solicitation, when expressed as divine speech, may sound less like a command than a seduction.[47]

Is Keller suggesting that God *seduces* chaos into a dynamic creation? If so, God's seductive utterances receive a passionate response from creation:

> The heavens are telling the glory of God;
> and the firmament proclaims his handiwork
> Day to day makes utterance,
> and night to night speaks out.
> there is no speech, there are no words, whose sound goes unheard;
> their voice goes out through all the earth
> their words to the end of the world.
> He placed in them a tent for the sun,
> who is like a groom coming forth from the chamber.[48]

Who was the sun making love to all night? This daybreak eroticism may be more than mere coincidence, arising in as it does the context of a tradition which envisions the relationship between Israel and God to be a marriage. Biblical tradition imagines God's generative speech as seductive indeed.

In biblical tradition God speaks the world into being—a truly generative act—and creation speaks or sings in response. As the above psalm alludes, the nonhuman world never ceases speaking, yet it does not speak in human words. Notions of divine speech and creation's response resonate with Latour's concept of the powers of speech and speech prosthesis. Presumably, the speech of nonhuman creation is audible to the God of the psalmist, if not to the average earthling of the twenty-first century. No doubt this God hears the groaning of a creation too long ignored by human sovereigns.

Keller does not necessarily envision a God who literally "hears," yet she nonetheless envisions a God who is affected by the material world. There is no sheltering God's omnipotence at the expense of God's relatedness.

---

47. Keller, *Face of the Deep*, 115.

48. Psalm 19, JPS translation; divine speech also figures in Psalm 50; creaturely speech of nonhumans also in Psalms 96, 97, 98 and 148; and God's responds to the speech of creatures "by awesome deeds" in Psalm 65.

Keller's panentheist God remains vulnerable to the vicissitudes of material becoming, as a God who responds to the groaning of creation must. In this vision, "creator and creature create, effect, each other; not from a prior nothing but from their shared preconditions." [49] If we are not to understand God as the unmoved mover, capable of acting unilaterally to assure a just outcome, how then can we understand God? Inspired by process philosopher Alfred North Whitehead, Keller asks whether we "might reserve the term 'God' . . . for a principle of limitation by which the possible becomes actual?" [50] This God would operate within the "bottomless ground of creativity" but yet not be identical with it.

Keller finds resonance with the term apophatic panentheism, in which the "'en' designates an active indeterminacy, a commingling of unpredictable and yet recapitulatory, self-organizing relations. The 'en' asserts the difference of divine and cosmic, but at the same time makes it impossible to draw the line." [51] And, more importantly, the "en" prevents anyone from reading history as necessarily the unfolding of God's immutable will. While God is within all things and all things are within God, this–crucially—does not mean that God is in control of all things.

At this point Keller's constructive maneuvers become resonant with the metaphysics of our epoch, not surprising since she remains conversant with a wide body of science studies, such as chaos and quantum theories. Influenced by the process thought of Alfred North Whitehead, whose metaphysics intentionally integrated early quantum theory, this is to be expected. There is commingling, indeterminacy, and a God present on the immanent plane—no unidirectional force, no transcendent guarantor of justice. One might suggest that Keller has stealthily crafted a theology espousing the (at least partial) immanence of the divine, yet retaining a transcendent source of valuation—even if it does not retain a transcendent guarantee of order. Yet, possibly the "comingling" will reveal an ethical framework despite Schmitt's insistence that immanence is devoid of a system of valuation.

But perhaps we are getting ahead of ourselves. From where in tradition does Keller retrieve the notion of a God entangled with creation? In part, she mines the text of Job, but is keen to note that she is not reading "into the book of Job a systematic process panentheism," which would be, in her words, anachronistic. [52] The text is best read, she insists, as parody.

---

49. Keller, *Face of the Deep*, 218.

50. Ibid., 238.

51. Ibid., 219.

52. Ibid., 140.

Nonetheless, she lingers on Job's testimony that he can now "see God with his eyes."[53] Keller observes that "there is no trace, no beard or backside, of a personal God who might be thus 'seen.' What Job 'sees' in the vision of God is only the creatures." Keller postulates that "to 'see' God is to see the creation," and speculates that the creation might be metaphorically readable as the body of God, as McFague elsewhere argues. This is but one example of a textual tradition articulating a divine dwelling in intimate proximity to creation, both affecting and affected by it, but not identical to it.

Rabbi Arthur Green echoes Keller's notion that the material world may be something in the way of God's self-expression. Green clarifies that when he refers to God he means "the inner force of existence itself."[54] He goes on to describe this God as "constantly evolving life energy," and the billions of years' history of the universe as "a *meaningful* process."[55] The endorsement of the universe as God's body, as perhaps purposeful divine self-expression, is simultaneously offensive to atheists and orthodox theists alike—atheists because they are allergic to the very word God, and theists because it seems to reduce God to the material universe. Keller insists that rereading the material world as the body of God need not "reduce Elohim to an impersonal force of nature."[56] Rather, it could carve an opening through which we could peer into a decidedly different concept of "divine purposes"—and of nature—which would then come to "suggest the purposefulness of a universe that against all statistical odds yields laws that work, rules of space, time, speed, and cohesion through which life continues to complicate itself and emerge undaunted."[57] This purposefulness does not take the form of a unilateral imposition of force, but as invitation to create beauty and order at the knife edge of chaos.

Keller insists that her *tehomic* return to a creation theology "is not a matter of coming full circle—another dream of closure—but of narrating the recapitulatory, iterative dynamic of becoming itself." Her aversion to closure reveals itself in *Apocalypse Now and Then: A Feminist Guide to the End of the World*, in which Keller took great pains to demonstrate the almost self-fulfilling nature of apocalyptic prophecies. Of particular relevance to the present study, she observes that:

---

53. Job 42:6, as quoted by Keller.

54. Green, *Radical Judaism*, 18.

55. Ibid., 20. See also Whitehead, *Religion in the Making*: "The purpose of God is the attainment of value in the temporal world" (100).

56. Keller, *Face of the Deep*, 139.

57. Ibid.

Expectations seek, after all, to realize themselves. The religious habit of imagining the world out of existence would not seem to be irrelevant to the material habits of world-waste running our civilization; in right-wing religious anti-environmentalism, for instance, the expectancy that Our Father will make us a shiny new world when this one breaks explicitly correlates with a willingness to dump this one.[58]

And indeed, reports of climate chaos and geopolitical upheaval are interpreted as precursors to promised messianic redemption by many on the religious right.

In Keller's deft analysis, anti-apocalypticisms disclosed themselves as no solution, as each is permeated with its own cryptoapocalypse. Keller concluded her volume with hope for "the development of a counter-apocalypse—itself not immune from occasional alternation between outsized ideas and skeptical deflations" but yet capable of sublating its eschatology to a pneumatology.[59] She urges us to "ease history back into a helical timefulness, a rhythm akin to the spiral nebula, the shifting seasons, the entrainment of relations."[60] The nonlinear matrix of Revelation provokes open-endedness, despite the static depiction of the New Jerusalem with which it closes.

What makes a theology of becoming so compelling for the current project is integrally connected to this spiral toward beginning, away from ending. Particularly in light of her own critique of apocalypticism and anti-apocalypticism, it would seem that political theologies tinted with shades of messianism or apocalypticism are likely to propel us toward precisely an end—and many political theologies possess a messianic streak.[61] All of the "endings" toward which both apocalyptic and anti-apocalyptic movements have propelled their followers have concluded not with a final ending. Oh, yes, wreckage, to be sure. But not *The End*. Human life, even the lives of those endorsing apocalyptic platforms, continued on despite the catastrophe. And new life was fabricated from this waste.

In our own scenario of climate change, on the one hand an end is near but on the other we cannot be certain how final the end will be, when, or for whom. Someone—someone human—may very well be left to eke out an

---

58. Keller, *Apocalypse Now and Then*, 2.

59. Ibid., 276.

60. Ibid., 275.

61. For example, Crockett, *Radical Political Theology*; Miguez, *Radical Political Theology*; Rieger and Sung, *Beyond the Spirit of Empire*; Moltmann, *God for a Secular Society*; and Northcott, *A Political Theology of Climate Change*.

existence in the aftermath. Furthermore, it is quite possible that we are already living *after* "the end"—as Bill McKibben's *The End of Nature* already declared in 1989. Writing in 2018, this end is already apparent: the very long era of predictably seasonable weather is over. We are living *after* the Green Revolution could legitimately promise us even more abundant harvests next year. Debate continues as to whether we have hit peak oil; therefore we may also be already living *after* the era of easily accessible crude oil, as well.[62]

Keller argues that "eschatology is discourse about the collective encounter at the edge where and when the life of the creation has its chance at renewal—that is, it is about the present."[63] This is decidedly not a reinvention of Eden, nor a regression to some mythological past that never was.[64] Keller's eschatology is about facing the chaos of the present moment with a resolution to coax a livable life for as many as possible out of the wreckage. Keller's eschatology informs a political theology of food oriented toward *creatio ex profundis*, creating out of the chaos following in the wake of yet another inconclusive apocalypse. If we are already living after the end, as I suggest above, we must be living into yet another beginning—ripe for a theology of becoming.

Drawing from the Christian tradition Keller argues that faith can never be reduced to assenting to propositional statements such as creeds. Neither does faith express itself as passive waiting. Instead, "in a world of open-ended indeterminacy . . . faith will approximate courage."[65] We must be the ones to "bear the fruit, use the talent, heal the sick, feed the hungry."[66] She notes that "Those who follow this activating gospel have been variously suspected of Judaizing, gnosticism, Arianism, Pelagianism, atheism, socialism, or feminism."[67] Despite these heretical monikers, the notion that humans are responsible for one another and the earth we live on—that God alone does not determine the outcome—has a long history in the tradition. Although Keller advocates active responses to the suffering of the world, she assures us that this "do-it-yourself message . . . has little to do with the self-sufficiency of a lonely ego."[68] Such efforts at self-containment would, in

---

62. Nafeez, "Former BP Geologist." Contrast with Russel Gold: "Why Peak Oil Predictions Haven't Come True." The Association for the Study of Peak Oil notes in its July 2016 blog entry that "Oil production is not falling as fast as predicted." Note that the last source does *not* say production is not falling at all—just not as quickly as anticipated.

63. Keller, "Eschatology, Ecology, and a Green Ecumenacy," 85.

64. See Provan, *Convenient Myths*.

65. Ibid., 139.

66. Ibid., 214.

67. Ibid.

68. Ibid.

Keller's formulation, block "the originary flow," truly sinful from the perspective of a theology of becoming.

But most people do not think systemically when they consider the question of sin. Instead, they ponder more private wrongs. According to Keller,
this is not accidental: "God's omnipotence was accordingly shored up to replace human responsibility for the world, while Christian morality was left to
monitor bodily openings and effluvia."[69] In other words, whereas for Schmitt
the doctrine of God's sovereignty legitimates human political sovereignty, for
Keller it places a boulder over the mouth of "the ocean of springs," in the process vacating much of the substance of religious life, "blocking out, keeping
outside our finite bodies, the very one to whom we cry."[70]

The notion of divine sovereignty disables us from rising to our responsibility to shape social structures in such a way that promotes lives of dignity
and worth for human and nonhuman alike. There is little need for us to
assume personal responsibility if God is ultimately responsible for the outcome. Keller goes on to say that "the logic of omnipotence lays upon naked
suffering the added burden of godforsakenness."[71] Not that Keller believes
they have *literally* been godforsaken; merely that the logic of omnipotence
implies that all events are under God's control, so one cannot help but surmise that the abject have been forsaken by God.

But the seven million people per year who die of starvation because
they don't have money to purchase food have not been forsaken by God.
They have been forsaken by people acting within social and economic
structures. The decisions of people operating within these structures clearly
become visible as a blockage of the originary flow of the force of life when
an analysis of suffering is infused with insights from Keller's theology of
becoming. Death by starvation or by metabolic syndrome becomes legible
as a diminishment of the good that the afflicted could have experienced and
contributed to the world. Animals in concentrated animal feed organizations who require massive doses of antibiotics because they are kept in such
close quarters have not been forsaken by God. Nor have marine creatures
killed as a consequence of fertilizer runoff from factory farms. All of these
beings have been forsaken by people operating within material-discursive
apparatuses that block the originary flow of life in numerous ways.

Keller suggests that accepting responsibility for the planet is enfolded
into the role of humanity as envisioned in Genesis. Part and parcel of this responsibility is that we develop "an economy and ecology serving the 'good'

69. Ibid., 214.
70. Ibid., 215.
71. Ibid.

of all other species."[72] Given the anti-oppression concerns surfacing as early as her introduction and reappearing throughout her text, no doubt Keller would prefer these economies and ecologies to also serve the good of more members of the human species as well, although here she is speaking specifically against an "unconstrained birthrate."[73] What applies to the birthrate is equally applicable to the economy as a whole:

> In its participation in an illimitable universe, a tehomic ecology underscores "the inescapability of limits." An endless becoming does not signify the unlimited expansion of any entity. Becoming unfolds within the constraining and sustaining context enfolding any individual—perhaps even a divine one. Yet limit functions not as container but as skin, permeable membrane, elemental body of mud, water, air, and fire. The endless becoming of the All takes place within a within: that of the milieu of milieus, in which no cost of "growth" can be concealed.[74]

If growth of the human species must be limited, that is presumably because the growth of the economies that provide for their needs at the expense of other species must similarly be limited. And it must be recalled that the bodies of the starving and obese, and the bodies of water, land and sky together suffer for the benefit of the capitalist promise of an ever-expanding economy.

Keller's vision of an immanently invested divinity does not rob the religious world of an ethical framework. Rather, it internalizes that framework: "the change of divine subject changes the subject of ethics: it *becomes* us."[75] We must right our own moral wrongs, correct our own systemic injustices, cease and desist from our own oppressive practices. To rely upon divine intervention is to relinquish moral accountability for the earth and for each other. Implicit in Keller's disavowal of divine omnipotence and assertion of human responsibility is an ethics of care, mindful of our persistent commingling with the world around us. When selfish actions diminish the creative potential of ecosystems and other peoples, an ethical violation has been committed.

In order to more fully explicate the ethical implications of Keller's apophatic panentheist theology of becoming, we will need to weave in the "apophatic" more tightly. Keller's most recent book, *Cloud of the Impossible: Negative Theology and Planetary Entanglement,* explores the apophatic with

72. Ibid., 222.

73. Ibid.

74. Ibid., 225–26.

75. Ibid., 140.

the rigor applied to panentheist becoming in *Face of the Deep*. She defines the apophatic as "speech as the most *knowing*, indeed erudite, sort of nonknowing."[76] Cusa, in particular, felt himself drawn into this learned unknowing when confronted with the tendency of truths to "undo each other." Cusa referred to this class of opposing truths as *coincidentia oppositorum*. Keller's genealogy of the apophatic tradition stretches as far back as the Jewish Philo of Alexandria, and winds through the texts of Gregory of Nyssa, Pseudo-Dionysius, and Nicolas of Cusa. Yet throughout the entirety of the text, Keller remains "haunted by [the image]" of Cusa's articulation of a God that "enfolds (*complicans*) and unfolds (*explicans*) the boundless manifold of the universe," Keller carries this vision through her own engagement with the apophatic tradition.

Keller is concerned throughout *Cloud of the Impossible* to develop an expansive ethics "that exceeds concern for the ones near and like us." She is inspired to stage this encounter between "a deconstructive apophasis and a prophetic relationalism" because it brings us to the edge of the unkown, where we nonetheless know that we remain inseparable from many Others. The ethical demand arises in this context of inseparable entanglement. Furthermore, this staging allows the oscillation between affirmation and negation, enfolding and unfolding, distinction and entanglement, that highlights "the very fold between our nonknowing and our nonseparatbility." This fold, Keller hopes, may begin to "appear as possibility itself," a possibility that fertilizes fecund becomings and planetary solidarity.

In the interest of illuminating the material dimension of our inseparability, Keller "examines certain layered explications—scientific, philosophical, and poetic—by which our ontological entanglement comes to matter."[77] Keller finds that, working perhaps from an opposite end of the spectrum, "scientists become engrossed in questions that deposit them at the outer edge of those 'limits of decidability'—right on the cloudy threshold of theology."[78] She notes that the "key problem for physics itself" is posed by precisely the same "classicism of a separable objectivism" which has similarly haunted theology. Keller does not hope to find proof of God in the *coincidentia oppositorum* that physics as a whole faces in the context of the clashing truths of classical and quantum physics. However, she *does* anticipate being rewarded with "material evidence of a universe so apophatically entangled as to escape the rival classicisms that pit science

76. Keller, *Cloud of the Impossible*, 2.

77. Ibid., 9.

78. Ibid., 131.

and theology against each other."[79] The rivalry may be abandoned, but the conundrums remain.

Quantum nonseparability, a term describing the fact that subatomic particles have been shown to affect one another across great distances, bolsters Keller's assertion that each of us is deeply entangled with innumerable others. The apophatic implication of quantum nonseparability consists in this: we can never fully know the scope or magnitude of our relational entanglements. The dark cloud of unknowing hovering over this relational field does not represent evil, no more than does the darkness hovering over the face of the deep in Genesis, Keller assures us. Rather, the dark cloud of unknowing hovering over this relational field signals "the deep variegations of nonknowing that it may do ill to ignore or to manipulate."[80] This sounds a note of caution to those who would fancy themselves capable of solving social problems once and for all.

In her engagement of Barad's agential realism (in conjunction with other quantum theories) Keller observes that "an agential cut does not cut the bond of entanglement but, we might say, makes decisions . . . *within* it."[81] In other words, as we decide the outer boundary of the collective, in good Latourian fashion, we must be mindful that the boundary itself is fiction. The collective remains entangled with whatever it has attempted to extrude. This decision is made within a matrix of becoming from which we can never extricate ourselves *or* banish any other Other. We remain entangled with, if inseparably distinct from, a panoply of beings.

Keller insists that the incalculabilty of their number, these others do not fade from ethical significance. Yet this unknowing need not paralyze us. Rather, Keller insists, "the subject mindful of its unknowing *minds* the world afresh. It minds, it is bothered by, the deformations of powers and knowledge, it minds oppressions. For it recognizes also the signs and eligibilities of its own largest life."[82] The subject mindful of unknowing, then, entertains the distinct possibility that her own life has been diminished by the casting of some Other into the role of *homo sacer*.

The capacity to love across differences, to act on behalf of not only ourselves of the myriad others with whom we are entangled constitutes a political strategy. It does not constitute a guarantee of security, as "a theology

---

79. Ibid., 132.

80. Ibid., 7. These "deep variegations" of relationality may bear upon what is at stake in the closure of the commons. As was suggested in the previous chapter, we remain inseparable from what is on the other side of the closure, and perhaps dependent upon it despite our failure to recognize this dependence.

81. Ibid., 151.

82. Ibid., 230.

of becoming" must "negotiate its solidities, its solidarities, within the flux." These negotiations are not undertaken with hope of a final security, nor with fear of disorder, but rather in the spirit of "responsible, flexible, and therefore steadfast forms of self-organization."[83] In this political love, Keller observes, "we gain the courage of our connections."[84]

And we will need both steadfast forms of self-organization and courage in order to persist in creating a good common world as climate catastrophes loom and food scarcity threatens for reasons other than merely economic.[85] Which is where a *tehomophilic* theology of becoming might just inspire not self-fulfilling apocalypticism, but constructive reimaginings of human social structures that intra-act creatively with the nonhuman in more sustainable ways. Birthing new ways of being may be daunting. As Keller testifies, "any beginning partakes of the irreducible"[86] The task of beginning again is nothing new. It could even be construed as a holy task.

In Keller's apophatic panentheist theology of becoming we find a theological model that simultaneously draws from traditional theological resources and is yet compatible with the metaphysical image of our epoch as revealed by science studies. This model does not posit an all-powerful God, nor does it lend credence to human enactments of Schmittian sovereignty. Furthermore, Keller's apophatic panentheism recommends caution as the Latourian collective sets about its task of creating the good common world. In fact, Keller's apophatic panentheism, perceiving the implications of quantum nonseparability, heightens awareness that no Other can ever be finally eliminated from the collective. Finally, and perhaps most importantly, it provides a model for ethically attuned creation in the context of chaos. And, as discussed in the previous chapter, chaos is likely to emerge with increasing frequency on a quickly warming planet.

She, too, is aware that time is of the essence. In her recent essay "Toward a Political Theology of the Earth" she not only embraces hers as a political theology, she recognizes the urgency of the climate crisis. Because too little time remains for us to "demythologize achievements . . . to deterritorialize

83. Ibid., 216.

84. Ibid.

85. Numerous authors noting the ominous projections for life on Earth in the context of radical climate disruption promote transformations of social relations and consumptions patterns, broadly speaking. See Diamond, *Collapse*; Dumanoski, *End of the Long Summer*; Klare, *The Race for What's Left*; Klein, *This Changes Everything*; Korten, *The Great Turning*; and McKibben, *Deep Economy*.

86. Ibid., 222. Reading Keller, it occurs to me that the problem with the law that Benjamin observes—it is too general, needs to be applied to individual cases, and eventually no longer applies at all—could in some way be circumvented if we viewed laws as provisional and iterative (which is what they are), rather than permanent.

the lingering theology of a false triumph" we must instead widen the net of our solidarities.[87] She urges us to build assemblages "strong enough . . . to take on the real foe: the neoliberal economics for which 'nature' appears only as resource or enemy."[88] Notably, this foe is not a particular person, group, or ecological circumstance; it could best be described as a set of material-discursive practices that are leaving deleterious marks on bodies.

Conclusion

A political theology of food joins Keller in seeking "an actually radical political theology" that permits entry to a multiplicity of gods, beliefs, and practices—including Abrahamic orthodoxies and heterodoxies in the task of recreating a sustainable world together. We must, as she claims, recognize our togetherness in this crisis. Whatever theological, spiritual, or moral commitments will allow us to hover over the abyssal *tehom* and speak generative language—audible or otherwise—until a new, more mutually abundant way of relating emerges will suffice.[89] Some of these commitments will doubtless be anchored in Abrahamic orthodoxies, and others inspired by sciences perceived to be more or less secular. All are welcome. What political models might prove consonant with Keller's theology of becoming, the metaphysical image of our epoch, and therefore also with a political theology of food?

87. Keller, *Intercarnations*, 178.

88. Ibid., 183.

89. For her notion of expressing "theologically the praxis of living close to the abyss" (6) and all that such praxis might entail in the context of climate change, which inspires my own thinking, I am indebted to Sidgridur Gudmarsdottir's *Tillich and the Abyss*.

Chapter 8

A Timely Popular
Sovereignty

DEMOCRACY IS COMMONLY UPHELD as a bulwark against the sort of totalitarian or fascist regimes into which absolute sovereignty can be said to devolve. Because it draws strength from a multiplicity, presumably, it thwarts the consolidation of power that leads to authoritarianism. Yet both liberal democracy and the popular sovereignty upon which it is based are critiqued from both the right and left ends of the political spectrum. Schmitt, it will be recalled, perceived both liberal democracy and versions of popular sovereignty as utterly lacking authentic sovereignty or the capacity to maintain order in the face of a crisis. Ironically, many progressives denounce liberal democracy for its affiliation with sovereignty and brutal imposition of order in its name.[1]

Recall, for instance, Clayton Crocket's argument, that popular sovereignty derives from monarchical sovereignty, as evidenced by the notion that "it is the unitary will of the people that is sovereign, not the individual whims of the multitude."[2] The tendency of liberal democracy to rely upon a unity contrasts with "the multiplicity of nature" and amplifies its potential for misuse of power.[3] Despite this potential misuse of power, Crockett laments the eclipsing of the will of the people by "political power" that has been "mediated in complex ways" permitting either "naked military force"

1. Such as Clayton Crockett, Jacques Derrida, Michael Hardt, Antonio Negri and many others.

2. Crockett, *Radical Political Theology*, 46.

3. Ibid., 46–47.

or "a more subtle sovereign wealth "to become the more potent political decision-makers.[4]

Crockett sees little difference between popular sovereignty and democratic sovereignty, which he finds unpalatable because of its connection to the nation-state.[5] He views democratic sovereignty as so tightly bound to the nation-state than one can scarcely imagine a democratic sovereignty independently of a state structure. He questions whether democratic sovereignty might be unthinkable without the nation-state: "democratic sovereignty is tied to the nation-state and perhaps cannot be thought without the state."[6] The tight linkage between democratic sovereignty and the concept of the nation-state is problematic for Crockett in part because "the state's legitimacy and authority is being called into question."[7] More specifically, it is sovereignty itself that is being called into question, and Crockett hopes to conjure a radical democracy unburdened by this concept.

Crockett cites Derrida's contention that all states are rogue states as evidence of this contestation. He goes on to argue that the crisis of both democracy and the nation-state are the result of their reliance upon liberalism, an ideology that is itself in crisis. In what can be seen as a prophetic moment, Crockett observes that two approaches to the crisis of liberalism confront us in our contemporary political climate:

> One can either abandon democracy in abandoning liberalism and embrace a Machiavellian neoconservatism where (American) might makes right, or one can try to recuperate or restore a vital tradition of democracy.[8]

It appears that with the 2016 election, the US generally opted for the former, although the latter may emerge as an upshot of the myriad discontents with the new administration. Crockett is pessimistic about the potentiality for restoring liberal democracy due to the neoliberal economic agenda with which it has become nearly synonymous. Crockett turns to the notion of radical democracy to denote a democracy disarticulated from liberalism, neoliberal economics, and ultimately sovereign power.

Crockett's theorization of radical democracy disarticulated from sovereignty bears some resonances with Keller's theology of becoming, and also with the metaphysical image of our epoch. However, Crockett stops

4. Ibid.
5. Ibid., 104
6. Ibid., 48.
7. Ibid.
8. Ibid., 93–94.

short of legitimizing a nation-state. The state in its current form is welded to neoliberal economics, and therefore hostile to efforts to create a truly equal society. Yet a legitimate nation-state is a demand of many in the food sovereignty movement. Can others grapple with Crockett's valid critiques in a way that *might* support this vital movement?

Political theorist William Connolly cuts right to the heart of the matter, at least as regards support for the nation-state. Certainly, nationalism or an undue emphasis on any particular identity is problematic in his eyes. Nonetheless, dissolution of the nation does not resolve the problems wrought by the nation in the first place. He supports efforts to reconsider concepts such as "freedom, belonging, and human exceptionalism in relationship to a host of planetary processes."[9] He is aware that climate change threatens earthlings with violent conflict and ecological catastrophes, which will disproportionately affect the already marginalized. To mitigate this threat, he calls for "vibrant pluralist assemblages" composed of a multiplicity of stakeholders representing a diversity of subject positions.[10]

One fear Connolly specifically names is the fear that these assemblages will not assemble themselves quickly enough to avert disaster. There is no guarantee we will come together at all, let alone come together quickly. In other words, those of us who are passionately concerned about climate change and its myriad effects—including impacts on food—may fail to unify in a timely fashion. Enter Paulina Ochoa Espejo's *Time of Popular Sovereignty: Process and the Democratic State*.

People as Process

Political theorist Paulina Ochoa Espejo begins with the observation that any assemblage that might go by the name of "the people" never, in fact, *does* unify. So perhaps fears of either excessive or delayed unification are misplaced. Espejo shares Crockett's concern about the theoretical linkage of "unitary will" with the concept of popular sovereignty, but her fear is unrelated to its potential for consolidation of power. Rather, her concern emanates from the possibility that the theoretical requirement for a "unitary will" in order to legitimize popular sovereignty might *unduly restrict* the power of the people, because "the populace changes constantly," neither the population of the people nor their will achieves unification at any point.[11]

9. Connolly, *Facing the Planetary*, 27.

10. Ibid., 148.

11. Espejo, *Time of Popular Sovereignty*, 2.

Popular sovereignty even more than monarchical sovereignty falls to critiques of dinunity. If such unification is impossible to demonstrate in the case of a single individual, then how much less likely is an entire populace to demonstrate unity? Since such unification of will cannot be shown to occur in a populace, how is it that those of us living in democracies can support the legitimacy of our governments? Espejo argues that the concept of popular sovereignty "gets its strength from . . . the promise of unification of the popular will" in some distant future, or alternatively from the notion that the popular will had been unified at the nation's inception.[12]

Complicating this disunity even further, not only are the members of the populace not of one mind, the members are not even the same members over periods of time. People die, others are born, some move away and new members arrive. At the most basic levels, then, "the people" remains indeterminate, never achieving stable form. How does one legitimize rule in the context of never-ending flux that fails to unify?

The challenge that democratic theory sustains in the face of this indeterminacy has so far been resolved via one of two unsatisfactory approaches, according to Espejo. The first is to sustain "democratic legitimacy" of the will of the people "while tolerating paradox" insofar as the people's will can never have been shown to be unified at any point. This opens any government claiming to operate democratically vulnerable to allegations that they have misappropriated "the name of the people to establish the hegemony of a group."[13] The second approach rejects the logical inconsistency, and with it the concept of "the people as a ground of legitimacy." Ultimately the second approach leads some—especially "philosophical anarchists and critics of liberal democratic politics," Espejo notes—to "dismiss the people as a dangerous fabrication that masks the realities of power." Both options have inherent weaknesses.

The first option, tolerating the paradox, could be said to lead to the sorts of totalitarianism and fascism typical of the Schmittian sovereign via an alternate route. Maintaining the paradox that the will of the people is never unified yet possesses democratic legitimacy requires maintaining a vacancy similar to that required by Barth's version of sovereignty. However, in the case of popular sovereignty, what is vacated is a precise definition of "the people." Espejo asserts that totalitarianism results from the need to produce a unified people in order to validate popular sovereignty. In this case, it is not the decision on the exception that leads to the devolution into

12. Ibid., 5. For example at the drafting of the constitution.

13. Ibid., 11. Nearly every presidential administration is guilty of such imposition, given no president in modern history has been unanimously elected, yet each behaves as if his priorities are universally endorsed by Americans.

totalitarianism. Rather, it is the persistent failure of "the People" to integrate "the people," as Agamben illustrated.

The second option, dismissing "the people" altogether, Espejo, derides as a failure of imagination curtailing hope of creatively imagining a desirable political order. There is little point in striving for a more just political order if one has already concluded that such an order is unobtainable. Democracy may be the "worst form of government, aside from all those other forms that have been tried from time to time," as Churchill quipped, but to abandon it altogether seems to be an "out of the frying pan into the fire" situation.[14]

Espejo observes that "the root of the indeterminacy problem is the demand made by theories of popular sovereignty that the people be a fixed and stable thing that seeks to conform to the ideal version of itself, such that its internal changes do not alter the essential nature of the state it founds."[15] Even if the people shift in membership or opinions, the state comes to represent "the will of the people" and as such is construed as both good and immutable. Thus, "the will of the people" is tinted with a more or less orthodox theological tone and dualist metaphysics much as is the case with Schmittian sovereignty.

The theological and metaphysical dimension of political theory is not lost on Espejo, who contends that the requirement for unification "depends on beliefs and metaphysical commitments that are seldom questioned, despite not often being justified in moral or political terms."[16] These metaphysical commitments cannot be easily abandoned, in part because they form the kernel of the contrarian arguments most often deployed to "legitimize the modern state."[17] Espejo asserts that much political philosophy is embedded in a dualist philosophy. By contrast, Espejo formulates her theory of "people as process" through an integration of nondualist process-oriented metaphysics with political theory.

Through recourse to process-oriented philosophies with an emphasis on dynamic becoming rather than static being, Espejo is free from a need to demonstrate the unification of the people. Further, she is also freed from the need to envision "the will of the people" as immutable or necessarily good. Rather, "the people as process is a source of democratic legitimacy that moors state institutions while remaining compatible with change, surprise, and innovation. It can both sustain democratic institutions and accommodate people's indeterminacy because it does not seek a

14. Jasieweicz, "The Churchill Hypothesis," 169.
15. Espejo, *Time of Popular Sovereignty*, 11.
16. Ibid., 12.
17. Ibid.

predetermined goal."[18] As such, it does not legitimize itself on the basis of past, present or future unification.

Yet Espejo's theory of the people as process retains the notion of a "general will . . . as a tendency defined by the expectations of many individuals."[19] The people as process is comprised of "a fleeting community of hopes, expectations memories and fraternal feelings, periodically subject to drastic and unexpected changes."[20] This community encounters institutions and sets of practices that condition and constrain their actions as individuals. Both "the people as process" and the practices and institutions with which they interact "are related in a process of becoming."[21] One hears echoes of Baradian agential realism in this description, not to mention Keller's theology of becoming.

If the open-ended indeterminacy and relational process of becoming characteristic of Espejo's people as process bears resonances to Keller's theology of becoming, that is because Keller and Espejo share an intellectual lineage. Espejo, inspired by her mentor William Connolly, draws from a philosophical lineage that includes Leibniz, Hegel, Bergson, Whitehead, Deleuze and others—the same intellectual wellspring from which Keller draws (and to which Keller contributes). Espejo does not feel compelled to convince her readers that processes are either "a product of cognition, the nature of life, or the nature of all material reality."[22] It will suffice for her purposes to claim that processes are a basic component of social life. To suggest that a people is a process means, to Espejo, that a people is a series of coordinated events involving a self-creative aim.

Espejo is quick to clarify that process thinking does not imply that everything is in such flux that identity is impossible. Some things do endure over time, and process philosophy permits the examination of entities from the perspective of both durability and fluctuation.[23] As a corollary, process thinking does not deny all forms of self-identity, although process thinking would contend that any "self" that existed across time was constituted as a temporally ordered series of iterative events, rather than as the persistence of a static condition. That is to say, although most things undergo transformation over time, they nonetheless remain recognizable "for as long as they

18. Ibid., 13.
19. Ibid.
20. Ibid., 13.
21. Ibid.
22. Ibid., 141.
23. Ibid., 143.

last." For example, a given person never ceases to change throughout their lives, yet they typically remain recognizable from day to day.

The key features of process thought that Espejo seeks to employ in theorizing "people as process" include "events," "coordination," and "self-creation." An event is an occurrence in a particular time and space. Using the term "event" allows Espejo to "describe social facts as activities and relations rather than substances or essences."[24] In order to qualify as events, the occurrences must be coordinated by conceptual goals (although these need not be conscious), causal limitations, and randomness" The conceptual goals motivating events do not consist of idealized, static forms awaiting actualization. Rather, the pattern unfolds iteratively and "it is always the result of concrete occurrences."[25] Events do not take place in absolute freedom, because they are constrained by other events.

Because Espejo is crafting a *political* people, not just any event will do. First of all, people events must be characterized by coordination. A political conversation at a coffee house and a democratic election alike could be "considered part of the people" because each is coordinated in relation to "practices of constituting, governing, or changing a set of institutions, which are the *highest* authority . . . for those affected by the institutions in questions."[26] By Espejo's standards, "political events restricted to your club, your city block, or your province don't count."[27] Incidentally, she is denies that the decision "whether to grill or broil chicken for tonight's dinner" could count as a people event. This is a standard I find troubling and about which I will say more shortly.

Participation in people events is not restricted along lines of citizenship, or even necessarily of geography. According to Espejo, participation is open to "all those individuals intensely affected by the supremely authoritative institutions and by the events that modify the institutions. A person is intensely affected by those institutions when they can coerce her and there are no alternative institutions that would allow her to continue her normal life."[28] This, she notes, is not a normative claim based upon entitlement of individuals. Rather, it is an ontological claim regarding the events and relations that comprise a people. By virtue of the impact

24. Ibid., 145.
25. Ibid., 146–47.
26. Ibid., 158.
27. Ibid.
28. Ibid., 159.

of particular institutions and practices upon one's life, one immediately "partakes of the people."[29]

Espejo is adamant that people as process is not about an aggregate of individuals. Rather, it is about the humans and nonhumans related in particular sets of coordinated events unfolding over time. A "coordinated series of events unfolding over time" would, in Baradian terms, be regarded as material-discursive apparatuses that specifically relate to the highest authority in one's life. These sets of material-discursive apparatuses are unavoidable. And because they are apparatuses, they leave marks on bodies. They shape the material conditions of one's becoming. Espejo's concept of "the people as process" is so expansive as to permit the inclusion of "related processes like the market, the environment, and international pressures" as among those highest authorities which constitute people events.[30]

Once one partakes of the people, one has a "good moral claim to certain rights over those people events" that affect one's life.[31] Espejo argues that even undocumented workers have good moral claims on the nation in which they currently reside. She cites the example of an indigenous servant living in colonial Peru. By Espejo's account, this servant was intensely affected by the Spanish empire, and therefore "partook of the people of Spain." Subsequently, had the Spanish Empire been otherwise configured—for example as a democratic republic—this servant would have had a legal claim to rights. Even in the absence of legal rights, however, Espejo insists that "he had a good moral claim to those rights."[32] The *moral* claim stands, despite the absence of *legal* rights in the context of the Spanish Empire.

If a Peruvian servant partakes of the peoplehood of Spain, the peasant farmers in developing nations who grow food for American citizens also, by Espejo's calculations, have a "good moral claim" to some rights from the transnational corporations and multilateral trade agencies setting agricultural agendas. They may, for example, have a moral claim to be freed from pressures to adopt high-input agricultural methods that are cost-prohibitive for smallholders in the short run and deplete the soil in the long run. A political theology of food demands that these claims be honored.

Organizations such as the Pachamama Alliance that support food sovereignty and indigenous rights in Latin America speak in terms of the "rights" of the nonhuman, raising questions as to whether Espejo's "people as process" might prove sufficiently elastic to stretch to nonhuman

29. Ibid.

30. Ibid., 161.

31. Ibid., 160.

32. Ibid.

"persons"—or even nonhuman nonpersons. In some cases, the nonhuman world may make moral claims upon human social, political, and economic structures as well, as the nonhuman world is also intensely affected by these structures. For example, what moral claims to freedom from abuse might be made by a cow *en route* to slaughter after enduring the confines of a concentrated animal feeding organization? What moral claims to freedom might a farm-raised salmon make? Or for that matter, the rivers and oceans that the salmon call home? Might there be a way in which these broader concerns, vitally important to a political theology of food, might find expression in the concept of people as process?

Let us revisit the decision whether to broil or fry chicken for dinner. Previously, Espejo suggested that this type of decision could not be considered a people event. Admittedly, it is possible that even within the context of food politics the decision between broiling versus frying is likely not a political decision, and may not qualify as a people event. However, I would suggest that decision whether or not to eat chicken at all *might* qualify as a people event.

Increasing numbers of people are now choosing vegetarian and vegan food plans in part because they perceive chickens and poultry workers as making a moral claim to better living and working conditions. These food plans are often preferred in part because of their lower carbon footprint as well. In response to nonhuman moral claims, there are those who find morally repugnant the inhumane treatment of poultry—confined to tiny cages, and selectively bred for breast size at the expense of the ability to even stand up. Concerns about the ethical integrity of our food system are not restricted to poultry. Many people are eating lower on the food chain in order to reduce their carbon footprint. Vegetarian options or locally raised, pastured, grass-fed beef are also preferred by many who acutely perceive their moral complicity in the treatment of livestock. Some, in recognition of the "good moral claim" to rights on the part of coffee growers purchase only fair-trade coffee.

As I cannot stress enough, ethical eating alone will not shift our food system toward ecological sustainability. Given that 40 percent of the food produced in the US finds its way to the dump, clearly demand has been divorced from supply such that alterations in demand are likely to be of little impact. Yet, as already discussed in chapter two, the financial, political, and agricultural institutions currently shaping our food system are the highest authorities in our society. Subsequently, if a political conversation in a coffee house counts as a people event, it is challenging in the present context to imagine that making an ethical decision regarding what to have for dinner does not also count. A political theology of food perceives ethical eating as a "people event" because it is coordinated in relation to "practices of constituting, governing, or changing a set of institutions," effectiveness or lack thereof notwithstanding. And, more to the point of nonhuman "rights," ethical eating can function as a people event that recognizes the "good moral claim" of the nonhuman world to be liberated from oppression by human systems.

Re-Membering the People

Espejo's "people as process" overcomes several problematic components of popular sovereignty that in many regards mirror those already identified with Schmittian sovereignty. Meanwhile her "people as process" validates the legitimacy of "the people" as rightfully capable of demanding some laws and structures, while resisting others. Espejo's "people as process" could be used to legitimate the moral claim of peasant farmers to some rights from the transnational corporations and multilateral trade agencies setting agricultural agendas, and also to highlight the political nature of ethical eating as a "people event."

My applications of Espejo's "people as process" seem to take her theory in directions she does not necessarily intend or endorse. They could, in fact be seen as diluting the potency of a people by virtue of the transnational, global tendrils of connection between "peoples" and some of the highest authorities in their lives—the transnational corporations and multilateral agencies determining how food is produced and distributed worldwide. Yet, this dilution of both moral accountability and political power seems inherent within the global food system.

And if "related processes like the market, the environment, and international pressures" are among the authorities that establish a people as process, then certainly the corporate food regime would seem to be a legitimate series of people events. Resituating a people by virtue of the "highest authorities" active in their lives in the context of transnational global capitalism re-collects, re-members, "the people" across national, geographic, and ethnic boundaries—boundaries staunchly defended by nationalists and fascists of many varieties. Perhaps this is a good thing? Espejo's theory at least begins to identify how we might view ourselves as political agents morally accountable to a myriad of other unknown Others, and how we might find ourselves in solidarity with them despite our various other markers of social location.

"People as process" further begins to shift our perception of these relations. We in the Global North are not reduced to the role of guilty oppressors. We are participants in a people. When some in the Global North learn about the injustices, the environmentally destructive practices, the animal cruelty, they want to divorce themselves from these practices. But once they seek alternatives, they are faced with their limited capacity to exit the global food system. They cannot afford to buy locally grown organic produce, or humanely raised grass-fed beef, because the production of these foodstuffs is not subsidized in the way that conventional agricultural products are subsidized. Or they may not live in an area where these items are available. The fact that we are in some regards constrained by the same institutions as are landless peasants could shift our self-perception from "oppressor in the Global North" to "someone in the Global North who also encounters oppression within the global food system." This shift is subtle, and as with all things process, this shift holds no guarantee. But perhaps there is something to the self-definition as "oppressor" that incapacitates effective political action, whereas identifying ourselves as also constrained suddenly clarifies our skin in the game.

The oppressions in the global food system are differential, to be sure, and we in the Global North are indeed privileged. Retaining a sufficient sense of privilege to give us hope of changing this system is a good thing. Simultaneously, we have to realize what is at stake. We are already losing access to nutritious food, and we are losing the capacity to make ethically and ecologically sound choices because the corporate regime has eclipsed our power. Since we are already losing these benefits—and stand to lose much more should climate crises suddenly disrupt our food system—we might gain greater commitment to genuine solidarity with landless peasants and migrant farm workers by recognizing the oppression that we, too, encounter.

"The people as process" also holds great benefit as regards the application of human rights language to the question of food. As discussed in earlier chapters, in the context of our climate-induced mass migration such rights are rather fragile, dependent as they are upon notions of citizenship for their enforcement. Some versions of popular sovereignty contend that both territorial boundaries and recognition of a people by a third party is required for the recognition of a people. However, "the people as process" does not view peoples as territorially or legally bounded, as do many conceptions of popular sovereignty.[33] The existence of "a people as process" arises in relation to "internal institutions and interactions, and they may be nested in one another, flow into one another, or separate from one another if the rate and intensity of interactions ceases."[34] From the perspective of

33. Ibid., 167.
34. Ibid.

"a people as process," climate refugees would not lose the moral right to food simply because they do not hold citizenship. Certainly, they will be intensely affected by a new set of highest authorities, and while this will not give them the moral claim to citizenship, it will nonetheless recognize their moral claim to food.

Espejo has devised a way for "a democratic people as process" to "rule itself democratically without unifying reason and will," yet even this process is not entirely self-determining.[35] Other events and forces impinge upon the outcome, for example: unconscious motivations of participants; other peoples; unanticipated consequences of decisions; and blind luck. Furthermore, a popular decision cannot be declared a "good" solely on the basis of its popularity. This is a significant qualification, and not to be passed over lightly. At the same time, this is true of every political decision and is the very reason why a transcendent source of valuation is so frequently sought. In summary, then, Espejo has theorized a model of popular sovereignty that avoids the hazards of requiring unification or transcendent validation.

Simultaneously this model *does* shine a spotlight on the less than democratic nature of our food system in a way that clarifies the limitations of its "goodness." This model inherently critiques our global food system as undemocratic, because, as Espejo writes, a democratic people only arises when "those individuals who partake in the people, and who are affected by its decisions, have an equal say in the process of making, governing, and changing the institutions that rule them."[36] The starving and the obese— along with peasant farmers—have been banned from substantive contribution to decision-making regarding agricultural production and distribution in the corporate regime. However, Espejo's "people as process" could potentially animate more robust political transformation of the food system if these groups could recognize their collective peoplehood.

Espejo concludes by agreeing "with the philosophical anarchist critics that all currently existing states are illegitimate," yet she believes that the state must be tolerated as a necessary evil. She does not go so far as to promise a utopic solution to the problems inherent in the state form, however. Nonetheless, she maintains "that if you don't have at least the logical possibility of legitimate government, then there is no good reason to try to improve it."[37] Espejo's tolerance of the state as a necessary evil awaiting our remediation directly counters Schmitt's perception of the sovereign as *katechon*, restraining the Antichrist until the solution descends from above to impose a lasting

35. Ibid., 185.
36. Ibid.
37. Ibid., 192–93.

order. By Espejo's account, the solution will arise from within "the experience of creative freedom."[38] Creative freedom will be much needed as we endeavor to coax new forms from wreckage of the old.

Tolerating the state as a necessary evil decidedly does not equal granting any nation-states (or their leaders) *absolute* sovereignty. Indeed, absolutes tend to fall by the wayside in a political theology of food with roots in process philosophy. Process philosophy recognizes both self-determination and limitation: a photon may appear as wave or particle in its interaction with an apparatus; it will not appear as a giraffe. The sovereignty of a "people as process" is an extension and expression of self-organizational potency in the context of causal limitation characteristic of all materializations. A nation-state becomes visible of one of many modes of self-organization, rather than an absolute good or absolute evil. The goodness of any nation-state hinges on its willingness to hold itself morally accountable to and for those impacted by its processes.

Reflecting back on Faser and Rimas's insistence that an effective solution to a pending food crisis (and corresponding civilizational collapse) is unlikely in the absence of effective legislation, it would seem that an intact nation-state could in fact be a good thing. That is, provided it views its national boundaries—both physical, territorial boundaries as well as the more or less bounded sets of material-discursive practices in which it engages—as somewhat provisional. All boundaries exhibit some degree of porosity and flux. They might better be regarded as surfaces of exchange with externalities, not merely defenses from them. In this context, legislation is one means by which a territorially organized people articulates its general preferences in relationship to deterritorialized transnational corporations. For if corporations are people and tax donations are political speech, certainly "the people" must have some way of collectively speaking back. The eating public may choose to speak on behalf of peasant farmers in this conversation, while selectively appropriating aspects of industrial agriculture.

Embracing the demands of landless peasants that the sovereignty of their nation-states be recognized simultaneously inscribes a limitation to the sovereignty of *other* entities, such as multilateral trade organizations, transnational corporations, and other nation states. To honor claims of sovereignty made by a people as process (such as the food sovereignty movement) is not synonymous with granting the movement absolute authority to determine how the rest of the world should farm. It is, however, to honor the decision of a sovereign "people as process" to use Espejo's descriptor—or the delineation of a collective, to use Latour's term. This "people as process,"

38. Ibid., 195.

having organized itself through a rigorous process of perplexity, consultation, hierarchization and institution—numerous "people events" large and small—has determined that transnational corporate agriculture has at best a limited role in their collective.

Conclusion

A political theology of food seeks modes of sociality capable of collecting humans and nonhumans across boundaries of nation, geography, ethnicity and religious affiliation for the purposes of promoting mutually abundant flourishing. These self-organizing collectives cannot base their claims to legitimacy upon their unity, or their ability to guarantee security and goodness, and especially not on their ability to suspend entirely the principles by which they have consented to collect. In other words, their legitimacy must be sought in an entirely different framework than that in which Schmitt's sovereign found his. Schmitt theorized sovereignty anchored by a dualist metaphysics that does not square with nondualist experiences of reality (disclosed by science studies). A political theology of food, emanating from a nondualist metaphysics and responding to the perils of climate change, sees excessive risk in the sovereign's suspension of law, its claims to unity, and its false promises to provide security.

Paulina Ochoa Espejo's "people as process" provides a sampling of the sorts of politics that would be resonant with the metaphysical image of our epoch as iterative and process-oriented and its valuation of the immanent material plane. Espejo has disarticulated the people's claims to legitimacy from claims to its unity. A "people" exists by virtue of their relationship to the authorities which impact their lives. A geographically distributed "people" impinged upon by the corporate food regime comes into sharper focus through this lens. Validity of moral claims is distinguished from the provision of legal protections, resituating human rights dialogue as a moral rather than legal question.

Espejo does not declare the decisions of a people good simply by virtue of their popularity—or presumably even their purported necessity for preservation of a people. The moral value of a people's decisions is related to the impact of these decisions upon participants (including those whose participation is largely involuntary). This shifts profoundly the context in which the friend/enemy distinction is made, and calls into question the validity of states of exception in ways that time does not permit me to explore here. Espejo does not grapple with issues of security, but a political theology of food insists that a people is only as secure as its commitment to the welfare of all of its participants. A "people as process" remedies some of the critiques of sovereignty regarding unity, the decision on the exception, and promises of security.

Espejo's political theory of popular sovereignty has the capacity to support food movements that resist the totalizing maneuvers of transnational corporate agriculture—even when these food movements demand national sovereignty. When applied to the question of food politics, this political theory might facilitate solidarity between the Global North and the Global South. We in the Global North, as part of the "eating public" participate in "people moments" with each forkful of food we eat. Meanwhile, Espejo's "people as process" redraws the political and ethical map such that we are not related solely by virtue of territorial boundaries or citizenship status. Most importantly, it clarifies the "good moral claim" of *homo sacer*, the Other who asks that we not let him die alone.

Conclusion

THE CONCEPT OF SOVEREIGNTY is historically entangled with the global food trade. The global food trade has long been characterized by asymmetrical flows of power and capital, and sovereignty has historically reinforced that asymmetry. Conceptually, political sovereignty shares structural parallels and historical lineage with the theological concept of sovereignty. Rarely has an analysis of the concept of sovereignty as it appears in global food politics been undertaken, despite the fact that global food trade has precipitated contestations over sovereignty since at least the latter part of the medieval era. Not only has sovereignty as a historical concept seldom been applied to global food politics, sovereignty as a theological concept has not been applied in this arena.[1] This political theology of food has undertaken the analysis of the concept of sovereignty as it appears in global food politics in part to address this lack.

The sovereign, modeled on a transcendent God, is characterized by unity; guarantees security for those under the auspices of his protection; decisively suspends the system of law in order to annihilate existential threats. When applied to global food politics the political concept of sovereignty fractures along those fault lines. Theologically, the claim that the theological concept of sovereignty can be secularized and transferred to a creaturely human is dubious at best. Unity is a condition that never quite obtains—certainly not in a nation-state and not even for a given individual. A new materialist analysis demonstrates that the materialization of the human body—and behavior and cognition along with it—arises as the result of its perpetual intra-actions with food and social structures. Whatever measure of security is established under the leadership of a sovereign, it is far from

1. At least as of the date of this writing.

absolute. Not only is it temporally limited, it is at best unevenly distributed to the sovereign's subjects.

Finally, it is unlikely to the point of being impossible that any human act of sovereignty will resolve the existential threat posed by climate change. This is all the more relevant in the context of global food politics, as the vulnerability of the food system is already being exposed in the early stages of climate change. Simultaneously, global food trade produces up to 30 percent of greenhouse gas emissions, magnifying its most significant existential threat rather than reducing it. The existential threat posed by climate change is likely to be perpetual, unpredictable and uncontrollable for the next several decades. Enactments of sovereignty are likely to worsen rather than improve the situation in part because these enactments prematurely simplify complex situations, expelling numerous factors from the good common world. These factors do not disappear; they return to haunt the collective, in the words of Bruno Latour.

And yet, the food sovereignty movement, operating as a radically democratic assemblage, demands sovereignty, both for the movement and its members and for their respective nation-states. Is it possible to defend the movement against the critiques that a Schmittian would likely level against their procedures? Likewise, is it possible to support their demand for a stronger nation-state despite the critiques of those on the left aimed at the nation-state and its abuses of power? Can we support their use of "rights" language despite its reliance upon problematic notions of citizenship and state, especially in light of the massive displacement of people likely to occur (and already occurring) as climate change progresses?

A political theology of food insists that the problems with Schmittian sovereignty are not eliminated simply by disbanding the nation-state. From this vantage point, the corporate food regime can be seen to enact an economic rendition of Schmittian sovereignty, yet this regime is not attached to any nation-state. It could be said to be a supersovereign, or at least a manifestation of the larger supersovereign that transnational global capitalism has become. This supersovereign claims to embrace the principles of democracy, but is shown to betray those principles with regularity.

Some of the greatest threats posed by this supersovereign are quite similar to those posed by the Schmittian sovereign as identified by Agamben's *Homo Sacer* and *State of Exception*. These threats arise due to the corporate food regime's (supersovereign and) manic obsession with unification and intolerance of differences. Only one economic system will do: neoliberal capitalism. Only one agricultural method can be legitimated: industrial high-input agriculture. As Agamben attests, what cannot be integrated in this push toward unification—agroecological methods, smallholders, peasant farmers—is often targeted for elimination. Socially, this is reflected in staggering amounts of oppression, persecution, violent conflict and dislocation.

Agriculturally, this is reflected in the mandate that developing nations retool their agricultural systems in order to produce cash crops for global trade at the expense of producing staple crops for local consumption. This further requires the use of industrial agricultural methods that deplete soil, poison waterways and contribute to global climate change. Could the carnage caused by a sovereign directly relate to size of the territory and population ruled? If so, contemplation of the potential for suffering is mind-numbing in the circumstance of a global supersovereign. It is to some degree a desire to ward off those threats that inspires the food sovereignty movement to demand nation-state sovereignty.

Although the concept of national sovereignty props up lethal totalitarian regimes, it simultaneously provides a stop-gap measure against an even *more* totalizing, absolute global sovereignty. A political theology of food rethinks sovereignty—popular and national—divorcing its validity from the concept of unification (either of God or sovereign) associated with many problematic outcomes of deployments of sovereignty. A political theology of food further urges that sovereignty not be construed as necessarily the unlimited authority to suspend law, as with Schmitt, or the capacity to resist, as with Crockett.

Instead, this political theology of food has argued for sovereignty as the power to do otherwise—perhaps even the power to embrace a multiplicity of options. We will need numerous options as extreme weather events proliferate, thwarting our best efforts to grow food in a changing climate. Additionally, this political theology of food has sought other ways to think about God—a concept that underwrites sovereignty—that are more reflective of the metaphysical image of our epoch as disclosed by science studies and described by new materialism. Images of God are potent models for political structures; it is in the public interest to generate and embrace more promising images.

Process and feminist theologies such as Catherine Keller's theology of becoming are more consonant with the metaphysical image of our epoch as disclosed by science studies than is the orthodox theology upon which Schmitt modeled his concept of sovereignty. Keller's God is intimately entangled with the fluctuating material world. Rather than overpowering it in order to assure security, this God seductively coaxes order from chaos again and again, and invites us to do the same. Keller articulates an immanent framework for ethical responsiveness capable of responding to Schmitt's assertion that the immanent domain does not provide such a source. Keller's is a particularly inspirational vision in the context of climate-induced chaos, from which we will need to coax order again and again if the human civilizations are to endure.

Resonant with Keller's theology of becoming because it is drawn from the same process philosophical wellspring, Paulina Ochoa Espejo's "people as process" provides a framework useful for navigating the paradoxical claims to sovereignty made by the food sovereignty movement. Espejo's model of popular soveriegnty liberates the sovereignty of a people from the concept of unity by refusing to legitimate the sovereignty of a people on the basis of past, present, or future unification. In fact, unification is not a goal. The goal is to permit those who are unavoidably affected by authoritative institutions to have an equal say in the decisions made by those institutions. Because the goal is not unification, this model sidesteps some of the pitfalls of traditional, Schmittian sovereignty.

Popular sovereignty based upon the notion of a "people as process" establishes a framework for resisting the totalizing maneuvers of transnational corporate agriculture. This framework is capable of establishing a "people" even across national boundaries, as a "people" is defined by the highest authorities in their lives, from whose grasp they cannot escape. In the context of the authority of the corporate food system, we in the Global North—whether geographically or socioeconomically—can find ourselves in a shared peoplehood with those in the Global South. On the one hand, we are relatively privileged, but at best relatively so, and we, too, will face catastrophes as climate change worsens. Yet because the sovereignty of a "people as process" does not require unification in the same manner that traditional models of sovereignty do, these differences do not eclipse our togetherness with people in the Global South.

A political theology of food supports the food sovereignty movement, its people and its platform. Validation of this movement does not therefore mean that all other approaches to agricultural production and distribution must be immediately abandoned. A political theology of food does not support unification around *any* single agricultural method. An abrupt unification around agroecological farming and local consumption would consign billions of people to starvation. However, continued unification around industrial agriculture *also* threatens billions of people as well as uncountable species. Diversification of nested local-regional-global food systems surfaces as an advantageous approach to a complex set of problems.

Above all, a political theology of food hopes to empower potent food activism. We need all hands on deck. Nothing in Espejo's concept of a people insists that differential positions within power structures thwarts the formation of a people. Transporting Espejo's people as process to the realm of global food politics demonstrates that Global North and Global South alike are subject to the authority of the corporate food regime and hence form a people. By calling attention to the increased vulnerability resulting from the sovereign decision, the intra-active becoming of human flesh, and the threat posed by climate change, a political theology of food illuminates what is at stake for all of us—even those of us in the Global North who are relatively food secure at the moment.

The news about climate change is bad, and the forecast even worse. Fortunately, the metaphysics of perpetual becoming disclosed by science studies means that change is not only possible it is inevitable—and it could even be change for the better. Various sociopolitical changes could potentially minimize the loss of lives, human and nonhuman alike. Because the global food system is both causative of and vulnerable to climate change, it is potentially a pivotal site for intervention. Might we capitalize on what Espejo calls "people moments" small and large—from the level of the food we choose to eat to the level of policies for which we advocate—in our intra-actions with the global food system to create changes for the better?

Bibliography

Agamben, Giorgio. *Homo Sacer: Sovereign Power and Bare Life*. Stanford: Stanford University Press, 1998.

————. *State of Exception*. Chicago: University of Chicago Press, 2005.

————. *The Time That Remains*. Stanford: Stanford University Press, 2005.

Aguilar, Maria, et al. "Prevalence of the Metabolic Syndrome in the United States 2003-2012." *Journal of the American Medical Association* 313 (2015) 1973–74. https://doi:10.1001/jama.2015.4260.

Ahmed, Nafeez. "Former BP Geologist: Peak Oil Is Here and It Will 'Break Economies.'" *The Guardian*, December 23, 2013, https://www.theguardian.com/environment/earth-insight/2013/dec/23/british-petroleum-geologist-peak-oil-break-economy-recession.

Alkon, Alison Hope, and Julian Agyeman. *Cultivating Food Justice: Race, Class, Sustainability*. Boston: MIT Press, 2011.

Allen, Edgar Leonard. *The Sovereignty of God and the Word of God: A Guide to the Thought of Karl Barth*. New York: New York Philosophical Library, 1951.

Antonello, Pierpaolo, and Roberto Farneti. "Antigone's Claim: A Conversation with Judith Butler." *Theory & Event* 12 (2009). Project Muse. https://muse.jhu.edu/article/263144/pdfAssociation for the Study of Peak Oil. "Peak Oil Review." Peak-Oil.org., July 18, 2016, http://peak-oil.org/peak-oil-review-18-jul-2016/.

Barad, Karen. *Meeting the Universe Halfway: Quantum Physics and the Entanglement of Matter and Meaning*. Durham: Duke University Press, 2007.

Barber, Dan. *The Third Plate: Field Notes on the Future of Food*. New York: Penguin, 2014.

Barth, Karl. *Community, State, and Church: Three Essays*. New York: Anchor, 1960.

————. *The Humanity of God*. Richmond: John Knox, 1946.

Bellio, David. "Can Climate Change Cause Conflict? Recent History Suggests So." *Scientific American*, November 23, 2009, https://www.scientificamerican.com/article/can-climate-change-cause-conflict/.

Benford, Robert D., and David A Snow. "Framing Processes and Social Movements: An Overview and Assessment." Annual Review of Sociology 26 (2000) 611–39.

Benjamin, Walter. "Critique of Violence." In *Selected Writings*, edited by Edmund Jephcott, 277–300. Cambridge: Harvard University Press, 1999.

————. *The Origin of German Tragic Drama*. Translated by John Osborne. New York: Verso, 1998.

Bennett, Jane. "Vegetal Life and OntoSympathy." In Entangled Worlds: Religion, Science, and New Materialisms, edited by Catherine Keller and Mary-Jane Rubenstein, 89–110. New York, Fordham University Press 2017.

————. *Vibrant Matter: A Political Ecology of Things*. Durham: Duke University Press, 2010.

Betcher, Sharon V. *Spirit and the Obligation of Social Flesh: A Secular Theology for the Global City*. New York: Fordham University Press, 2014.

Beus, Curtis E., and Riley Dunlap. "Conventional versus Alternative Agriculture: The Paradigmatic Roots of the Debate." *Rural Sociology* (1990) 590–616.

Black, Richard. "Climate 'Is a Major Cause' of Conflict in Africa." *BBC News*, November 24, 2009, http://news.bbc.co.uk/2/hi/science/nature/8375949.stm.

Bleich, J. David. "Vegetarianism and Judaism." In *Judaism and Environmental Ethics*, edited by Martin D. Yaffe, 371–83. New York: Lexington, 2001.

Boyarin, Daniel. "The Jewish Life of the Logos: Logos Theology in Pre-and Pararabbinic Judaism." In *Border Lines: The Partition of Judeo Christianity*, by Daniel Boyarin, 89–127. Philadelphia: University of Pennsylvania Press, 2004.

Britt, Brian. "The Schmittian Messiah in Agamben's The Time That Remains." *Critical Inquiry* 36 (2010) 262–87.

Brooks, David. "A Return to National Greatness: A Manifesto for a Lost Creed." *The Weekly Standard,* March 3, 1997, http://www.weeklystandard.com/what-to-do-about-iraq/article/2064.

Butler, Judith. *Giving and Account of Oneself*. New York: Fordham University Press, 2005.

————. "Is Judaism Zionism?" In *The Power of Religion in the Public Sphere*, edited by Eduardo Mendieta and Jonathan Vanantwerpen, 70–91. New York: Columbia University Press, 2011.

————. *Precarious Life: The Power of Mourning and Violence*. New York: Verso, 2004.

Carr, Deborah, and Michael A. Friedman. "Is Obesity Stimatizing? Body Weight, Perceived Discrimination, and Psychological Well-Being in the United States." *Journal of Health and Social Behavior* 46 (2005) 244–59.

Center for Disease Control. "Obesity and Socioeconomic Status." NCHS Data Brief 50, December 2010. https://www.cdc.gov/nchs/products/databriefs/db50.htm.

————. "Stats of the State of California." CDC.org., 2014. https://www.cdc.gov/nchs/pressroom/states/california/california.htm.

Chokshi, Niraj. "Stop Bashing G.M.O. Foods, More Than 100 Nobel Laureates Say." *The New York Times,* June 30, 2016. https://www.nytimes.com/2016/07/01/us/stop-bashing-gmo-foods-more-than-100-nobel-laureates-say.html.

Chu, Jennifer. "Study: Air Pollution Causes 200,000 Early Deaths Each Year in the U.S." *MIT News*, August 29, 2013. http://news.mit.edu/2013/study-air-pollution-causes-200000-early-deaths-each-year-in-the-us-0829.

Cline, William R. "Global Warming and Agriculture." *Finance and Development* 45 (2008). https://www.imf.org/external/pubs/ft/fandd/2008/03/cline.htm.

Cobb, John. *Process Theology as Political Theology*. Philadelphia: Westminster, 1982.

————. "Theology, Perception, and Agriculture." In *Agricultural Sustainability in a Changing World Order*, edited by Gordon K. Douglas, 205–17. Boulder, CO: Westview, 1984.

Cohn, Avery, et al. *Agroecology and the Struggle for Food Sovereignty in the Americas.* New Haven: Yale School of Forestry and Environmental Studies, 2006.

Connolly, William E. *Facing the Planetary: Entangled Humanism and the Politics of Swarming.* Durham: Duke University Press, 2017.

———. *The Fragility of Things: Self-organizing Processes, Neoliberal Fantasies, and Democratic Activism.* Durham: Duke University Press, 2013.

———. *Why I Am Not a Secularist.* Minneapolis: University of Minnesota Press, 1999.

Conversi, Daniele. "Sovereignty in a Changing World: From Westphalia to Food Sovereignty." *Globalizations* 13(2016) 484–98.

Copely, Gregory R. "The Big Picture Take on Geopolitical Instability." *Time,* January 14, 2016, http://time.com/4180507/geopolitics-big-picture/.

Counihan, Carole, and Penny Van Esterik. *Food and Culture: A Reader.* New York: Routledge, 2013.

Crockett, Clayton. *Radical Political Theology: Religion and Politics After Liberalism.* New York: Columbia University Press, 2011.

Crockett, Clayton, and Jeffrey W. Robbins. *Religion, Politics, and the Earth: The New Materialism.* New York: Palgrave MacMillan, 2012.

Dayen, David. "Trump Sides With Big Agriculture Over Family Famers: Even Some Republicans Are Upset Over This Corporate Handout." *The Nation,* October 18, 2017, https://www.thenation.com/article/trump-sides-with-big-agriculture-over-family-farmers/.

de Vries, Hent. "Introduction: Before, Around, and Beyond the Theologico-Political." In *Political Theologies: Public Religions in a Post-Secular World,* edited by Hent de Vries and Lawrence E. Sullivan, 1-88. New York: Fordham University Press, 2006.

de Wilde, Marc. "Meeting Opposites: The Political Theologies of Walter Benjamin and Carl Schmitt." *Philosophy and Rhetoric* 4 (2011) 363–81.

Derrida, Jacques. *The Beast and the Sovereign: Volume I.* Chicago: University of Chicago Press, 2008.

———. "Force of Law." *Cardozo Law Review* (1990) 920–1045.

———. *Rogues: Two Essays on Reason.* Stanford: Stanford University Press, 2005.

Diamond, Jared. *Collapse: How Societies Choose to Fail or Succeed.* New York: Viking, 2005.

Dumanoski, Dianne. *The End of the Long Summer.* New York: Crown, 2009.

Engelbrekt, Kjell. "What Carl Schmitt Picked Up in Weber's Seminar: A Historical Controversy Revisited." *The European Legacy* 14 (2009) 667–84.

Espejo, Paulina Ochoa. "Between a Rock and an Empty Place: Political Theology and Democratic Legitimacy." In *Common Gods: Economy, Ecology, and Political Theology,* edited by Melanie Johnson-DeBaufre, Catherine Keller, and Elias Ortega-Aponte, 307–25. New York: Fordham University Press, 2015.

———. *The Time of Popular Sovereignty: Process and the Democratic State.* University Park: The Pennsylvania State University Press, 2011.

Fairbairn, Madeleine. "Framing Resistance: International Food Regimes and the Roots of Food Sovereignty." In *Food Sovereignty: Reconnecting Food, Nature and Community,* edited by Hanna Wittman, Annette Aurelie Desmarais, and Nettie Wiebe, 5–30. Oakland: Food First, 2010.

Farid, Mai, et al. "After Paris: Fiscal, Macroeconomic, and Financial Implications of Climate Change. Staff Discussion Notes," Washington, DC: International Monetary Fund, 2016.

Faser, Evan D. G., and Andrew Rimas. *Empires of Food: Feast, Famine, and the Rise and Fall of Civilizations*. Berkeley: Counterpoint, 2010.

Ferdman, Roberto A. "The Decline of the American Family Farm in One Chart." *The Washington Post*, September 16, 2014, https://www.washingtonpost.com/news/wonk/wp/2014/09/16/the-decline-of-the-small-american-family-farm-in-one-chart/?utm_term=.ee058583d464.

Feuer, Alan. "Occupy Sandy: A Movement Moves to Relief." *The New York Times*, November 9, 2012, http://www.nytimes.com/2012/11/11/nyregion/where-fema-fell-short-occupy-sandy-was-there.html.

Field, C. B., et al. "2014: Summary for Policy Makers." In *Climate Change 2014: Impacts, Adaptation, and Vulnerability.Part A: Global and Sectoral Aspects. Contribution of Working Group II to the Fifth Assessment Report of the Intergovernmental Panel on Climate Change*, edited by C. B. Field, V. R. Barros, D. J. Dokken, K. J. Mach, M. D. Mastrandrea, and L. L. White, 1–32. New York: Cambridge University Press, 2014.

Food and Agriculture Organization of the United Nations. "Livestock's Long Shadow. Executive Summary." Rome: FAO, 2006.

———. "The State of Food Security of the World." New York: United Nations, 2015.

Fox, Jonathan. *Politics of Food in Mexico: State Power and Social Mobilization*. Center for US-Mexican Studies, 1993.

Friedmann, Harriet. "International Political Economy of Food: A Global Crisis." *New Left Review* (Jan/Feb 1993) 29–57.

———. "Moving food regimes forward: reflections on symposium essays." *Agriculture and Human Values* (2009) 335–44.

Friedmann, Harriet, and Philip McMichael. "Agriculture and the State System: The Rise and Decline of National Agricultures, 1870 to the Present." *Sociologia Ruralis* 29 (1989) 93–117.

Gearhardt, Ashley N., et. al. "Neural Correlates of Food Addiction." *Archives of General Psychiatry*, 2011.

Gilbert, Natasha. "One-Third of Our Greenhouse Gas Emissions Come from Agriculture." *Nature*, October 31, 2012, http://www.nature.com/news/one-third-of-our-greenhouse-gas-emissions-come-from-agriculture-1.11708.

Gold, Russel. "Why Peak Oil Predictions Haven't Come True." *Wall Street Journal*, September 14, 2014, http://www.wsj.com/articles/why-peak-oil-predictions-haven-t-come-true-1411937788.

Green, Arthur. *Radical Judaism: Rethinking God and Tradition*. New Haven: Yale University Press, 2010.

Griffin, David Ray, John B. Cobb Jr., Richard A. Falk, and Catherine Keller. *The American Empire and the Commonwealth of God*. Louisville: Westminster John Knox, 2006.

Gudmarsdottir, Sigridur. *Tillich and the Abyss: Foundations, Feminism, and Theology of Praxis*. London: Palgrave Macmillan, 2017.

Gupta, Akhil. "A Different History of the Present: The Movement of Crops, Cuisines, and Globalization." In *Curried Cultures: Globalization, Food, and South Asia*, edited by Krishnendu Ray and Tulasi Srinivas, 29–46. Los Angeles: University of California Press, 2012.

Hardt, Michael, and Antonio Negri. *Commonwealth*. Cambridge: Belknap/Harvard University Press, 2009.

———. *Empire*. Cambridge: Harvard University Press, 2000.

Hauter, Wenonah. *The Battle Over the Future of Food and Farming in America*. New York: New Press, 2012.

Henig, Ruth B. *The Weimar Republic 1919–1933*. London: Routledge, 2002.

Herberg, Will. "Introduction: The Social Philosophy of Karl Barth." In *Community, State and Church: Three Essays, by Karl Barth*, 11–67. New York: Anchor, 1960.

Holt-Giminez, Eric. *Campesino A Campesino: Voices from Latin America's Farmer to Famer Movement for Sustainable Agriculture*. Oakland: Food First, 2006.

Holt-Giminez, Eric, and Raj Patel. *Food Rebellions! Crisis and the Hunger for Justice*. Oakland: Food First, 2009.

"Hunger and World Poverty." Poverty.com. n.d. http://www.poverty.com/.

Hunger Notes. 2013 World Hunger and Poverty Facts. May 7, 2010. http://www.worldhunger.org/articles/Learn/world%20hunger%20facts%202002.htm.

Hyman, Mark. "How Malnutrition Causes Obesity." *Huffington Post*, March 3, 2012. http://www.huffingtonpost.com/dr-mark-hyman/malnutrition-obesity_b_1324760.html.

International Diabetes Foundation. "IDF Worldwide Definition of the Metabolic Syndrome." idf.org. 2006. http://www.idf.org/metabolic-syndrome.

International Monetary Fund. "IMF Factsheet: Climate, Environment, and the IMF." Washington, DC: International Monetary Fund, 2016.

Isovich, E., M. J. Mijnster, G. Flugge, and E. Fuchs. "Chronic Psychosocial Stress Reduces the Density of Dopamine Transporters." *European Journal of Neuroscience* (March 12, 2000) 1071–78.

Jasieweicz, Krzysztof. "The Churchill Hypothesis." *Journal of Democracy* (1999) 169–73.

Johnston, Sarah, and Jeffrey Mazo. "Global Warming and the Arab Spring." *Global Politics and Strategy* 53 (April 2011) 11–17.

Kagan, Robert, and William Kristol. "What to Do About Iraq." *The Weekly Standard*, January 21, 2002. http://www.weeklystandard.com/what-to-do-about-iraq/article/2064.

Kahn, Victoria. "Political Theology and Fiction in The King's Two Bodies." *Representations* (Spring 2009) 77–101.

Kalechofsky, Roberta. *Vegetarian Judaism: A Guide for Everyone*. Marblehead, MA: Micah, 1998.

Kantorowicz, Ernst. *The King's Two Bodies: A Study in Medieval Political Theology*. Princeton: Princeton University Press, 1997.

Kaplan, Gregory. "Power and Israel in Martin Buber's Critique of Carl Schmitt's Political Theology." In *Judaism, Liberalism & Political Theology*, edited by Randi Rashkover and Martin Kavka, 155–77. Bloomington: Indiana University Press, 2014.

Karl, Marilee, and Rocio Alorda. "Inseparable: The Crucial Role of Women in Food Security Revisited." *Women in Action* 1 (2009) 8–19.

Keith, Lierre. *The Vegetarian Myth: Food, Justice, and Sustainability*. Crescent City, CA: Flashpoint, 2009.

Keller, Catherine. *Apocalypse Now and then: A Feminist Guide to the End of the World*. Boston: Beacon, 1996.

———. "Be a Multiplicity: Ancestral Anticipations." In *Polydoxy: Theology of Multiplicity and Relation*, edited by Catherine Keller and Laurel C. Schneider, 81–101. New York: Routledge, 2011.

———. *Cloud of the Impossible: Negative Theology and Planetary Entanglement*. New York: Columbia University Press, 2015.

————. "Eschatology, Ecology, and a Green Ecumenacy." *Ecotheology* 2 (1997) 84–99.

————. *Face of the Deep: a Theology of Becoming*. New York: Routlege, 2003.

————. *From a Broken Web: Separation, Sexism, and Self*. Boston: Beacon, 1986.

————. *God and Power: Counter-Apocalyptic Journeys*. Minneapolis: Fortress, 2005.

————. *Intercarnations: Exercises in Theological Possibility*. New York: Fordham University Press, 2017.

————. *On the Mystery: Discerning Divinity in Process*. Minneapolis: Fortress, 2008.

————. "Talking Dirty: Ground Is Not Foundation." In *Ecospirit: Religions and Philosophies for the Earth*, edited by Laurel Kearns and Catherine Keller, 63–76. New York: Fordham University Press, 2007.

Khare, R. S. *The Eternal Food: Gastronomic Ideas and Experiences of Hindus and Buddhists*, Albany: State University of New York Press, 1992.

Klare, Michael T. *The Race for What's Left: The Global Scramble for the World's Last Resources*. New York: Metropolitan, 2012.

Klein, Naomi. *This Changes Everything: Capitalism vs. the Climate*. New York: Simon and Schuster, 2014.

Knight, Nika. "Leader of Honduran Campesino Movement Assassinated." Commondreams.org. October 19, 2016, http://www.commondreams.org/news /2016/10/19/leader-honduran-campesino-movement-assassinated.

Knorr, Dietrich Knorr, and Tom R. Watkins. *Alterations in Food Production*. New York: Van Nostrand Reinhold, 1984.

"La Via Campesina and Allies Push for the Declaration on Peasants' Rights in Geneva." Viacampesina.org. September 23, 2016, https://viacampesina.org/en/ index.php/main-issues-mainmenu-27/human-rights-mainmenu-40/peasants-right-resources/2146-la-via-campesina-and-allies-push-for-the-declaration-on-peasants-rights-in-geneva.

"La Via Campesina Europe in solidarity with Colombian farmers." Viacampesina. org., October 7, 2016, https://viacampesina.org/en/index.php/main-issues-mainmenu-27/human-rights-mainmenu-40/2154-la-via-campesina-europe-in-solidarity-with-columbian-farmers.

Lakhani, Nina. "Fellow Honduran activist Nelson Garcia murdered days after Berta Caceres." *The Guardian*, March 16, 2016, https://www.theguardian.com/ world/2016/mar/16/berta-caceres-nelson-garcia-murdered-copinh-fellow-activist.

Lappe, Frances Moore. *Getting a Grip: Clarity, Creativity and Courage in a World Gone Mad*. Cambridge, MA: Small Planet Media, 2007.

Latour, Bruno. *Facing Gaia: Eight Lectures on the New Climatic Regime*. Medford, MA: Polity 2017.

————. *Politics of Nature: How to Bring the Sciences into Democracy*. Cambridge: Harvard University Press, 2004.

"League of Nationalists." *The Economist*, November 19, 2016, http://www.economist. com/news/international/21710276-all-around-world-nationalists-are-gaining-ground-why-league-nationalists.

Long, Cheryl. "Industrial Farming is Giving Us Less Nutritious Food." *Mother Earth News*, June/July 2009, http://www.motherearthnews.com/nature-and-environment/nutritional-content-zmaz09jjzraw.aspx#axzz3124Fj5lk.

Magalhaes, Pedro T. "A Contingent Affinity: Max Weber, Carl Schmitt, and the Challenge of Modern Politics." *Journal of the History of Ideas* 77 (2016) 283–304.

Maier, Harry O. "There's a New World Coming! Reading the Apocalypse in the Shadow of the Canadian Rockies." In *The Earth Story in the New Testament*, edited by Norman C. Habel and Vicky Balabanski, 166–79. New York: Sheffield Academic, 2002.

Mares, Teresa M. "Engaging Latino Immigrants in Seattle Food Activism through Urban Agriculture." In *Food Activism: Agency, Democracy, and Economy*, edited by Carole Counihan and Valeria Siniscalchi, 31–46. London: Bloomsbury Academic, 2014.

Martel, James R. *Divine Violence: Walter Benjamin and the Eschatology of Sovereignty.* New York: Routledge, 2012.

McDonald, Bryan L. *Food Security.* Malden, MA: Polity, 2010.

McKenna, Erin. "Feminism and Farming: A Response to Paul Thompson's the Agrarian Vision." *J. Agric Environ Ethics* 25 (2012) 529–34.

McKibben, Bill. *Deep Economy: The Wealth of Communities and the Durable Future.* New York: NY Times, 2007.

McMichael, Philip. "A Food Regime Geneology." *The Journal of Peasant Studies* 36 (January 2009) 139–69.

———. "Global Development and the Corporate Food Regime." Symposium on New Directions in the Sociology of Global Development. XI World Congress of Rural Sociology, Trondheim. July 2004.

Mendez-Montoya, Angel F. *The Theology of Food: Eating and the Eucharist.* West Sussex: Wiley-Blackwell, 2009.

Merchant, Carolyn. *Reinventing Eden: The Fate of Nature in Western Culture.* New York: Routledge, 2004.

Miguez, Nestor, Joerg Rieger, and Jung Mo Sung. *Beyond the Spirit of Empire: Theology and Politics in a New Key.* London: SCM, 2009.

Miles, Tom. "Four Famines Mean 20 Million People May Starve in the Next Six Months." *Reuters*, February 16, 2017, http://www.reuters.com/article/us-un-famine-idUSKBN15VoZO.

Moltman, Jürgen. *God for a Secular Society: The Public Relevance of Theology.* Minneapolis: Fortress, 1999.

Moore, Carla J., and Solveig A. Cunningham. "Social Position, Psychological Stress, and Obesity: A Systematic Review." *Journal of the Academy of Nutrition and Dietetics* 112 (April 2012) 518–26.

Morley, Ruth, and Alan Lucas. "Nutrition and Cognitive Development." *British Medical Bulletin* 53 (1997) 123–34.

Mortada, Dalia. "Let Them Eat Baklava: Today's Politics Are Recipes for Instability in the Middle East." *The Economist*, March 17, 2012, http://www.economist.com/node/21550328.

Muers, Rachel. "Seeing, Choosing and Eating: Theology and the Feminist Vegetarian Debate." In *Eating and Believing: Interdisciplinary Perspectives on Vegetarianism and Theology*, edited by David Grumett and Rachel Muers, 184–97. New York: T. & T. Clark, 2008.

Muers, Rachel, and David Grumett. *Eating and Believing: Interdisciplinary Perspectives on Vegetarianism and Theology.* New York: T. & T. Clark, 2008.

———. "Introduction." In *Eating and Believing: Interdisciplinary Perspectives on Vegetarianism and Theology*, edited by Rachel Muers and David Grumett, 1–14. New York: T. & T. Clark, 2008.

Nace, Ted. *Gangs of America: The Rise of Corporate Power and the Disabling of Democracy.* Oakland: Berrett-Koehler, 2003.

Nelson, Jack. *Hunger for Justice: The Politics of Food and Faith.* Maryknoll, NY: Orbis, 1980.

Northcott, Michael S. *A Political Theology of Climate Change.* Grand Rapids: Eerdmans, 2013.

Obesity Society. "Obesity, Bias and Stigmatization." Obesity Society. n.d. http://www.obesity.org/obesity/resources/facts-about-obesity/bias-stigmatization.

Olorunnipa, Toluse. "Trump Signs Executive Order to Impose Additional Layer of Oversight on Regulations." *Bloomberg News,* February 24, 2017, https://www.bloomberg.com/politics/articles/2017-02-24/trump-order-imposes-additional-layer-of-oversight-on-regulations.

O'Rahilly, Stephen, and I. Sadaf Farooqi. "Human Obesity: A Heritable Neurobehavioral Disorder That Is Highly Sensitive to Environmental Conditions." *Diabetes* 57 (2008) 2905–10.

Palmer, Tom G. "Carl Schmitt: The Philosopher of Conflict Who Inspired Both the Left and the Right." *Foundation for Economic Education,* November 6, 2016, https://fee.org/articles/carl-schmitt-the-philosopher-of-conflict-who-inspired-both-the-left-and-the-right/.

Pani, L., A. Porcella, and G. L. Gessa. "The role of stress in the pathophysiology of the dopaminergic system." *Molecular Psychiatry* 5 (2000) 14–21.

Parenti, Christian. *Tropic of Chaos: Climate Change and the New Geography of Violence.* New York: Nation, 2011.

Patel, Raj. *Stuffed and Starved: The Hidden Battle for the World Food System.* Brooklyn, NY: Melville House, 2012.

———. "What Does Food Sovereignty Look Like?" *Journal of Peasant Studies* 36 (2009) 663–706.

PBS NewsHour. "Did Food Prices Spur the Arab Spring?" September 7, 2011. https://www.pbs.org/newshour/world/world-july-dec11-food_09-07.

Peeke, P. M., and G. P. Chrousos. "Hypercortisolism and Obesity." *Annals of New York Academy of Science* (Dec 29, 1995) 665–76.

Peters, K. A`., et al. "Disseminated intravascular coagulopathy: manifestations after a routine dental extraction." In *NCBI: Oral Surg Oral Med Oral Pathol Oral Radiol Endod* 99 (2005) 419–23. https://www.ncbi.nlm.nih.gov/pubmed/15772592.

Pollan, Michael. *Omnivore's Dilemma: A Natural History of Four Meals.* New York: Penguin, 2006.

Poole, Martin. "Dirt Poor: Have Fruits and Vegetables Become Less Nutritious." *Scientific American* (April 27, 2011). http://www.scientificamerican.com/article/soil-depletion-and-nutrition-loss/.

Provan, Iaian. *Convenient Myths: The Axial Age, Dark Green Religion, and the World That Never Was.* Waco, TX: Baylor University Press, 2013.

Raine, Nigel E., and Richard J. Gill, "Tasteless Pesticides Affect Bees in the Field." *Nature* (May 7, 2015) 38–40.

Ray, Krishnendu, and Tulasi Srinivas. *Curried Cultures.* Oakland: University of California Press, 2012.

Robinson, Jo. "Breeding the Nutrition Out of Our Food." *New York Times,* May 25, 2013, http://www.nytimes.com/2013/05/26/opinion/sunday/breeding-the-nutrition-out-of-our-food.html?pagewanted=all&_r=2&.

Robinson, Thomas N., Dina L. G. Borzekowski, Donna Matheson, and Helena Kraemer. "Effects of Fast Food Branding on Young Children's Taste Preferences." *Archives of Pediatric Adolescent Medicine* 161 (August 2007) 792–97.

Roser, Max. "Agricultural Employment." Our World in Data, 2016. https://ourworldindata.org/agricultural-employment/.

Rossing, Barbara. "For the Healing of the World: Reading Revelation Ecologically." In *From Every People and Nation: The Book of Revelation in Intercultural Perspective*, edited by David Rhoads 165–82, Minneapolis: Fortress, 2005.

Ruether, Rosemary Radford. *Gaia and God: An Ecofeminist Theology of Earth Healing.* San Francisco: HarperSanFrancisco, 1992.

Santos, Esperanza "Pangging" A., and Margie Lacanilao. "Women Contributing to Food Sovereignty through Sustainable Agriculture." *Kasarinlan: Philippine Journal of Third World Studies* 26 (2011) 447–51.

Schanbacher, William D. *The Politics of Food: The Global Conflict Between Food Security and Food Sovereignty.* Denver: Praeger Security International, 2010.

Scheer, Roddy, and Doug Moss. "What Causes Ocean 'Dead Zones'?" *Scientific American*, n.d., https://www.scientificamerican.com/article/ocean-dead-zones/.

Schiavoni, Christina M. "Competing Sovereignties, Contested Processes: Insights from the Venezuelan Food Sovereignty Experiment." *Globalizations* 12 (2015) 466–80.

Schmitt, Carl. "The Age of Neutralizations and Depoliticizations." https://www.docdroid.net/cNhoLIH/the-concept-of-the-political-carl-schmitt.pdf#page=8.

———. *The Nomos of the Earth in the International Law of the Jus Publicum Europaeum.* Translated by G. L. Ulmen. New York: Telos, 2003.

———. *Political Theology: Four Chapters on the Concept of Sovereignty.* Chicago: University of Chicago Press, 1985.

———. *Political Theology II: The Myth of the Closure of Any Political Theology.* Cambridge: Polity, 1970.

Schwab, George. "Introduction." In *Political Theology: Four Chapters on the Concept of Sovereignty*, by Carl Schmitt, xxxvii–lii. Chicago: University of Chicago Press, 1985.`

Sen, Amartya. *Poverty and Famines: An Essay on Entitlement and Deprivation.* Oxford: Oxford University Press, 1981.

Sielen, Alan. "The Devolution of the Seas: The Consequences of Oceanic Destruction." *Foreign Affairs* (December 2013). https://www.foreignaffairs.com/articles/global-commons/2013-10-15/devolution-seas.

Smith, Gregory A., and Jessica Martinez. "How the Faithful Voted: A Preliminary 2016 Analysis." Pew Research Center. November 10, 2016. http://www.pewresearch.org/fact-tank/2016/11/09/how-the-faithful-voted-a-preliminary-2016-analysis/.

Snyder, Timothy. *Black Earth: The Holocaust as History and Warning.* New York: Tim Duggan, 2015.

Soelle, Dorothy. *Political Theology.* New York: Fortress, 1974.

Southgate, Christopher. *The Groaning of Creation: God, Evolution, and the Problem of Evil.* Louisville: Westminster John Knox, 2008

Spielmaker, Debra, and Mark Lacy. "Growing a Nation: The Story of American Agriculture." *Agriculture in the Classroom*, June 12, 2006, https://www.agclassroom.org/gan/timeline/17_18.htm.

Statistic Brain Research Institute. "World Hunger Statistics." May 7, 2013. http://www.statisticbrain.com/world-hunger-statistics/.

Strong, Tracy B. "Foreword: The Sovereign and the Exception: Carl Schmitt, Politics, Theology, and Leadership." In *Political Theology: Four Chapters on the Concept of Sovereignty*, by Carl Schmitt, vii-xxxv. Chicago: University of Chicago Press, 1985.

Taubes, Jacob. *The Political Theology of Paul*. Stanford: Stanford University Press, 2004.

Taylor, Mark Lewis. *The Theological and the Political: On the Weight of the World*. Minneapolis: Fortress, 2011.

Tirosh-Samuelson, Hava. "Religion, Ecology, and Gender: A Jewish Perspective." *Feminist Theology* 13 (2005) 373–97.

Thompson, Helen, and Pieter Oomen, eds. "Hazards of Pesticides to Bees." 11th International Symposium of the ICP BR Bee Protection Group, November 2011, Waginingen, Netherlands.

United States Environmental Protection Agency. "Draft Inventory of U.S. Greenhouse Gas Emissions and Sinks: 1990-2015." EPA.gov. February 15, 2017. https://www.epa.gov/sites/production/files/2017-02/documents/2017_chapter_5_agriculture.pdf.

Union of Concerned Scientists. "High and Dry: Why Genetic Engineering Is Not Solving Agriculture's Drought Problem in a Thirsty World (2012)." Ucsusa.org. May 2012. http://www.ucsusa.org/food_and_agriculture/our-failing-food-system/genetic-engineering/high-and-dry.html#.WMYYHPLUog4.

Unitarian Universalist Association of Congregations. *Ethical Eating Study Guide*. Boston: UUA, 2012.

United States Department of Agriculture. "Foodwaste FAQs." Office of the Chief Economist, n.d., https://www.usda.gov/oce/foodwaste/faqs.htm.

United States Holocaust Memorial Museum. "Documenting Numbers of Victims of the Holocaust and Nazi Persecution." Holocaust Encycolpedia, n.d., https://www.ushmm.org/wlc/en/article.php?ModuleId=10008193.

University of Texas. "Study Suggests Nutrient Decline in Garden Crops over Past 50 Years." *University of Texas News*, December 1, 2004, http://www.utexas.edu/news/2004/12/01/nr_chemistry/.

Viacampesina.org. "La Via Campesina and Allies Push for the Declaration on Peasants' Rights in Geneva." September 23, 2016, https://viacampesina.org/en/index.php/main-issues-mainmenu-27/human-rights-mainmenu-40/peasants-right-resources/2146-la-via-campesina-and-allies-push-for-the-declaration-on-peasants-rights-in-geneva.

————. "La Via Campesina Europe in solidarity with Colombian farmers." October 7, 2016, https://viacampesina.org/en/index.php/main-issues-mainmenu-27/human-rights-mainmenu-40/2154-la-via-campesina-europe-in-solidarity-with-columbian-farmers.

Via, Michael. "The Malnutrition of Obesity: Micronutrient Deficiencies that Promote Diabetes." *Endocrinology* (March 2012) 1–8.

Walker, Margaret Urban. *Moral Understandings: A Feminist Study in Ethics*. New York: Oxford University Press, 2007.

Walsh, Bryan. "Can GM Crops Bust the Drought?" *Time*, September 10, 2012, http://science.time.com/2012/09/10/can-gmo-crops-bust-the-drought/.

Waskow, Arthur. *Down to Earth Judaism: Food, Money, Sex, and the Rest of Your Life*. New York: W. Morrow, 1995.

Weber, Samuel. "Taking Exception to Decision: Walter Benjamin and Carl Schmitt." *Diacritics* 22 (1992) 5–18.

Westervelt, Amy. "Does climate change really cause conflict?" *The Guardian*, March 9, 2015, https://www.theguardian.com/vital-signs/2015/mar/09/climate-change-conflict-syria-global-warming.

Whitehead, Alfred North. *Process and Reality*, 3rd Edition. New York: Free Press, 1979.

———. *Religion in the Making*. New York: Macmillan, 1926.

Wirzba, Norman. *Food and Faith: A Theology of Food*. Cambridge: Cambridge University Press, 2011.

World Food Programme. "Zero Hunger." Wfp.org, n.d. http://www1.wfp.org/zero-hunger.

World Health Organization, "Double Burden." http://www.who.int/nutrition/double-burden-malnutrition/en/.

World Hunger Education Service. "2015 World Hunger and Poverty Facts." May 10, 2015, http://www.worldhunger.org/articles/Learn/world%20hunger%20facts%20 2002.htm.

Zurayk, Rami. "Use Your Loaf: Why Food Prices Were Crucial in the Arab Spring." *The Guardian*, July 16, 2011, https://www.theguardian.com/lifeandstyle/2011/jul/17/bread-food-arab-spring.

Index